Hermann Lotze, Bernard Bosanquet

Logic in three books

Of thought, of investigation and of knowledge. Vol. 2

Hermann Lotze, Bernard Bosanquet

Logic in three books
Of thought, of investigation and of knowledge. Vol. 2

ISBN/EAN: 9783337219079

Printed in Europe, USA, Canada, Australia, Japan

Cover: Foto ©Thomas Meinert / pixelio.de

More available books at **www.hansebooks.com**

𝕮𝖑𝖆𝖗𝖊𝖓𝖉𝖔𝖓 𝕻𝖗𝖊𝖘𝖘 𝕾𝖊𝖗𝖎𝖊𝖘

LOTZE'S SYSTEM OF PHILOSOPHY

PART I
LOGIC

London

HENRY FROWDE

New York

MACMILLAN AND CO.

Clarendon Press Series

LOGIC

IN THREE BOOKS

*OF THOUGHT, OF INVESTIGATION
AND OF KNOWLEDGE*

BY

HERMANN LOTZE

ENGLISH TRANSLATION, EDITED BY

BERNARD BOSANQUET, M.A.
FORMERLY FELLOW OF UNIVERSITY COLLEGE, OXFORD

Second Edition, in Two Volumes
VOL. II

Oxford
AT THE CLARENDON PRESS
1887

[*All rights reserved*]

CONTENTS OF VOLUME II.

BOOK II.
Applied Logic.

CHAPTER VI.

FALLACIES AND DILEMMAS.

	PAGE
240. Premises must be true in order to *prove* a conclusion	1
241. And must not covertly involve the conclusion	2
242. Preposterous Reasoning confuses the principiatum as causa cognoscendi with the principium as causa essendi	3
243. Ambiguity of middle term mostly due to the confusion of a relative with an absolute truth	4
244. Illustration of the above from moral precepts, all of which have their exceptions	5
245. As have also mechanical formulae, which become unmeaning, when pushed to extremes	7
246. Fallacies of too wide or too narrow definition	10
247. Fallacy of incomplete explanation illustrated by the popular idea that lapse of time destroys motion	10
248. Incomplete disjunction the cause of much philosophical and other onesidedness	12
249. The fallacy in Zeno's paradoxes about reality of motion	14
250. Examples of classical dilemmas stated and explained	17

CHAPTER VII.

UNIVERSAL PROPOSITIONS AS DERIVED FROM PERCEPTIONS.

251. Inductive methods are based on results of deductive Logic	22
252. Connexions of elements revealed in sensible experience are mostly impure	23

253. The universality of a pure connexion or its character as a law of nature guaranteed by the law of Identity . . . 24
254. The raw matter of Inductions consists not of passive impressions but of perceptions already articulated by thought as subject and predicate and ranged under general conceptions 25
255. They are so ranged by an incomplete analogy, based on a distinction of essential from non-essential remarks, which logical theory cannot assist 28
256. In reaching universal inductions we must argue ad subalternantem 31
257. The truths of Geometry are universal because the diagram is used as a symbol only of our conception . . . 33
258. The highest inductions not categorical but hypothetical judgments 35
259. Terms which are exclusively cause and effect of each other are related as ground and consequent 37
260. Experiment merely subsidiary to observation and has no peculiar virtue of its own 38
261. Typical cases of the relation in which two phenomena C and E may stand to one another 40
    (1) C and E Co-Exist always.
    (2) C and E frequently concur.
    (3) Absence of C not involving absence of E. Criticism of the canon 'cessante causa cessat et effectus.'
    (4) Presence of C not involving presence of E. Difference of relation of cause and effect and of ground and consequent.
    (5) Absence of C involving absence of E.
    (6) Presence of E involving presence of C. Criticism of Newton's canon 'effectuum naturalium ejusdem generis eaedem sunt causae.'
    (7) Absence of E involving absence of C.
262. Whether the phenomenon C is or only contains the cause of E can only be decided by analysis of both into their elements and observation of which elements of the one involve which elements of the other. Typical examples of such analysis 52
263. The exact nature of the causal nexus inferred from any of the above relations to exist between C and E can only be apprehended by observation of the quantitative changes they cause in one another. Examples of such quantitative correspondences 60

CHAPTER VIII.

THE DISCOVERY OF LAWS.

264. Science not content with discovering a mere connexion between two phenomena seeks to know the law of this connexion 67
265. Laws of nature are universal hypothetical judgments and not assertions of universal matters-of-fact 68
266. A law expresses an objective and intelligible connexion of phenomena, a rule is a mere subjective method of thought 71
267. The ultimate criterion of sense-perception to be found in sense itself 73
268. Facts as they appear are not only relative to one another but to the standpoint of the observer, and must therefore be grasped as projections of ulterior and truer facts . . 76
269. A law always transcends the given, being an extension to cases not given of what holds good within the given. A truly universal law is not a demonstrable truth . . 79
270. Laws based on statistics are mostly partial truths . . . 84
271. The law which prima facie best fits in with observed facts need not therefore be the truest expression of their interconnexion 85
272. Simplicity no guarantee for the truth of a law. The simplest law only preferable where it is the sole conceivable one . 87
273. A *postulate lays down* the conditions under which alone the given appearance is conceivable. A *hypothesis* is a *suggestion* of conceivable facts fulfilling the demands of the postulate and so explaining the appearance. A *fiction* views the given as an approximate realisation of a known law, in the absence of a known law to which it can be simply referred 90
274. Rules for framing of hypotheses not to be laid down beforehand, but none to be rejected because beyond reach of refutation if false 94
275. Hypotheses must satisfy their postulates and supply the conditions of the appearances to be explained . . . 97
276. An old hypothesis not to be hastily set aside but modified to suit the new and discrepant facts 99
277. A hypothesis must limit itself to asserting what is possible, i. e. what can be conceived or pictured as matter-of-fact . 101

CHAPTER IX.

DETERMINATION OF INDIVIDUAL FACTS.

	PAGE
278. In determining facts which transcend the immediate impression we must be guided by probability . . .	104
279. In view of the complexity of things a principle of explanation must not be too simple and abstract . . .	105
280. And on the other hand it must involve as few presuppositions as possible. Positive evidence preferable to negative .	107
281. The mathematical determination of chances assumes that they are all equally possible, but that one of them must occur	109
282. (1) Mathematical chance no positive prediction of events. It measures our expectation of their occurrence .	113

    (2) theory of composite chances.
    (3) dependent chances.
    (4) probability of alternative causes.
    (5) probability of an event's recurrence.
    (6) mathematical expectation.
    (7) moral expectation.

283. Calculus of chances not only presupposes the laws of all calculation such as law of Identity and doctrine of disjunctive judgment, but also an ordered universe of interdependent events	127
284. Mathematical chance is our subjective expectation of an event, and not a permanent property thereof. The resulting chance improbable only as compared with the sum of its alternatives, not as compared with any *one* of them	130
285. Success of attempts made to test by experiment the calculus of chances	133
286. Such successful results not fraught with intelligible necessity, but the result of constant conditions operating among variable ones, which in the long run neutralise each other	135
287. Use of the calculus in cases where constant and variable causes of an often repeated event are unknown. Nature of so-called statistical laws	139
288. Use of the calculus in determining the probable accuracy of our observations of magnitude. The method of the least squares	142

CHAPTER X.

OF ELECTIONS AND VOTING.

		PAGE
289.	Conditions presupposed by a logical treatment of the problem of expressing a collective will	148
290.	Defects of absolute majority	149
291.	The weight of votes. A majority of majorities may be a minority of the whole constituency	149
292.	Voting so as to express intensities of Volition	153
293.	Election by elimination	157
294.	When *order* of putting proposals to the vote is important	159
295.	Rejection of innovations *as such*. 'Order of the day'	161
296.	Amendments and substantive motion. Order of putting proposals to the vote	162

BOOK III.

On Knowledge (Methodology).

INTRODUCTION.

297.	Analytic and Synthetic methods practically inseparable	166
298.	Correspond respectively to Investigation and Exposition; are more general than 'methods' of applied Logic	169
299.	But applied Logic, like common thought, rests on untested bases	170
300.	And so does science as we have it	171
301.	Methodology however as treatment of Knowledge is enquiry into sources of certainty	173

CHAPTER I.

ON SCEPTICISM.

302.	Scepticism presupposes Truth and Knowledge	176
303.	But doubts whether our Knowledge is Truth. Descartes	179
304.	This doubt invoves the assumption of a world of things which our thought should copy	182
305.	But any decision postulates the competence of thought	184
306.	Which *can* only be guided by conceptions in our minds	185
307.	Our delusion could only be revealed by fresh *knowledge*	187
308.	Which must be related to the old. *Things* are not *knowledge of things*	189

		PAGE
309.	That Things may not be what they seem, as a mere general doubt, is self-contradictory	192
310.	Sceptical arguments in Sextus Empiricus	193
311.	They involve the above difficulties	196
312.	Error in 'we *only* know phenomena'	198

CHAPTER II.

THE WORLD OF IDEAS.

313.	Genesis of Plato's doctrine of 'Ideas'	200
314.	The Ideas as Universal conceptions	202
315.	Possible knowledge of Ideas apart from question of Things	204
316.	Distinction between Existence, Occurrence, Validity	206
317.	Confusion of Existence and Validity in case of the Ideas	210
318.	Ideas in what sense eternal, and independent of things	211
319.	Aristotle on the Ideas. *His* universal too is οὐσία	214
320.	Modern counterparts of the Ideas. Validity a difficult notion	216
321.	'Ideas impart no motion' criticised; importance of *Judgments*	218

CHAPTER III.

THE A PRIORI AND THE EMPIRICAL METHODS.

322.	Judging of knowledge by our notions of its *origin* an illusion	223
323.	Attempt to find a starting-point for knowledge. 'Cogito, ergo sum'	226
324.	Innate Ideas; but are they *true?*	229
325.	Action of one thing on another implies Spontaneity in order to Receptivity	231
326.	Nature of mind is contributory in *all* elements of knowledge	232
327.	Both in simple Perception and in such ideas as that of causal connexion	234
328.	External reality must be criticised on ground of knowledge	236
329.	Universality and Necessity as marks of *a priori* knowledge	239
330.	Universal validity not derivable from repeated perceptions alone	241
331.	There may be spurious self-evidence, which is tested by thinking the contradictory	243
332.	Use of psychological analysis in establishing first principles	246
333.	Even modern Psychology hardly helps Logic	248

CHAPTER IV.

REAL AND FORMAL SIGNIFICANCE OF LOGICAL ACTS.

	PAGE
334. Thought must have *some* Real significance	252
335. Comparison and distinction as acts resulting in Relations .	254
336. Thought is symbolic and discursive	256
337. How can a relation of *ideas* be objective	259
338. Only as independent of individual mind. The case of *Things*	260
339. A universal cannot be realised, but has objective validity .	264
340. Nominalism and Realism confuse Existence and Validity .	267
341. The Reality of general notions is only validity . . .	268
342. Conception not akin to object in structure, but in net result .	270
343. Degrees of subjectivity in kinds of Judgment . . .	273
344. Subjective character of Syllogism and Induction . . .	276
345. Terms antithetic to 'Subjective' and 'Formal' . . .	279

CHAPTER V.

THE A PRIORI TRUTHS.

346. The world of Knowledge and the world of Things . .	283
347. 'Actual Reality'; adequacy of Judgments to it . . .	286
348. Applicability of thought to the course of events involves (1) Some *given* reality, which thought cannot create .	288
349. (2) The Universality of Law in the Real world; ultimately a matter of faith	290
350. And (3) synthetic judgments *a priori*, as basis of knowledge of particular laws	294
351. Hume's restriction of judgment destroys *all* judgment . .	295
352. Mathematical reasoning is not covered by the Law of Identity	297
353. Illustration by Kant's arithmetical instance	299
354. And by his geometrical instance	303
355. Meaning and value of apprehension *a priori* . . .	305
356. Self-evidence of universal Truths	307
357. Intuition is opposed to discursive thought—means immediate apprehension	309
358. Self-evident Truths require to be discovered by help of analysis	311
359. Pure Mechanics in what sense *a priori*	313
360. Gradual formation of pure ideas of Motion and Mass . .	316
361. Mechanical principles, like those of Arithmetic and Geometry, at once identical and synthetic	319

362. In higher Mechanics, Proof is one thing, and the *Ratio legis* another 323
363. Analytical Knowledge as the ideal, means the simplest synthetical knowledge 325
364. The simplest ultimate Truth need not be a mere datum of experience, though it must be Synthetic 327
365. A synthetic yet necessary development the supreme goal of science 329
APPENDIX 331
INDEX 333

CHAPTER VI.

Fallacies and Dilemmas.

240. TRUE conclusions, as Aristotle has observed, can be correctly drawn from false premises. Every Laplander is a born poet, Homer was a Laplander, and therefore—by the first figure—a poet. All parasitic plants have red flowers, no rose has red flowers, therefore—by the second figure—roses are not parasitic plants. Metals do not conduct electricity, all metals are non-fusible, and hence—according to the third figure—non-fusible substances exist, which are non-conductors of electricity. Alter Laplander into Greek, plants which have red flowers into plants which have exploding seed-vessels, and write glass for metal, and in each example one premise will be true, while by inserting a new middle term in each case you may make both premises true, but in every case the conclusion follows with neither more nor less validity. Let T be a perfectly true proposition, S its subject, and P its predicate; then a middle term M may be chosen at random so long as the terms are arranged in both premises on the model of an Aristotelian figure: if this is done the conclusion T will always follow according to the figure.

We shall see why this is universally true, if we take as our middle term an abstract symbol M, instead of a concrete term: thus, all M are poets, Homer was an M; all parasitic plants are M, roses are not M; all M are non-conductors, all M are non-fusible. What these symbolic premises tell us is the relations in which S and P must stand to *some* middle term, if their conjunction SP is to be valid in the conclusion: and conversely these premises tell us that given *any* middle term M to which S and P are related as required, then the proposition SP must be valid. If the M is found and so both the required premises established, then SP is valid not merely in fact but now also of necessity; on the other hand if we could show that there exists no M to which S and P can stand in the requisite relation, we shall know that SP was impossible, for no experience could give us SP as a fact: but if we have merely chosen a wrong M then the case is different. The premises we have chosen will not do, but that is no reason why there should not be some other M, the insertion of which will render the premises correct and so necessitate the conclusion SP. If again we have correctly drawn a conclusion SP and that conclusion is unsound, there must be something false in the premises, from which it follows. In a word in all cases where T is not given in direct perception, but deduced from premises, what really depends on the correctness of those premises is not the truth of T, but only our insight into that truth. Without correct premises T cannot indeed be *proved*, but nevertheless it can be true and its truth is independent of any errors we may commit, when reflecting about it, and subsists even when conclusively deduced from premises materially false. This point deserves notice, for it is a common mistake in reasoning to take the invalidity of the proof which is offered for T as a proof of the falsehood of T itself, and to confuse the refutation of an argument with the disproof of a fact.

241. A proposition T is valid if it is rightly drawn from valid premises, but it is not proved unless these premises are valid independently of itself. If T itself or any proposition T^1, whose validity presupposes the validity of T, appears disguised in the premises, T is correctly deduced, but is not proved at all. This fallacy is called *petitio prin-*

cipii or *circulus in demonstrando*, and in its naked form seems easily avoided. Yet it is frequently committed, especially where the conclusion is reached by a long chain of deduction and depends on the constructions of the scientific imagination as well as on the relations of abstract ideas. In such a case we are often able to deduce T with formal accuracy by first presupposing some indirect and distant consequence of T, which consequence of T is then taken as an independent truth from which T' follows. There are no rules which will enable us to avoid this mistake, but it may be well to remember that we are peculiarly liable to it when we attempt to prove by a direct and progressive argument propositions which contain some final and underivative element of our knowledge. In such cases, whether the element be a necessity of our thought or a fact universally valid in our perception, apagogic and regressive methods alone are applicable.

242. The second kind of fallacy is called *Hysteron Proteron*. It is so like the first (the argument in a circle) that we often have no reason to distinguish it therefrom. It consists in using a proposition, which both calls for and admits of proof, to demonstrate another, which not only needs none, but is itself actually the proper ground from which to prove the first proposition. We are told for example that God's will is holy, that the moral dictates of our conscience are the expression of the divine will within us, and *therefore* they too are holy and binding on us. But we cannot help objecting that if the holiness and binding force of our moral dictates were not felt by us as an independent fact and irrespectively of the origin of those dictates, the argument would fall to the ground. Upon other grounds no doubt we might continue to believe in a mere supreme being, but the idea of holiness would not and could not suggest itself to us, and hence the major premise of the argument proposed could never exist. The transition from God's will to our conscience is therefore no proof; but

although inadmissible as a sequence of thought it is perhaps the right way of giving expression to the truth. For in a great many cases that which is in fact the consequence or *principiatum* may be for us a means, and often the only means, of knowing that which in itself is the *principium* or real ground of the possibility of the former. When we have acquired knowledge, by way of induction especially, and are exhibiting the result systematically, it is evident that we always take the universal statement, which we really know only from the particulars, and placing it at the head of them use it to prove those very particulars. Hence it is of importance alongside of this method to employ another mode of exposition which shall set out the items of our knowledge in the order in which they can actually be proved by the help one of another. We often allow ourselves to commit a *hysteron proteron*, when we are trying to prove a point, either in the course of conversation, or in the rapid reflexion by which we seek to assure ourselves of the truth of some proposition which we desire to employ in an enquiry. The inference in these cases is *ex concessis*, from premises whose truth we presuppose but do not discuss. In an enquiry the implication of these premises with the rest of our knowledge is taken as a sufficient guarantee, and in conversation we may find it easier to get these premises admitted than it would be to gain acceptance for the truth from which in reality they follow.

243. The commonest fallacy is ambiguity of the middle term, *quaternio terminorum* or *fallacia falsi medii* more or less disguised. The Greek sophists were the first to remark the chain of thought which appears in the syllogism and to notice its linguistic expression, and a great number of these fallacies were at that time exhibited. They are classified in the Aristotelian work on the subject, but many of them have no value at the present time, even in the light of pleasantries. There are yet some which remain as abiding sources of danger, and among these we may signalise the double fallacy *de dicto simpliciter ad dictum secundum quid* and *de dicto secundum quid ad dictum simpliciter*. Two general modes of fallacious thought are developed by the habitual commission of these fallacies and illustrate them on a grand scale. The first is doctrinairism, the second narrow-mindedness. The doctrinaire is an idealist, who refuses to see that though ideas may be right in the abstract, yet the nature of the circumstances under which and of the objects to which they are to be applied must limit not only their practicability but even their binding force. The narrow-minded, on the other hand, can recognise and esteem no truth and no ideal, even the most universally valid, except in that special form to which they have become accustomed within a limited circle of thought and personal observation. Life is a school, which corrects these habits of mind. The parochially-minded man sees things persist in spite of himself in taking shapes, which he considers unprecedented, but he finds the world somehow survives it and learns at last that a system of life may be excellent and precious, but that it is rash from that to argue that it is the only proper mode of orderly existence. And the enthusiast for ideals, when he sees the curtailment which every attempt at realisation inflicts on them, learns the lesson which the disjunctive theorem might have taught him. Every universal P changes in the act of being applied from something that held *simpliciter* into something that holds *secundum quid*,—changes from P to $p^1 p^2$ or p^3: to refuse to accept it in any one of these, which are its only possible shapes, is to ask that it be realised under a condition which even logic pronounces impossible.

244. One of these fallacies consists in our taking a P, which holds good of M in the abstract, and asserting it of M under new conditions which make it no longer applicable. The other and opposite mistake transfers to M taken absolutely predicates, which are only true of M under certain conditions. In both we have an ambiguity of the middle term, which wavers in its meaning between the unlimited M and the determinate conditioned M^1. Examples present themselves and could be given in great numbers, but there is one worth dwelling on from its own special interest. I refer to the question of the morality of lying. On principle we condemn all lies, but in practice almost everyone allows there are exceptions, a confession which points to some mistake in the way in which the principle is laid down. In fact the particular lies which, apart from the influence of education, we find hateful are those whose object is to make others chargeable for our faults, wantonly to do mischief, or to wound the self-esteem of another by entangling him in false ideas in order to exalt ourselves. It is these secondary features that rouse our indignation against an untruth, and it is only these that make us call an untruth a lie. The *secundum quid* and its influence on our judgment is quite plain in these cases, and on the strength of them apart from other considerations we should be wrong to conclude that every falsehood, when the intention is not bad, is immoral. Other considerations do however exist. We communicate with our fellows in order to waken in all alike ideas of the same reality, and our object in doing this is that when we work together our efforts may coincide, and when we work apart we may avoid collisions, and in general we desire to avoid undertakings which are not in accordance with the nature of things. But failure would be certain, if everyone made it the rule to lie; everywhere the truth is one, but possible falsehoods are innumerable. The interchange of falsehoods therefore ensures no meeting-point for common action, so that however good our intentions we should ever be missing the mark. False assertion is thus contrary to the essence of assertion, to the moral end which all communication aims at, and therefore we set it down broadly as a thing in itself reprehensible. The untruths of poetry, jesting and courtesy are exceptions, they are not real assertions, and on these points we make a silent reservation.

Here comes in the fallacy. We think that we can now unconditionally assert the badness of falsehood; that we have got rid of the old *secundum quid* and have got the *simpliciter*. Unfortunately the *simpliciter* is ambiguous; it may mean that false-speaking is wrong *in itself* and can be justified only *secundum quid*, i.e. for special reasons in particular cases. But it may mean that falsehood is *universally* bad, so that no special considerations can ever justify it. These versions of the *simpliciter* practically collide in our consciences, and it is that which makes our opinions about falsehood so self-contradictory. The logical premises from which we here started justify only the first version. What we started from was that universal false-speaking would frustrate our moral aims and therefore we said it was bad; but where the aim is immoral it may be right to frustrate it, and admitting our premise it is therefore still possible that a lie may be justified. To prove the *simpliciter* in the sense of without exception other premises would be wanted. It would be the business of ethics to discuss them, we are here concerned with only the logical side of the question, and our object has been to show that *fallacia falsi medii* arises not only through confusion of *simpliciter* and *secundum quid*, but also that the *simpliciter* itself in the example we discussed and in many others beside is the seat of an ambiguity. A thing true *simpliciter* may be true *by itself* alone and not under all conditions, i.e. it may be true only in general, but not always and in all particular cases. But it may equally well be true *by itself* in the sense of being true independently of conditions and hence always and necessarily true in every particular case; universally, that is, not merely in general.

245. We may consider here some examples, where an universal proposition is extended to instances which can formally be brought under it as exceptional cases, but where the conditions which make it applicable have disappeared. If the terms of the proposition are variable quantities, and if these are followed to their limits at zero or infinity, we get such examples. With a lever the work done remains the same, so long as the product wl of the weight w into the arm l is unaltered. Thus the more l is increased, the less weight w is wanted to do the same work; hence, it has been subtly argued, at an infinite distance from the fulcrum, a mass $=0$ would suffice to balance any weight whatever on the other arm of the lever; and this conclusion has been urged against the validity of the general formula. It is natural simply to dismiss the idea by remarking that the formula contemplates cases where real forces are applied to the lever, and is not true where that condition is wanting. This removes our doubts on the question of fact, but hardly settles the logical problem. For we do not always dismiss these cases; we have no hesitation in taking $\cos 0 = 1$, although the idea of a cosine is in its origin without meaning except for a real arc ϕ, from the extremity of which a perpendicular may be drawn to the semi-diameter through the initial point, and we pass from this case to the limiting value $\phi = 0$. Now since the law of the lever remains valid at every stage of approximation to the values $l = \infty$ and $w = 0$, it would be well if it admitted of being interpreted for these limiting cases in such a way as to show what is the second meaning which it assumes after the first becomes inadmissible, or failing this it would be desirable that the formula itself should exhibit its own invalidity. This it would do not merely by producing conclusions, which from a point of view external to the formula we can judge to be incredible, but still more by becoming destructive of itself. The force which a wedge exerts varies inversely with the breadth of its back; let this sink to nothing and we get the same dilemma: the formula gives an infinite effect, while the effect is in fact nothing at all. But here we might answer, though more in jest than in earnest, that as a matter of fact it *would* need an infinite force to keep a geometrical plane, such as we have now reduced our wedge to, from penetrating a block of wood; and it might be proved with equal show of formal rectitude that this would not require the block to be cleft.

I cannot at present as decisively settle the doubts which some have about the lever; though I should deem it irrational to postpone any consideration of the principle of the lever till one had solved the problem which arises in connexion with an arm of infinite length, for surely it is intrinsically absurd to think of the mass $= 0$ at an infinite distance as having any effect at all; the very idea, as it admits of no interpretation in fact, must be self-contradictory. And so it is, for the law has no meaning except as ascribing to a definite mass w at a definite distance l from the fulcrum a definite effect, which alters as l alters. Now why should a mass $= 0$ produce an effect at an infinite distance other than it would produce at any finite distance we like to take? How would the case of a mass $= 0$ acting at the end of a lever of infinite length differ from that of a mass $= 0$ acting at any other point in the lever, or from a third case, which would properly always coexist with the other two, viz. that in which we suppose the nothing to be applied at all points in the lever and—what is more—to act in any direction we like? Thus the attempt to retain the law of the lever for $wl = 0 . \infty$ fails, not merely because it gives incredible *results*, but because the law loses all its *meaning* inasmuch as things become indistinguishable whose distinction is essential to that meaning. Other paths lead to the same conclusion. wl is no constant quantity, so that w should vary inversely as l, but the effect varies for every and any l with the variation of w, and w is quite free to vary as it will consequently the effect becomes $= 0$, when w sinks to 0, no matter what l may be; it follows that $wl = 0 . \infty$ can only have the value 0 and no other.

246. There is another fallacy which is akin to that of too wide or too narrow definition and in general arises from it. T being the point to be proved, the mistake consists in proving too much or too little either as to the qualities which T includes, or the extent to which it is applicable. The conclusion which proves too much may be correct and may err simply in going further than was required. For instance you may prove correctly of all animals what you wanted to prove only of men, and in such a case the ground is valid and has simply been applied more generally than was requisite. But in other cases a conclusion may be false as well as too wide, and here the mistake lies in using a wrong ground of proof, so throwing doubt upon the narrower conclusion instead of proving it. In the argument which proves too little, the mistake is again of two kinds. In the first case the ground of inference may be a true and general proposition quite wide enough to prove T, and the mistake lies in taking this ground in a particular form which will not do so; it is corrected simply by using the ground of inference in the general form in which it proves T. But the second form of the fallacy is more serious. A special case of T may have been correctly proved from certain premises, but those premises may be quite inadequate to establish T as an universal. To sum up, any argument which does not exactly tally with the proposition to be proved must leave us in doubt as to its applicability; *nihil probat qui nimium probat* is as true as *nihil probat qui parum probat.*

247. It would be easy to supply illustrations, but I prefer to consider another fallacy, that of incomplete explanation. This is often to be met with in the speculations of amateurs, but does not generally take the form of demonstration. It consists in assigning a general cause for some phenomenon without enquiring if the cause assigned will account for the particular modifications, to which that phenomenon is subject. It is perhaps not possible to deduce the law of the persistence of motion from any more universal principle; but at any rate the vulgar opinion that every motion ceases with the lapse of time is impossible in itself, and can be used to prove the law by a *reductio ad absurdum*. That diminution of motion arises from real obstacles existing in time is true and is quite conceivable, but it is quite inconceivable how *mere time* should cause a diminution. No doubt our own bodily movements are enfeebled as exhaustion increases, and this might suggest to us the idea that mere lapse of time can destroy all motion; yet we are undeceived when we reflect that if this really happens it must happen either earlier or later, at some one particular time or another, but that there exists no law and no reason to connect it with any particular time. For assume that each of the absolutely similar moments dt has the same constant consuming power, and takes from every unit of mass the velocity q,—no doubt one can understand on this assumption, how it is that swifter motions of the same mass persist longer than slower motions. But on the other hand so long as q is a finite quantity we can still think of motions, whose velocity during dt regarded as one period is less than q, and these movements could on such an assumption never take place in reality at all. Or shall we assume that the consuming force of time is proportional to the velocity to be consumed? Then the question remains as to the ratio. But I refrain from any further hypotheses. In the first place since time and mass are utterly disparate things one sees at once how hopeless it is to try to determine a unit of mass, for which q would measure the arresting power of a time dt. In the second place we can equally conceive of innumerable different ratios as existing between the velocity and rate of retardation, and it is evident that mere time can of itself afford us no reason for preferring one of these ratios to another. But apart from all this there is an objection which would render all such attempts idle. For supposing that a time dt removes some part of the motion, the question remains—whence comes the residue, the motion which has not been removed? It is clear that in case of this residue the law of the persistency of motion has been presupposed. If we had not tacitly presupposed the law to be valid for it, we should have to say that the whole motion was arrested by the first period dt. What it comes to then is this. Either motion does not take place at all but vanishes[1] the moment it gives a sign of intending to endure through a time dt; or if motion gradually diminishes, the law of persistence is the primary law, and the diminution of motion is secondary, the result of external obstacles. These obstacles we shall now naturally seek only in what is homogeneous with itself, viz. in opposed tendencies to motion.

I will merely call the reader's attention to the connexion of this proposition (that every ground of explanation must establish not merely T in general, but also the possibility of its modifications) with the doctrine of the disjunctive judgment. It would take us too far afield into mathematics, if we followed up this clue; it is sufficient just to notice that this logical requirement has found a special and fruitful expression of itself in the principle of the homogeneity of the functions to be combined in an equation.

248. *Incomplete disjunction* is a fallacy which often occurs in collective and indirect arguments. In order to prove T, these arguments attempt either to show that that holds in all particular cases of T, which it is desired to affirm universally, or to establish T as the sole remaining possibility by first disproving all cases of non-T. Neither task is very easy. In practical life especially we often find it very difficult in laying down a rule to examine beforehand all the possible cases to which it may be

---

[1] [Compare Metaph. § 163.]

applied and to see whether the proposed regulation would always be desirable or tolerable; and it is common again to find that after considering every course which seems conceivable, and after concluding all but one to be impossible, a momentary inspiration will suggest some other way out of the difficulty, which we had quite overlooked. In theory the most fruitful source of the fallacy is the dominant influence of some one order of ideas. Instead of setting out all the possible alternatives we are led silently to the one which consorts best with our own one-sidedness. For instance our sensations are subjective states excited in us; it is easy to show this; and further according to a view now widely accepted the forms of space and time in which we arrange the manifold matter of sensation are subjective also, they are modes in which our minds perceive. From this point we are easily led on to regard the idea of unknown things and processes underlying phenomena as a creation of our mind, which is compelled by its constitution to adopt this means of giving unity to its singular perceptions. The subjectivity of *all* elements of knowledge is thus established, and finally we venture on the inference that therefore there is no objective real world answering to the world of our ideas. But the inference is false: for supposing that this real world does exist, it is easy to see that things would be just the same to us as we find them. If real elements exist they can never pass into us bodily: they can do nothing but excite in us sensations and ideas, and these though caused by external impressions and our reaction against them would still be a creation of our subjective nature. An objective space may exist or may not exist, but at all events the perception of it must be the product of our subjective faculties. So too with causality: whether the law has objective validity or no, in either case equally we are forced to recognise it only so far as we think it and perceive its content to be in harmony with the laws of our thinking. Thus we see the complete subjectivity of all the elements of our knowledge proves nothing whatever as to the existence or non-existence of an objective reality. The best preservative against this kind of fallacy is the existence of hostile opinion. It is indispensable, besides developing our own doctrine, to familiarise ourselves with ideas which proceed from points of view opposed to our own.

249. *Sophisms* are distinguished from *paralogisms*. The latter are involuntary mistakes in inference, while the former are intentionally fallacious arguments, whose object is to confuse or deceive. It is thus obvious that in cases where the intention is doubtful we cannot tell a paralogism from a sophism. Zeno's arguments against the reality of motion may be taken as either. I shall not here discuss those real difficulties in the idea of motion which they touch upon, but will exhibit the arguments as examples of fallacies that are difficult to classify. The first argument tries to prove that an arrow in flight is at rest. It starts with the assumption that time consists of indivisible moments, and then infers that the arrow cannot move in any one of these moments. For if it moves, it must now be at one place and then at another, but in each indivisible moment there is no now and then, no before or after. Therefore the arrow is at rest in each, and if in each then in all; hence it is always at rest. To this we may answer simply that rest also is impossible unless a thing is at one and the same place both now and then, both before and after; and since in an indivisible moment there is no before or after the arrow can no more rest in it than move. And this conclusion accords with the ordinary theory of motion. So long as dt is a length of time the arrow passes in it through a small space $v.\,dt$, but as soon as ever dt ceases to be a quantity and becomes a mere dividing point in time with its definite position in the series of time—then no doubt in dt the arrow passes through no space at all; still it does not rest in it, but goes through it with a velocity v. But apart from this objection, what right has Zeno to maintain that in each successive moment of the arrow's flight it is at rest in the *same* place as it was at rest in before? There is nothing, I admit, in the idea of a moment or an arrow as such from which the idea of a change of place could follow. But it surely is involved in an arrow's *flight*. No doubt there is a difficulty as to the nature of that impulse which makes a body in motion different[1] at every moment from a stationary body, even if the moment be conceived as indivisible. And this is the point against which a sophism might have been directed with effect. But, failing this and failing any proof that velocity could not exist, Zeno had no right to start with the flying of an arrow,—so assuming velocity,—and then in his proof to drop the idea out of sight. All his argument shows, if you take it as it stands, is that rest is not motion and that motion can never be compounded out of rest. Had he retained the idea of velocity Zeno could at least have deduced such a successive change of place as proceeded by jumps from moment to moment; the conception of continuous motion he could not get at so long as he held by the notion that time is made up of indivisible moments.

Another of his arguments was that if the snail has a start the swift-footed Achilles can never catch it up, inasmuch as before ever he can overtake it he must first reach the place it has just left before and so on for ever. The argument might be simplified by omitting the fact of the snail's movement, which for the particular paradox is superfluous. Did the snail remain still Achilles would yet never reach it. Nothing which is in motion—this is the real basis of the argument—can ever come to the end of any given space however small. To do so it must first accomplish half the given distance, then half the remainder, then half the remaining quarter and so on for ever, so as never to reach the

[1] [Compare Metaphysic, § 171.]

end of the space. The argument assumes that the halving process can go on for ever *ad infinitum*, and so presupposes that the space is infinitely divisible or already consists of an infinite number of parts. It further assumes that an indivisible moment of time is required for the transition from one point of space to another; and so concludes that an infinite number of moments must elapse before any space whatever is got over, since any space contains an infinite number of parts. The conclusion, if we admit the premises, is so far quite correct; but it is quite an arbitrary assertion that this aggregate of infinitely numerous moments would form an infinite length of time; seeing that they are indivisible each of them must contain no sooner or later, unless, as Zeno does here, we foist in between every two moments a real lapse of time or represent these moments as following each other at definite intervals in a sort of secondary time, which we imagine as filling up the background. It is not even necessary to object to Zeno, what Aristotle's remark on the subject amounts to, that (according to our modes of expression) the integral of an infinite series of quantities continuously passing into one another may still be a definite finite quantity, and that therefore the aggregate of moments of time may be a finite length of time. The indivisible moments of time are conceived by Zeno not only as being each for itself without quantity, but also as so detached from each other, that there is no question of a transition, in virtue of which they would become constituents of time at all. The sum of all these nothings is therefore itself nothing; it is only an unwarranted complaisance on the part of our better-instructed fancy which allows it to be passed off on us as a quantity at all and then as an infinite quantity. Achilles requires no doubt an infinite number of moments of time to get from *a* to *b*, but these do not make up any *length* of time at all; it would be truer to say that Achilles consumes no time at all than that he consumes an infinite time; indeed it remains hard to say what end is served in this connexion by the consumption of indivisible moments of time or what it means.

250. Besides these fallacies the ancients have handed down to us many interesting dilemmas, i.e. conjunctions of thoughts from which follow opposite conclusions, equally necessary and equally impossible. One dilemma nicknamed Pseudomenos dates from Epimenides, who being a Cretan himself asserted that every Cretan lies as soon as he opens his lips. If what he asserted was true, he himself lied, in which case what he said must have been false; but if it is false it is still possible that the Cretans do not always lie but lie sometimes, and that Epimenides himself actually lied on this occasion in making the universal assertion. In this case there will be no incongruity between the fact asserted and the fact that it is asserted, and a way out of the dilemma is left open to us. Not so however if we drop Epimenides and the Cretans and instead of these two subjects, one of which is only contained in the other but not identical with it, put an identical subject: 'I lie now.' If my assertion is true, i.e. if I am lying, what I assert is false, and I am not lying. But what I assert is that my assertion is untrue: if it is false to say that my assertion is untrue, my assertion becomes true again and I am lying, and the whole chain of self-destructive consequences begins afresh. The reason of them is easily detected. Logically of course what is asserted is true or false, quite apart from the fact of its being asserted; it may be asserted or it may not: but the only sort of truth or untruth which the assertion can have, is what it acquires through the truth or untruth of what is asserted, which is independent of it. Thus we get contradictions, some of which are formally insoluble, when what is asserted is such as to involve something in regard to the fact of its assertion which makes the assertion impossible or untrue. The difficulty vanishes if instead of saying: I lie, we say: I lied. Just as little can we say in the present tense, I am silent, though we can quite well use the future, I will be silent, for then our assertion refers to another fact than itself, to a fact which is not in conflict with it.

There are many other instances of the sort, though none so classical as Pseudomenos. If a person answers yes, when he is asked if he be asleep, he sets his assertion in the same sort of conflict with what he asserts; so does a person, who calls out to an unwelcome visitor, that he is not at home. Lastly there are other cases resembling these, cases in which one subject has in an impossible manner to form both terms at once of a relation, which can only exist between two different subjects: Jean Paul's dwarf for instance, who only reached up to his own knees, not to mention other people's; or the inscription over the elephant's booth: this is the biggest elephant in the world, itself excepted; or lastly we may instance Munchausen's kind service to himself, when he pulled himself out of the bog by his own hair. Equally curious is the old dilemma of the crocodile: quoth the brute to the wailing mother: I give you back your child, if you tell me truly whether I am going to give it back or no. It would all be plain-sailing had the mother only to guess, if the crocodile intends *at that moment* to give or not give it back. If she guesses *right*, there is nothing to prevent the child being restored according to agreement; for even were it true, that the crocodile does not just then intend to restore it, still, if her guess is that he does not intend, he may yet fulfil the contract by changing his intention or giving it up against his will. But if she guesses *wrong*, she loses all claim to have her child back again. For whatever may have been the animal's real intention—which she guessed wrong—he need not in his actions bind himself by his then intention; he need only observe the terms of the contract, and this now that she has guessed wrongly forbids him to return the child. But the question asked of the mother, whether she is going to get her child back or no, need not refer to the animal's intentions; we may conceive of this future as a predestined to-come, so that in itself it is already a settled matter, which of the two possible events is going to occur. Interpreting the question in this way, we get an insoluble perplexity for obvious reasons; for we cannot without absurdity make an issue, which unconditionally impends, depend on a condition, whose fulfilment would necessarily be as ineffectual to bring about—as its non-fulfilment to bar—the inevitable. There is thus but one way out of the dilemma. If the restoration of the child is the event which is going to occur, and if the mother guesses this, all will end happily, yet not because her assertion in any way *conditioned* the happy result: her assertion in itself is quite ineffectual; it has only chanced to agree with the inevitable result and the terms of the bargain. If she had made any other answer, that would only have served to reveal more plainly the utter impotence of a bargain, which because it tries to condition the unconditioned must of necessity be violated. But the old form of the dilemma starts from yet another supposition, different from both of these: it supposes that it is not determined beforehand which of the two alternatives is going to occur, i.e. whether the child is going to be given back or not; that is to be settled by what the mother says. Now logic teaches that in any hypothetical judgment the validity of the consequent rests on that of the antecedent; but the latter must be independently fixed and unambiguous and must neither in its meaning nor its validity be conditioned by the meaning and validity of the consequent. In the case before us this absolute requirement is contravened. For the condition fixed upon here is not an assertion made by the mother but the truth of her assertion, and further not the truth of an assertion which refers to some third fact independent of the future result and which could therefore be true or untrue no matter what this result may be; on the contrary what she asserts is that this result will either occur or not occur,—a result which is connected with no other conditions at all,—and so its own truth depends on the very thing, which should depend on it. Consequently on this supposition as on the former there is only one case which logically admits of a satisfactory issue; the mother must answer, you are going to restore my child; and then its actual restoration at once makes her answer true and fulfils the agreement. In that case the issue is a happy one, but it was not conditioned by the answer she gave. Suppose after all the crocodile does not give back the baby, the very fact of his not doing so makes her answer a false one and at the same time the animal becomes justified according to the terms of the agreement in not giving it back. If however the mother is so unfortunate as to answer: you will not give it back, '*then*' the crocodile must say 'I cannot give it back; the agreement forbids me to, since if I did your answer would become a false one; no more could I restore the child even if your answer could be correct, seeing that by the very fact of my returning it it would become false.' The mother then objects: 'you must in any case give it me; on the score of the agreement, if my answer was correct; but no less if it was incorrect; for it would become a correct answer, if you refused to give it back.' There is no way out of this dilemma; as a matter of fact however both parties rest their cases on unthinkable grounds; for the answer really given can as little be true or untrue independently of the actual result as could the answer she might have given, an answer which only differs from this in being more fortunate.

The dilemma of Protagoras and Euathlus rests on a similar misuse of hypothetical conjunctions of thoughts. Euathlus is to pay for the instruction he has received as soon as he wins his first case; but as he engages in no suits, Protagoras gets nothing and sues him on that account. Now whether Euathlus wins or loses *this* suit, the verdict must in any case either oblige him to do that which the contract releases him from doing or release him from doing that which the contract obliges him to do. Various solutions of the difficulty have been attempted on the supposition that Euathlus is allowed to win this his first suit because he has won no previous suit, and so had not yet become obliged to pay. It was then open to Protagoras to institute a fresh suit, which must have this time led to his pupil being condemned to pay. This would be shifting an absurdity off logic, in order to make a present of it to jurisprudence. I will not anticipate the decision of the latter, but I suspect it would say that in acting as he did Euathlus had fraudulently prevented a certain condition from being realised, according to which he would have been forced to fulfil an obligation. If therefore it could fix a date, after which no other interpretation could be put on his conduct than that it was fraudulent, then though Protagoras no doubt could not base a suit on the contract, the law might well go behind it and taking its stand on the obligation, under which Euathlus really put himself by receiving the instruction, condemn him to pay, just as if the ambiguous agreement had never existed.

CHAPTER VII.

Universal propositions as derived from perceptions.

251. THE ideas which we ourselves have put together are completely open to our inspection and we can review their content and manner of conjunction. And hence the conclusions we draw from them are necessary and the process of conclusion is proof or demonstration, the essence of which is to descend from the more to the less universal and starting from a general truth to end with a particular application thereof. But the conjunctions of phenomena in the world outside us do not carry on their faces the universal laws and conditions of their connexion. They are individual experiences to be severally expressed in particular propositions, and though each embodies an universal principle, yet the path up to that principle must be a matter of search. The simplest form of this ascent in thought is a process with which we have become familiar as the inductive syllogism, and hence it is the custom in our day to collect into one body the numerous operations which assist us in ascending to generals and to call this inductive logic and to set it against the deductive or demonstrative logic along with much disparagement of the latter. Such disparagement rests on a mistake. The inductive methods it is certain are the most effectual helps to the attainment of new truth, but it is no less certain that they rest entirely on the results of deductive logic. It is the theory of the validity of syllogisms, the convertibility and contraposition of judgments, and of the forms of proof, that is the source of each provision and precaution by which so far as may be we secure each step of our paths as we ascend by induction from given perceptions to the universal laws of the real world.

252. The first step of this ascent is barred we are told by an insuperable obstacle. Experience we are told cannot give us universal cognitions, and in one sense no doubt this well-worn saying is true : but if we take it to assert a difference in validity between two sources of knowledge, experience on the one hand and an *a priori* certitude on the other, then the saying is true no longer and is the opposite of truth. Every experience, whose contents in their connexion can be expressed without deficit or surplusage in the form S is P, must *ipso facto* rank as an universal judgment, even if this experience stands absolutely alone. The law of identity guarantees that if the same S were once more perceived in a second experience it would be impossible that the same predicate P should be absent or should be replaced by some other predicate Q. On the other hand it is no less true that experience does not directly present us with perceptions which fulfil this condition. Our perceptions do not give us a subject S in conjunction with a predicate P and nothing more or less than this subject and this predicate. The real and true subject with which the phenomenon we observe is essentially connected is not S but Σ. It has elements s absolutely necessary to the production of the phenomenon and which notwithstanding we do not perceive. What we do observe, S, is a residue and what is more an impure residue, for it comes to us indissolubly joined with elements σ, which have nothing whatever to do with the production of the phenomenon. It is the same with the predicate. The true predicate which attaches to Σ, the true subject, is Π and it we do not perceive. It has features p which are invisible, and the residue P which we do perceive is bound up with other circumstances Π, the results of conditions which have no influence on the matter in question though they are operative at the same time. A complete expression of the actual fact demands addition and subtraction and would run thus $S + s - \sigma$ is $P + p - \pi$ or Σ is Π, while our first defective observation set down S is P as the fact. Only for the complete proposition Σ is Π (supposing this were given in a peculiarly fortunate perception) would universal validity be guaranteed by the law of identity,—not for the incomplete proposition S is P, which puts together what is not really thus connected.

253. It is important to bear this in mind, for apart from it we cannot understand a right, which science claims and which is essential to her development. If the question is as to a predicate Π, which we do not yet know and which we expect to find in a subject Σ, then wherever we are sure that we perceive this subject Σ whole and complete, and nothing else but Σ, we are equally sure that a single observation, which acquaints us with Π, has an universal import and that in every possible case, where the same Σ is repeated, the same Π must unalterably present itself. When the chemist is instituting an experiment, if he only can be sure that he is dealing with one definite substance and applying to it one definite reagent and has excluded the possibility of any foreign conditions influencing the result he is going to observe, then he never doubts that the reaction observed in this single experiment will exhibit itself identically whenever the same circumstances are repeated. He at once assigns to a single perception the rank of an universal truth. When the physicist undertakes a measurement he takes care first of all to eliminate the sources of error, with which, as he well knows, he is beset, but when once he has purified his observation he never dreams of regarding the fact that it comes ultimately from sensible experience as a reason for accounting it valid merely for this one occasion. It never enters into his head that under similar conditions the same object might perhaps on another occasion have a different magnitude. We need not enlarge on this head. Once suppose that a single observed case· is valid only for itself and not for its repetitions in like cases —that the record of an instrument is correct for the one occasion in which it is noted and not equally correct for a second occasion under identical circumstances—once suppose that with like object and like conditions a different result may be true, and there is an end to all possibility of developing universal truths from experience; there is an end not merely to the discovery of laws but to the use of the word 'law' with any intelligible meaning. The art of induction, which is to bring us to universal laws, rests wholly on the acumen shown in developing pure and self-connected propositions of the form Σ is Π out of the impure and confused material of our perceptions, which come to us in the form S is P.

254. Let us try to sketch in a connected series the steps essential to that development. The countless impressions which we receive in succession or together may be taken as an indiscriminate mass Ω. How do we come to distinguish in the mass of them groups A, B and C and to regard each group as a self-connected perception? It is because the impressions we so gather into one are permanently conjoined and thus raise themselves above the level of the shifting background, or again because by their simultaneous appearance at intervals they contrast with the uniform background formed by the others. This first step is a necessary one, but there is so far no act of thought. The mechanical course of our ideas is the agency which singles out these perceptions and first makes them objects of our involuntary attention and of our future thinking. And the result thus reached is proved by subsequent consideration to be wrong as often as right. The really connected is too often but incompletely conjoined and mixed with that which in no way belongs to it. We are impelled in like manner to the second step which consists in splitting up the sum of impressions contained within each of the gronps *A, B* and *C* and in taking one part of each sum as a subject and the remainder as a predicate attaching itself to the subject. It is our psychical mechanism which accomplishes the beginning of this step also. Thought indeed actively intervenes before long and intensifies this mere conjunction of two ideas—this mere adherence of one idea to another—by transforming it into an objective connexion and by establishing an opposition between the subject and predicate, between the former as essentially independent and the latter as dependent and simply attributed. Still it is the mechanical course of our ideas which always guides us in the application of this added principle of thought and which settles in each case which group of impressions is to rank as subject and which as predicate.

Thus articulated the whole content of a perception *A* or *B* might now be expressed in the form of a judgment,—but a singular judgment only. The subject which we here distinguish as s^1 or s^2 is nothing but a perfectly determinate group of single impressions, such a group being the sole possible object of immediate perception, and the thought that either s^1 or s^2 may be taken as the example of an universal conception *S* is an added thought. It cannot originate in an individual perception, but only in the comparison of many which soon begins. And here again, when out of the several subjects $s^1 s^2 \ldots$ the smaller group of attributes common to them all is forced upon our attention till it emerges as a general picture, which is now denoted by the name *S* and which takes the place of those several subjects in our memory,—this also is at first the result of the course of our ideas which is conditioned in a mechanical manner by universal laws. Here too thought adds a new depth, it transforms the general *picture*, which only represented what was found common to the various individuals, into a general *conception* which has the force of a law and joins what is essentially connected: but still it is the course of our ideas that determines the first applications of this added thought, and settles for us which elements of the subjects we compare are to be united in the general picture or again in the conception and which are to remain excluded. The elements which are felt to be modifications of one universal and are at the same time more lively as impressions are accepted, and those which excite our involuntary attention less strongly or reciprocally destroy one another are rejected.

And the result of this process is on the whole more often right than wrong. This is not the place to pursue in greater detail the psychological development of our conceptions, but there is one point worth mentioning. In the sensible impressions, which are the ultimate components of every perception, it is from the first not the differences of the actual impressions that are of prominent importance so much as the differences in their relations and in their manner of union. The mere child can neglect the differences of colour and sees that the characters shown him in red are the same as those he has learned in black. His general pictures of trees and animals are drawn as yet but from few examples, but they already comprehend the essential traits with such accuracy that when he afterwards perceives a new and unusual shape, it readily takes its place in the series. Errors however do occur: how these are corrected is what we have now to consider. We have tried in the foregoing to make clear our starting-point, which is this:—the inductive process deals with individual perceptions and its object is to establish a further connexion between them, but these perceptions are more than mere *impressions* that we *passively receive*. On the contrary they have already been so far worked upon by thought that not only have their contents already been divided by us into subject and predicate, but besides that we have already brought the subject under the head of a general conception S or at least meet it with a selection of such conceptions under one of which we try to bring it.

255. Let us take the last case first. Suppose that a singular subject s^m, new and not yet known, is presented in a perception through the sensible impressions $p^m q^m r^m$, and suppose we have a perfectly clear image both of these particular marks and also of their conjunction. The image if we do not go beyond it does not contain one doubtful element and yet it does not satisfy us. We cannot rest until we know what the new object may be called, whether animal or plant. Our desire to know this is based on a twofold interest. Pure thought is interested; for it is only by subordination under a general conception that the mere coexistence of the observed characteristics is transformed for thought into a well-grounded coherence. But what weighs much more with us is the practical wish to go beyond the observed fact and to justify ourselves by the general conception in filling in what we have not observed. For the name plant or animal would be for s^m a barren title had we not reserved the right to found upon it a claim to a number of properties as belonging to s^m, which no immediate perception has shown to belong to it. We constantly find ourselves in this position towards real objects. For every perception howsoever accurate, let it even apprehend every single mark that s^m now has, is limited as to time. No perception can tell us the future with the present; it can never say what our object will eventually do or become, and can only seldom and incompletely show us how it will alter with altering conditions. The gap that perception leaves in our mind we fill up by subordinating the observed s^m to the conception of plant or animal. These conceptions have sprung from countless observations and they comprehend the whole collection of coexistent attributes, which can scarcely ever, and the successive attributes which can never be exhausted in a single perception. But it is only by the union of all these that we can adequately determine the real nature of s^m, while a single perception of it gives us only an inexplicable fragment of a connected whole.

This process on its formal side is an *incomplete analogy*, and since so considered it argues *ad subalternantem* from the observed sameness of some attributes in S and s^m to the sameness of all, it must be pronounced invalid by the canons of pure logic. None the less our whole daily life depends on the application of this incomplete analogy. We rest secure on it in dealing with substances useful or deleterious; it alone persuades us of the existence of minds like our own and assures us that their actions flow from inner motives such as we feel. And in fact our dependence on it scarcely needs to be mentioned, so plain is it. The practical question is as to the means by which the bare probability of these inferences can be made to approximate in value to certainty. The sameness of all the marks is what logically justifies the subordination of s^m to S, and the natural conclusion from this fact is that the probability of a subordination being correct rises as the number of identified marks is increased. But it is evident at once that the value of this conclusion is much lowered by the necessity of taking into account the difference in value which exists among these marks. And this is not the whole difficulty. It is idle, it is a mere form to bid us direct our attention to the likeness above everything else of the essential marks, when as yet we have no means of distinguishing them from the non-essential. It is experience and experience alone which enables us to distinguish, and the few general rules we can lay down are all drawn from experience. There are attributes, which arise indifferently from the operation of widely-diffused causes on objects vastly heterogeneous, and consequently these marks cannot serve as criteria because not characteristic of the distinctive content, which any one conception connects, and again the modifications of these marks can produce no essential difference in any such content. But how should we know this except from experience? How but from experience should we know that mere quantitative differences in the marks are in the main but of slight importance and that diversities in the forms of conjunction and in the respective positions of those points in which relations centre are a matter of far greater moment? There are universal conditions in the world, which tend to produce similar alterations in different substrata which they encounter, and this gives us a test for the real and exclusive peculiarity of any kind of things. For each genuinely peculiar kind by reason of the specific mode, in which diverse centres of relation are united in it, exhibits unexpected forms of reaction against the universal conditions. Thus specific reaction against non-special conditions is the sign of a genuine kind—but this sign is the teaching of experience. And it is experience once more that informs us that these rules have their exceptions in the case of some object that we perceive. There may be marks that seem unessential and whose variations may appear of no moment, and yet there may be in such trifles the sign of a radical difference pervading the whole nature of two groups of attributes connected under two different conceptions.

In conclusion we must not forget that in trying to range new objects of perception under old universal conceptions we are not unfrequently driven by utterances of the same experience to quite an opposite result. These universal conceptions themselves—animal, plant, body—are altered, their boundaries are widened or contracted as our knowledge of things grows. On the one hand we may find in doubtful instances, which seemed to fall under one of these conceptions, points in which their habit permanently differs from that of the undoubted instances; or again instances which seemed to be excluded may be found to exhibit a gradual and uninterrupted approach to what is the character as a whole of the known and undoubted species. Thus it will be seen that we trust not to universal logical rules but to a knowledge of things for the correct carrying out of the imperfect analogy, by which we class a perceived object s^m under a general conception S. In fact we must distinguish applied logic itself as a theory of science from its application as a scientific activity. The theory can do no more than lay down general points of view, of which we should never have become conscious had we not exercised the activity. Logic therefore cannot step forward and claim to impose its rules on the whole domain of real thought, as if the whole work of the latter was about to begin for the first time; it is of no use to the mind, which has as yet no conceptions at all, but only to the mind, which is already in possession of a manifoldly articulated world of ideas, acquired through its own experience or by tradition. No doubt much interest attaches for the psychologist to the task of explaining how all these conceptions have arisen, but this task does not fall to the theory of science. *Its* rôle is only to establish what is true and certain in these ideas now we have got them; and in as much as many errors and defects must still cling to these rough and ready results of long intellectual development, theory must also point out how these shortcomings may in future be remedied and that which is still doubtful be brought near to certainty.

256. Now if, as we at present assume, the individual perception is so far logically formed, that we at once apprehend the particular object s^m which it portrays as an example of a general conception S, it will engage our attention no further provided that we find in s^m none but marks which belong to S, no matter whether all or only some of them. We shall however be led on to take a fresh step, when we find bound up with s^m in the perception a mark M, which does not belong to the group of attributes conjoined in S, so far as we know S. Experience (here, as I said just now[1], the only authority) teaches us to discriminate three possible

[1] [Section 255.]

cases. In the first place altering conditions or accidental circumstances may have temporarily invested the s^n of our perception with a property, real or merely apparent, which under other circumstances it would not display. Wise with the knowledge we have already won we quietly neglect many points of this kind: the same object wears different aspects according to its position, attitude, movement, distance or illumination, but we do not allow such differences to shake us in our conviction of its identity and its agreement with the general conception S; cases where there is more room for doubt we decide by trying to make observations of the same object under different conditions; it is only an M which adheres to it under all circumstances that is regarded as a permanent mark of its nature. But we still leave it unsettled, whether this M owes its presence to the individual nature of this subject s^m, which after all remains a particular subject, or to the universal nature of the general concept S, of which the observed s^m is a species or an example. To decide between this second and third case we resort to what is called *imperfect induction*; that is we compare s^m with other examples s^1, s^2.. of the same universal S with which we are familiar. In most cases what leads us to make the induction is that a number of individual perceptions $s^1 M, s^2 M, s^3 M$ thrust themselves one after the other on our notice, so waking in us a suspicion that the ground of M is universally to be found in the nature of S, in various examples of which we observe it. This presumption is rebutted, if we find a single subject s^q, which has not the mark M when placed under the same variety of conditions, under which that mark attached to the subjects of the other perceptions. On the other hand all instances of S which have so far been accessible to our perception may possess this predicate M, without our presumption in favour of the truth of the universal proposition, all S are M, being *ipso facto* corroborated. For when we argue that what is valid in a number of particular cases however large is therefore valid universally we always argue *ad subalternantem* and such inference is to the last unsound. Still placed as we are we must hazard such inferences, for even if perception could embrace all existing examples of a genus, those that are yet to be will always evade our senses. Here too then all we can do is to heighten so far as we can the probability of this imperfect induction. In order to this we shall find two rules of kindred import of great use. In the first place the individual subjects from the observation of which we start must be very numerous; the greater the number of such s the more manifold must the outward conditions be which act upon them, and of which we thus eliminate the force and influence. Any M which all these subjects retain in common in spite of such variety of conditions must owe its presence to no extrinsic causes but to the intrinsic nature of these subjects. Secondly we must so choose the subjects we observe that their specific or individual differences shall be the greatest possible within the limits of the genus or the species, the universal S; we thus eliminate the influence which particular resemblances between the observed subjects, which are independent of the nature of the universal S, might have in producing the common predicate. The M which they all unite in retaining in spite of these differences will have its ground solely in the character of the genus itself, and the universal proposition, all S is M, which we wished to arrive at, will thus be justified.

257. Pure logic raised a distinction between analogy and induction. If two subjects agree in respect of several of their marks, we gather that they will agree in all. This is reasoning by analogy. We make an induction on the other hand, when we argue that because several instances of a kind behave in a certain way, therefore all instances of the kind will behave so. We have used the words in the same meanings here, and it was accordingly an induction, by which we drew from the given premises s^1M, s^2M... the universal conclusion SM. But this procedure may be regarded more simply. Suppose we have made a number of observations and have found that all their individual subjects $s^1, s^2 \ldots$ agree in possessing on the one hand all the marks belonging to an S, on the other hand the one mark M; we may then conclude immediately by analogy that every subject s^q, even though we have not observed it, will yet, provided only it like them possesses all the marks of an S, possess also the particular mark M. By such an analogy is it that we supply the premises $s^m M, s^n M \ldots$ not given in the perception, the subjects of which premises together with the subjects of the $s^1 M, s^2 M \ldots$, which we have observed, exhaust the whole compass of S. The business of induction then consists in merely summing up the single propositions thus either given or supplied in the universal proposition: all S are M. We see from this that it is hardly worth while to separate in such applications of logic the part played by induction from the part played by analogy; nor is it worth while to find fault with the loose usage which confounds the two expressions; it is useless in short to try to refer to simple types of pure logic all the operations of thought, which may be broadly included under the name of an inference. One who has time to waste may perhaps enquire whether a voyager, who has sailed all round a land, concludes by induction, analogy, or subsumption, that it is an island. What does interest us here is rather the question, how we arrive at any universal proposition T about triangles. We prove T by constructing the triangle s^1; but this triangle, which we thus set before our eyes, is always a particular triangle, never more. It would seem as if T can in the first instance be true only of it, and always true of it so often as we construct it in the same way. Now we may of course change our mode of drawing it; still even if we found the proposition T corroborated in a thousand different triangles $s^1, s^2, s^3 \ldots$, this number would dwindle to nothing, when compared with the infinite number of possible triangles, which we have no opportunity of testing.

It is not therefore by any summing up of particular perceptions, which we create for ourselves in these constructions, that we reach the conclusion that T is true universally of all triangles whatever. We must be justified in regarding each single triangle we draw as a *symbol* for all, so that what holds of it holds of all the others which it represents. And our justification does not lie in the peculiar nature of spatial perception; that merely supplies the content of T; it does lie in the fact, that we only pay attention in our reasonings to those features, characteristic of the triangle drawn, which we have produced through the very process of constructing it, that is, to its property of being a plane figure, included by three straight lines. The figure actually drawn can never exhibit this property in the abstract and apart from other properties. It can only do so by having sides of definite length and a sum of angles distributed in a certain way. But we do not let these special qualities have any influence on our conclusions; suppose we have unintentionally constructed our triangle with right angles or equal sides, we shall set aside propositions which are valid because of these qualities and these alone, as having nothing to do with the subject of predication which we had in mind. Psychologically no doubt it is the unanalysed impression of resemblance, which prompts us at once to transfer to all triangles by analogy the proposition T proved of the particular triangle we have drawn. Our logical justification for doing so is twofold: first it lies in our consciousness that all triangles, whether already constructed or no, may still be classed under the universal conception of a triangle, which conception we have symbolised in our construction; secondly in the consciousness that in that single symbolic representation we saw the proposition in question flow solely from this conception without any appeal being made to any other conditions.

258. In attaining to universal propositions of the form all S are M, induction has reached its first goal, and it is possible to rest content with the result, especially when we are dealing with a question of practical life; for in such questions we can go without a reason, so long as we are certain that as a matter of fact M is really true of all instances of S, say of all men; we do not care so much to know why it holds of them, and why only of them and not perhaps of animals as well. The theoretic impulse however is not satisfied with merely joining M to its proximate subject; it would fain seek out within the limits of S the narrower group of attributes, which contains the ground of this conjunction, and which conditions the same attribute, wherever it may occur, perhaps even outside S. Then the induction is pushed further; we use a series of universal propositions of the form: SM, RM, TM ... as our new premises and try to deduce from them an universal conclusion of the form all Σ are M. In this new conclusion we understand and denote by Σ the true subject or the conception of the genus, or, to put it in another way, that complex of attributes, on which the predicate M in all cases depends and from which it results. Thus in our first induction we shall reach the proposition SM: in all mammals an exchange of gas takes place in respiration; in a second induction, in which S is successively replaced by birds, fishes, and amphibia, we shall reach the conclusion ΣM, all animals require an exchange of gases. This new conclusion at once throws light on the earlier one, by showing that what we had hitherto only observed as an isolated fact is really necessitated by the universal nature of animal life; a third induction sets alongside of ΣM a new premiss to the same effect, viz. all plants display though in another way the phenomenon of a change of gas; its conclusion $\Sigma^1 M$, all organic beings whatever find themselves in like case, shows us the phenomenon in question bound up with a still more universal subject; and lastly by comparing the behaviour of bodies which resemble organic bodies in structure towards the surrounding atmosphere we might be led to the thought that under the conditions prevalent on the earth's surface, such an exchange of material is absolutely necessary to the development of those interdependent processes of change, which make up organic life. In all this it is to be noticed that the further we advance these inductions, the less do we care to obtain as our result a *categorical* judgment of the form S is P; we are no longer seeking the highest general conception, to which a given phenomenon attaches a predicate; what we are in search of is a *hypothetical* judgment, which will acquaint us with the most general *condition* C, upon which the phenomenon always depends and of which it is the consequence whenever it occurs. And this new problem of discovering the conditions under which the content of a perception coheres is of such preponderating importance in applications of the inductive method, that we shall henceforth in our investigation of that method confine ourselves to the form which it assumes in order to the solution of that problem.

259. Let C and E respectively denote two groups of observed events; we will suppose that something or other in the way in which they appear has awakened in us the presumption—to be subsequently confirmed or corrected—that the two groups are really connected, and that C is or contains the cause of E, and that E is or contains the effect of C; lastly, let us bear in mind the remark we made at the beginning of this chapter (sect. 252), to the effect that C will seldom really contain the full cause of E and nothing but it, E seldom contain the whole effect of C and nothing but it. We may then indicate our problem thus: to discover from the impure observations $C\,E$ the pure case $B\,F^1$ of two terms belonging together of their own nature and related as condition and conditioned; and if we have to define the conception of this pure case we shall say, that in it B is the adequate ground of F, and the ground of nothing else beside F, while on the other hand F is the full consequence

[1] ['Bedingung' and 'Folge.']

of B without being at the same time the consequence of any other ground. In applying this definition we may abate somewhat of its rigour according to the different interests which from time to time rule our investigations. For instance we may be content to know that B as often as it is given produces F, no matter whether it conditions anything else besides F, or whether F can be produced by any other antecedent as well as by B. We shall only be content with such a result, however, where we are merely concerned to know the real *causes* which produce the effect in question. When the question is not as to the real causes, but a theoretical question as to the *ground*[1], owing to which these causes condition that effect as their necessary *consequence*, we shall always have to determine B and F with all the precision aimed at in the definition; even where F may be due to different but equivalent causes it is not that in which these differ that is the true ground of this consequence, for each cause has besides F other and separate effects; only what is common to all of them is the true ground B, and this B has then no other consequence than just this F.

260. From a single impure case $C\,E$ the pure case $B\,F$ can only be guessed by an accidental and happy inspiration: it can be demonstrated with certainty only by a comparison of several different cases. If we can observe a sufficient variety of cases we shall be able to detect elements, which do not really belong to each other and are merely accessory, by the variety and change of the relations they bear to one another. We can then let these unessential elements drop away and retain in its pure form the pure relation $B\,F$, which they all involve. These impure cases form the raw material, on which we go to work, and are mainly supplied by *observation*; but the course of things if left to itself presents us in but few fields of research with the full

---

[1] [Cp. 'Metaphysic,' sect. 51, on the distinction between 'Cause' and 'Ground' or 'Reason.']

number of cases that we should require in order to complete that elimination. It requires long epochs far transcending a single individual's range of observation for many natural processes to unfold the whole series of aspects which one should know in order to grasp the coherence of their conditions. But there are other obstacles to observation besides length of time; in the case of many actual products it is impossible to see how they have become what they are, because they never of themselves permit of being regressively analysed into the conditions out of which they arose. It is not often that we find ourselves so favorably situated as in the case of astronomy. This science has never met with more than accidental obstacles in its accumulation of numberless data in regard to an interdependent and periodic play of events. Yet even astronomy requires, in order to satisfy all its wishes, to be supplemented by observations of the past, and of these it finds but an inadequate supply.

Wherever we can by our own agency influence the object we are investigating we can remedy this want by *experiment*. We can institute at will a certain group of conditions C, and so compel the causes which are really at work to respond with an effect E, which would otherwise perhaps have never come within the domain of our senses. By varying at will the quantity and composition of that C we can bring about in E a series of changes in quantity and kind, which were still less likely to offer themselves unsolicited to our observation. Again we can break up C into its component parts, and in each experiment allow but one of them, or a definitely assignable group of several of them, to take effect, at the same time cutting off the rest from action. The constituent elements of the result E admit of being separated in the same way, so that we learn which of them depends on which element of the compound C. Thus experiment is the practical means by which we furnish ourselves with observations in such number and involving such mutual differences and affinities, as is requisite in order to the elimination of what is unessential in them and the derivation from them of a pure case BF. Defined in this way it is clear that experiment only has an advantage over observation in so far as it is capable of supplementing the usual deficiencies of the latter; its function is to furnish us with suitable and fruitful observations instead of the unsuitable and unfruitful ones which offer themselves. But it would be perverse to ascribe to it any other and mystical use in addition to that; we cannot set it over against observation as a new method of knowledge; it is merely a way of preparing and setting before ourselves phenomena which it is of importance that we should observe. And for the same reason experiment must not be unqualifiedly set above mere observation. In our day it is a prejudice of half-culture to suppose that anything that can be observed in broad daylight, without any preparation, ready to hand and in the gross, remains as a matter of course open to question; that alone is supposed to be true which can only be perceived in microscopic fashion, on a minute scale, after all manner of preparation and under conditions which render it very difficult to perceive at all. Such an assumption is paradoxical, and if elevated into a general principle becomes absurd. Still it is a just assumption to make in certain cases. In particular we can only ensure accuracy in our determinations of quantities by such artificial means, never by coarse observation alone. We must grant all this, but conversely observation often acquaints us with broad characteristics of phenomena, which in experiment would have been obscured by special conditions.

261. I shall now attempt to lay before my reader the various kinds of relation between C and E, with which observation and experiment acquaint us, not in the hope of exhausting them, but in order to illustrate by examples how many and various are the possible cases and the consequences to be drawn from them.

1. The case $(+ CE)$. C and E may be continually

present in reality and continually together; still their mere coexistence, however uniform, does not warrant our concluding that they are so related as to condition each other, though such a relation may perhaps exist between them. Iron and silver and all the other chemical elements are always present in the world together; but it does not follow from this that one of them is the condition of another's existing, or that all of them collectively are joint effects of a single cause. At best the philosopher, for certain speculative reasons, which we cannot enter into now, may question the possibility of there being a plurality of elements coexisting yet unconditioned in any way by one another. But the primary use of induction is to understand nature, and the scientific understanding refuses to accept mere coexistence as evidence of an ulterior connexion. We find, moreover, that in each single one of these elements various properties or modes of action are uniformly combined. For example, all have in common the property of gravitation, and each in particular has as well its special affinities to all the rest. This case is not the same as the last; here we have one and the same subject, with different properties coexisting in it as its own. This oneness of the thing forbids us to suppose that the several attributes found in it have no reference to one another, and there is thus awakened in us the natural tendency of thought to explain one of these properties by the other or both by a third original one, which under different conditions transforms itself into those two. We will not at present fix the goal to which this logical impulse may lead us in the future; for the present it remains just an impulse which leads to nothing so far; for so long as our observations reveal to us nothing else than the perpetual coexistence of both predicates, they do not supply us with the means of showing the nexus of conditions, which perhaps exists between the two or between them and a third.

2. The case $(+C+E)$. C and E are present together,

not uninterruptedly, but in frequent recurrence. In such a case it may be mere coincidence that brings them together without there really being any reciprocal connexion between them, each resulting from a separate condition. This is what we shall conclude with regard to the many mischances which befall us on Friday, and with regard to countless other superstitions of the sort. But we do not acquiesce in such a conclusion, if we can conceive of any real connexion between the C and E thus found together, and if there is any hope of finding out their connexion. We never think of acquiescing in it unless we shortly afterwards learn from further observations that their association is quite exceptional and abnormal. In itself the hypothesis of mere coincidence is the least probable of any; whenever phenomena occur frequently and repeatedly together there is probably a causal relation; it only remains difficult to decide whether one of the two C and E is cause or effect of the other, or whether both are not mere co-effects of a third cause Z. This doubt remains even when C' and E appear not simultaneously, but after one another in a definite sequence in all cases of repetition. In that case C may no doubt be the cause of E, but both may also be joint effects of a third Z, which is not uniform, but undergoes changes, which succeed one another in a definite order. Day and night always follow on each other in this way, yet they do not produce one another, but are successive joint effects of the earth's revolution on its axis. Lastly, it may happen that E has always remained unnoticed, and only meets our observation when C occurs; thus the heart always beats in a living person, but a healthy man hardly ever feels it, unless a special excitement C supervenes; then C is not indeed the cause of E, but the condition of its meeting our observation.

3. The case $(-C+E)$. Doubts are left unsolved by the last case, which can only be settled by further observations which present themselves or are procured by experiment.

We may find that E also occurs without C, or that C may be experimentally suspended, without at the same time suspending E. In such a case we cannot of course conclude that C is not the cause of E, though we may conclude that it is not its sustaining cause. The former conclusion would be a hasty one; we should appeal in justification of it to the principle: *Cessante causa cessat effectus*, but the only clear meaning which can be given to this principle is that with the cessation of a cause will cease those effects which the cause would have continued to produce had it continued to exist. That effects once generated are not all alike in this respect is shown by the simplest examples; a movement continues after the shock has ended, which produced it; the boiling of water ceases when the supply of heat abates, which produced it and is required as its constant sustaining cause. A child does not die with the death of its parents, the sole causes of which its existence could be the effect; but the equilibrium of a supported weight is lost when the supports are withdrawn. We need not at present analyse these cases any further; we can refer them all to an universal law of persistency[1], which in reference to our present problem we thus express: every reality, which has once been produced, of whatever kind it may be, continues to last, unless counteracting causes annul it. The effects which a cause produces do not therefore stand in need of a cause to sustain them so long as they consist in states of a subject which are in equipoise not only with the permanent nature of that subject, but with the external conditions under which it exists. They do require such a sustaining cause however, if there prove to be either in that nature, or in those conditions, forces which by their influence tend to transform it. If therefore E lasts on after C has ceased to be, three cases are possible: either there is no causal interdependence between the two at all, or else C is indeed the cause which produced though not

---

[1] [Cp. 'Metaphysic,' sect. 162.]

the cause which sustains the effect E, and in this case again C is either a productive cause alongside of other productive causes, or it may be the sole cause capable of producing C.

4. The case $(+C-E)$. C may be observed to occur without being followed by E, but there is of course nothing in that to attract our notice, unless it conflicts with our usual experience, i.e. unless C and E have been observed, as a rule, to occur in conjunction with each other. In such a case it may be that C is not the cause of E, and we then, by drawing this new conclusion, correct the earlier one, which we had formed from our observations to the contrary. The connexion of causes and effects in reality however is not the same as that between ground and consequent in the field of abstract thought. There every ground, which holds at all, bring about its consequence not partially but wholly, and also in such a way that the whole of it can be perceived in the result. Two grounds may be operative at once, e.g. a quantity g may have as its conditions two equations determining its relation to x and must satisfy both. The influence of the second equation will then always show itself in this way, that of the many values of g, which the first alone left possible, it will leave over but a single one or a definite number of these conjoined in a regular manner. A change E on the other hand, which must follow in reality from the cause C, can always be set aside by a countercause Z so that it is lost to perception. We cannot say that Z annihilates the capacity which C has of producing an effect, for C can only be restrained from producing its effect E, so far as it reacts itself on the restraining Z; in this Z it always brings about another effect E^1, instead of E, which we expected, or it assumes itself, under the joint influence of Z and of its own tendency to produce an effect, a state E^1, which it would not otherwise assume. But this E^1 is very often of such a nature as wholly to withdraw itself from direct observation; in that case E seems to be altogether absent,

while C is present; as a matter of fact E has only changed its form. This is invariably the case when moving forces meet with a fixed obstacle; they then seem to have no effect, whereas they really exert a strong pressure on the resisting body. If then we find that E fails to follow on C, it may be of course that there is a want of any causal connexion between the two at all, and in that case we must put a different interpretation on the sequences of C and E, which we have observed. But C may also be one or even the sole cause producing E and yet be prevented from bringing about E by a counterforce Z. This shows how much need there is of being circumspect, of looking round in every case of the sort to see, whether in place of E we cannot discover an effect E^1, which but for the obstacle it reveals would be absent. Lastly, when we institute C experimentally, and do not find that E ensues, and at the same time can find no trace of a E^1 taking its place, we are justified in concluding that C is not a cause capable of producing E at all.

5. The case $(-C-E)$. So far as mere observation goes the simultaneous absence of C and E will seldom strike us as noticeable, and when it does it will be because it conflicts with what we remember experiencing in the past. If however C has been constantly present and we find that when it ceases to appear E vanishes as well, the most natural thing to suppose is of course that C is at least the condition which sustains if not the condition which produces E, or may be that C and E are both joint effects of a third cause Z, and they both vanished because it has ceased. If E ceases to appear when we suspend C experimentally, the former alone of the two alternatives seems possible; still it may be otherwise. When we talk of a cause which has been active hitherto being suspended we may mean something more than that it just ceases. To effect such suspension we often have to take positive precautionary measures, and the new influence thus brought

into operation may, while suspending C, at the same time create new conditions paralysing the further action of causes, to which though quite distinct perhaps from C, the presence of E was all along really due. Such new conditions would result in the suspension of E as well. There was a prolonged controversy between those who maintained that infusoria are generated from an infusion of organic matter without germs of their own kind being present beforehand, and those who contended that their generation was conditional on the presence of spores or seeds adhering to the organic substance itself, or conveyed by the atmosphere, or contained in the water. The only way to settle the dispute was to show that the generation E of infusoria ceases when all access C of spores or seeds capable of producing life is cut off. They cut it off by boiling the water along with the organic substances and introducing air through red-hot tubes. The use of such means no doubt ensured the absence of living germs from all the three bodies concerned in the result; at the same time they were so violent that in excluding the germs they might also have rendered inoperative the causes which the counter theory assumed, viz. the inherent capacity of organic matter of developing into living organisms. The experiment therefore required to be modified in such a way as to eliminate the doubt.

6. The case $(+E+C)$. In none of our conclusions thus far have we established more than that C is a cause of E; that it is the sole cause, so that the converse of the proposition is true, and every E is the effect of a C, could only be ascertained by some method of exclusion, by which we could make sure that no other conceivable causes have the effect E. This exclusion is never possible with regard to the countless *proximate* causes, which are to be found at work in nature. We could not think of it till the elaboration of our perceptions was so much advanced as to have revealed to us a number of universally operative

forces, which could be exhausted in a complete disjunction, to some modification of which forces every result whatever would be wholly due. Nevertheless inductive science frequently arrives at such convertible propositions; when in several cases it has found C to be the cause of E, it assumes that an E, of which it does not observe the cause, is to be referred as an effect to the same C. Logicians cannot be gainsaid when they declare it to be wrong to do so according to the canons of formal logic. For it is quite clear that the particular judgment, many E are effects of C, in no way warrants our concluding *ad subalternantem*, that all E are effects of C. Nor can the hypothetical judgment, if C exists, E exists, be converted simply into the judgment, if E exists, C exists. But we would remind those who would lay too much stress on this fact that the scientific enquirer in drawing the conclusions here impugned does not pretend to be following the abstract ideal of a perverse logic. His knowledge of things and of the universal ways in which natural events do as a matter of fact usually occur, is so ample that he feels himself justified in making good any short-comings, which such conversion may have in respect of formal logical validity. There *might* be in nature, he would say, a hundred similar effects due to a hundred different proximate causes, only it is not so in fact; as a matter of fact similar effects flow from causes which do not resemble each other merely in being *able* to produce these similar results, but this ability itself depends upon an ulterior similarity between the causes.

We hardly need dwell on this any longer. In order to make up for what our conclusions lack in point of mere logical cogency, we appeal to the fulness of the knowledge we have already actually acquired, and such an appeal must obviously carry with it enormous weight. On the other hand we must bear in mind that the justification so derived has its limits. Newton has expressed the principle in question in his second rule as follows: 'effectuum naturalium ejusdem generis eædem sunt causæ.' I think we may without lessening our respect for his immortal genius confess that this formula by no means fulfils from a logical point of view those requirements of precision, which as a mathematician he knew so well how to satisfy. We do not forget that this rule is not put forward as a logical law, but just as a rule or practical maxim of natural philosophy, probably called forth by the brilliant discoveries which it preludes. But even as such it is not a little indefinite and every single one of its terms needs to be explained. To begin with, the words *idem genus* require to be defined, so that we may know what *effectus naturales* belong to the same and what to a different genus. I do not lay much stress upon that, nor can we even in logic altogether dispense with some such vague impressions; for the rest we interpret it in this connexion in the sense that merely quantitative differences would not make a difference of kind between processes resembling each other in form. But what are *effectus naturales*? If by these words we understand every natural event so far as it is referred as an effect to any cause whatever, the whole proposition which ends with the words *eædem causæ* is evidently untenable, so long as this last conception is left indefinite. If in the *idem genus* we include as we did just now quantitatively different results, these can only have *causas ejusdem generis*, not *causas easdem*; the causes no less than the effects must differ from each other in respect of quantity. But this is not all; the necessity of their being *ejusdem generis* is rebutted by the most common experiences, which teach us that causes may often differ widely from each other and yet be equivalent and bring about one and the same kind of effect. Suppose the velocity with which a body B approaches a point C to be uniformly accelerated, this much is of course clear and necessary, that some force must act on it able to produce this and just this effect; but of how many different kinds may the forces be which do this! They can act as a pull *a fronte* from the point C, they may also act on B as a push *a tergo*, so as to drive it towards C. The former mode of effect may be due to the forces of electricity or gravity, the latter to a series of self-accumulating shocks. If we persist in regarding all these causes as *easdem* or as *ejusdem generis*, because in spite of their essential differences in other respects they all agree in producing just this one effect, we not only use words in a very improper way, but we turn the rule into a trivial tautology. For it is obvious that all causes, which are to have effects of the same kind, must at least be so far themselves of the same kind as to be each and all of them capable of producing these effects; they must therefore be equivalent as regards this effect. This is a mere deduction from the law of identity and as such requires no special maxim of physical science to enforce it; such a maxim should it is evident represent something as in point of fact true, which on formal logical grounds is *not* necessary; that is to say, in this particular case, such a maxim will assert that the causes of similar natural processes are not only similar in reference to these events, but are also similar independently of them. But as we have just seen, there are experiences which prove that what *this* maxim asserts cannot be universally true.

There is still another sense however in which the words *effectus naturales* may be used; they may mean not so much natural processes as processes in nature, that is to say not such events as incidentally arise on a petty scale out of the application of physical laws to fortuitous groupings of conditions, but such processes as have their abiding place in the grand theatre of nature, processes which would be considered ends of nature by anyone, who felt himself justified in using this conception. There is nothing in Newton's language to force us to interpret it in this way, but that something of the sort was before his mind is probable from the prominent position he gives his rule in the introduction to a work, which was intended to embrace in one vast intuition those very abiding, all-embracing, and all-determining events of nature as a whole, which we have described,—we mean the revolution of the planets, the path our earth pursues, and the unceasing tendency of bodies to fall or press toward each other. Viewed in this light the above proposition would not be a direct rule to guide us in our investigations, but the expression of an actual fact, of which the existence has indirectly a controlling influence on the path investigation will strike out; we mean of the fact that there are at work in the world not an infinite number but a very small number of highest and most universal mutually independent causes, to one of which every group of interrelated effects is in the gross to be referred, though in detail one and the same effect is not always due to the same cause but may be due to very diverse equivalent proximate causes. It would still be difficult to fix the line of demarcation separating those great causes from these petty ones; nor would it be less difficult to make out what part of the proposition thus interpreted most deserves to be insisted on, that which points to the sameness in kind of the highest or that which points to the difference in kind of the proximate causes. Anyhow the scientific praxis of Newton is so admirable, that we do better to try to emulate it than to make a superfluous parade of its general maxims.

I will return to an instance. A chemist observes that a particular element C yields the reaction E; he then finds that a strange body, which he is examining for the first time, exhibits the same reaction E; he infers from this that the body in question is C, and this inference so far from being based on the simple conversion of that observation rests on the consciousness, which he has, of having already tested all the elements to be found on earth, and of having got this particular reaction E from none of them except from C. This proof by exclusion is not in a formal sense absolutely safe, but yet carries with it great probability.

If a new element C^1 is discovered, which gives the same reaction as C, he is so much the wiser, and forthwith looks about for some other test, by which to distinguish the two. Not quite the same amount of probability attaches to the conclusion drawn from spectrum-analysis. It is argued that materials, which in the spectra of the heavenly bodies produce the lines E, are identical with those terrestrial elements, which in a gaseous state display the same lines E in their spectra. Now we have not experimented with those non-terrestrial substances, and so we cannot be sure as we were sure in the former case that there are not several elements, differing in other respects yet agreeing in having this one reaction E. It is very probable there are not, because we know of no instance of one terrestrial element having the same lines in its spectrum as another without being the same element, besides which the bodies of our solar system may be regarded as connected fragments of what was once a single mass. Many bodies that are chemically quite different display the same colors in a light which falls upon or passes through them, and this proves that the capacity in question, i.e. the capacity of reflecting, absorbing, and transmitting different waves of light, does not cohere quite simply with the chemical nature of substances. On the other hand two elements are not attended with peculiar effects E or E^1, merely because the one is called or is Potassium, the other Sodium. The truth is that the only reason for their being or being called the one or the other is that the universal forces, with which bodies assert themselves against one another, occur in the two bodies in question with specific coefficients of different magnitude. But, it may be objected, there are conditions, which we cannot reproduce in any experiment. Under such conditions,—e.g. in the temperature prevailing on the sun's surface,—might not one of these coefficients, by the combination of which one element is characterised, assume a value which under terrestrial conditions it would only exhibit for another element? The result would be that different elements might occasionally exhibit the same lines in their spectra. All this is not so utterly unlikely, and so we cannot banish all doubt from our minds as to the glimpse into the constitution of the heavenly bodies, which spectral analysis has vouchsafed to us.

7. The case $(-E-C)$ would agreeably to our use of symbols mean, that we argue backwards from the absence of an effect E, which in other observations we found to follow on C, to the absence of C. There is no need of further explanation; all we can correctly infer from the absence of E is this, that although there may possibly be many different causes C^1, C^2, C^3 . . ., all capable of producing E, no one of them has been actually operative, either because no one of them existed or because each and all of them met with obstacles, which rendered the production of E impossible; the latter alternative is settled as before, according as traces are or are not to be found of another effect E^1, which takes its place.

262. Now supposing that in one of the ways described it has been set beyond a doubt that C either is or contains the cause of E, this last question can only be answered by repeated observations and experiments, by which we shall test one after another the several elements of C and see what is the effect of each. We may have no difficulty in distinguishing these elements, or we may only be able to separate them by means of artificial arrangements. In order to this we substitute for the cause C and effect E two equivalent composite groups consisting of the events $a+b+d$ and $\alpha+\beta+\delta$ respectively. The relations which result are manifold. The following are some of the simplest cases and will serve as examples.

1. The case $(C-a=E)$. The material analogy conveyed by these symbols is plain. They signify that the absence or experimental suspension of one part a of the cause C produces no change in the effect E. If this be

really the case, if, that is to say, the E now observed be exactly the same as the E formerly observed, we shall naturally conclude and shall be perfectly justified in concluding that a has nothing to do with producing the effect. But this is just what we do not always find; we are now dealing with all these cases simply with regard to the manner in which they appear to our observation, and we must remind the reader that very often the effect, so far as we can observe it, remains unchanged, whereas in fact the real effect has through the suspension of a undergone a change into E^1. Suppose six cords of equal length are fastened to the corners of a regular hexagon, on which is slung a weight. If we then remove the first, third, and fifth cords, the weight will, if the remaining cords are strong enough, not only remain hanging, but will appear to maintain its absolute place in space. Yet the latter is certainly not the case; the tension of the three remaining cords is increased, and as they have stretched a little the weight itself has sunk slightly in a vertical direction, and herein consists just the new effect E^1, which has taken the place of E; the difference between the two is lost to a superficial observer; who is led to conclude wrongly that the three other cords contributed nothing to the original effect E, whereas in point of fact the work which they did before has but been vicariously undertaken by the other constituent parts of C. It is hardly requisite to notice how common an error it is to suppose, because an effect is so minute as almost to escape our notice, that it therefore does not exist at all. Such an error always avenges itself on us later, and the risk we run of falling into it is so obvious that all kinds of methods are resorted to in order to magnify these slight effects and bring them within the range of our perception.

2. The case $(C-a=-E)$. It is found that on a vanishing in the observation or on its being experimentally suspended the whole of E vanishes. In such cases we naturally incline to the assumption that a alone is actively

concerned in bringing about or at any rate in sustaining E. That this may be the case, but is not so universally, we learn by comparing this with other observations; let us instead of a cause the other parts of C to vanish one after the other; then we shall often find that the whole E disappears in exactly the same way with the intermission of b and d; from which we gather that it depends not upon a single part of C, but upon the simultaneous presence and conjunction of all or at any rate of several of them. Every complex machine, every living body affords an example of this; in both there are many parts the lesion of any one of which is enough to put an end to the motion of the one and the life of the other, although no one of them by itself would have been able without the co-operation of the rest to produce and sustain motion and life. The fact that with the destruction of a single part of the brain a a definite spiritual function ceases is no proof that just this single part was the organ, which produced that function; even the counter experience, that no lesion of other single parts has the same result, does not render this conclusion perfectly certain; it always remains possible, that a was no more than the indispensable part, in which the effect of all the rest took just this form E. The function must then cease just as much when a is hampered as when all the remaining parts besides a of the brain are hampered in the discharge of their functions. In order to settle whether it is so or not, we must try to observe the changes of E into E^1, which arise when a is left undisturbed, while the functions of the remaining organs are checked in their action.

3. The case $(C-a=E+\alpha)$. The part a disappears in our observation from C or is by experimental means made to lapse, whereupon the effect E acquires a new element α which it had not before, or anyhow an effect α now arises for the first time; we may then conclude that the remaining parts of C involve the ground to which α is due, but that a hindered that ground from taking effect in such a way that

on the removal of a, α can for the first time exhibit itself. But the observation does not entirely justify the conclusion; for it remains open to doubt, whether when a disappeared a new and hitherto unnoticed condition Z did not enter, which alone has to do with the production of α, a being capable neither of producing α nor of arresting it. We set aside this doubt by an experiment, which makes us sure that the means we took to suspend a really produced no other or further effect than this negation of a, and did not at the same time contain a positive influence Z, to which the appearance of α can be attributed. Whenever a state of equilibrium is destroyed by removing one of the forces which preserved it, we have an instance of this; in the economy of living functions also Physiology meets with a variety of such cases. Suppose the severing of a nerve elicits violent movements, and that we can make sure, as in this case we can, that the act of severance has not produced any lasting and positive excitement, but has only annulled an influence which was active before; in such a case we cannot help believing that the organisation is so planned that one function holds another in check, and we therefore refer the movements observed to the removal of the check. There is much in history, which, if we consider it, leads us to take the same view. Of course there are positive stimuli, which have driven mankind along a certain path of historical development, but the majority of great and violent revolutions are due to the removal of checks, which prevented ever present tendencies and feelings from unfolding themselves; and even those positive impulses for the most part only guide events for a while in their particular directions; after a time everything takes another turn, because unwittingly and unintentionally the given impulse has removed or weakened the checks which restrained forces of quite a different kind and of a different tendency.

4. The case $(C-a=E-\alpha)$. This case does not require considering afresh, but has already been dealt with under

the second and third heads. If the suspension of a part a of C occasions the disappearance of a part α of the effect, a and α must necessarily be connected as cause and effect, and a may be the exclusive cause of α and α the exclusive effect of a, so that a is the cause adequate to produce or sustain α; but it may be that a is only either the one or the other combined with the remaining parts of C, and this last may continue to be the case, even when counter experiments shew that any other part of C may be suspended without α being annulled in the same way, for the parts which still remain may serve as substitutes for the parts set aside. And this is not all. It may be that a does but indirectly condition α, as in the third case; then another part of C, perhaps $d+f$, is the cause which produces and sustains α, only a third part b arrests the action of $d+f$, while finally this check in turn is balanced by a in such a way that the removal of a enables the counteracting force of b to suppress α. All the other conditions of life C may be left unimpaired, yet if only oxygen a be withdrawn, the living functions of the animal body are suspended, without so visibly altering its structure in other respects as a different cause of death might alter it. No one has ever ventured to infer from this fact, that oxygen by itself produces life; it was plain that it could only produce life in union with the constituent parts of the body, that is, as a stimulus acting upon these, or as one collateral cause among many. There were some however who ascribed to it a more positive *rôle*; it was they declared the very stimulus, which by its direct influence awakens and elicits those organic movements, of which life is the totality. It has been impossible to confute this interpretation of the facts altogether; but it is certainly not the whole truth; it only shares in the truth along with another view according to which the influence of oxygen consists in the removal of obstacles, which these functions themselves throw in the way of their own further continuance, owing to their consumption of the organised materials.

5. The case $(C+a=E)$. If a fresh cause a be added to C without having been before contained therein, the aggregate effect E can only remain unmodified under certain conditions, which are the same as those under which, in the first case, the lapse of a constituent part a until then contained in C left E unaltered. Two cases are possible. Either there is to be found in the observation, while a is present in it, a Z which escapes our notice although it cancels the effect of a, or our experiment is at fault and we have not succeeded in introducing a in such a way that it can exhibit its effect. If however a is really active the aggregate E must be really altered into E^1, but this change may either withdraw itself from observation or it may not affect the particular part of the aggregate E, to which in our negligence we alone directed our attention, in which case it will equally pass unnoticed.

6. The case $(C+a=E+\alpha)$. A fresh element a, on being added to the causes C which have thus far operated, gives rise to the fresh element α in what was the effect E. It may then be that a is by itself the sufficient cause which would produce the effect α in the objects in question. But it may also be the case that a, like the last drop which makes a cup overflow, is no more than the cause which completes the tale, so that neither those previous causes without it, nor it without them, would have brought about this result. Lastly, it may happen, that the effect E or more generally the fact E, which by being augmented by α passes over into E^1, is neither a mere state nor an event ever repeating or continuing itself in the same way. It may itself be a process of development or growth, which once generated by a group of causes C is forthwith constrained by the nature of the objects, on which these causes act, to transform itself from E into E^1; in that case a is an idle addition to C, or such an addition as may no doubt have its effect on other occasions, but on this has nothing to do with the entrance of α. When we introduce into a patient's system the drug

a we are left in doubt, whether the favourable turn *a* taken by the disease is due to the reputed efficacy of the drug, or whether the disease would not have taken the same turn without *a* at all. It is not altogether easy to settle such a doubt, because in this case the possibility of experiment is confined within such narrow limits. If we have once observed that in several cases the desired result has ensued upon the introduction of *a*, we shrink from the experiment of omitting what may be but is not certainly superfluous. On the other hand counter experiences may offer themselves unsought and seem to prove that *a* is not wanted, and yet not remove the ambiguity. The cases compared are seldom of quite the same kind, and it can hardly be proved that the *a* which is now left out has not found a substitute in some Z of equivalent influence. We meet with similar embarrassment in dealing with social and historical phenomena; it is difficult to decide whether a new turn taken by events is to be attributed to a measure or occurrence *a*, which is observed to precede it. Still harder is it to discover wherein the efficacy of *a* in all cases consists, and what collateral conditions involved in C favour it and render it possible.

7. The case $(C+a=C+b)$. The causes have an element C in common, but have also distinct elements *a* and *b* which differentiate them. It is impossible that two such causes should have exactly the same effect, but it is quite possible that of their aggregate effect a certain portion on which we fix our attention is the same, or lastly that so much of this portion as falls within our observation is the same. Such is the case which I denote by the above formula. The most obvious conclusion to draw from it is of course that both causes produce a like effect in virtue of their like element, and that so far as regards this effect their dissimilarity is without influence. I hardly need say that this conclusion is very often the correct one, even when two or more causes have nothing else in common than just

a few attributes, while *a* and *b*, in which they disagree, dilate into clusters of very many attributes. But it may be that C by itself alone never produces or sustains the like effect we spoke of; in order to do so it may always require to be backed up by *a* or *b* or *d*, in which case we must regard the latter elements as equivalent and companion causes of E. It may even be the case that the part C, which remains the same in different causes, is quite inoperative as regards E and that E is entirely dependent on the unlike elements of the two. Let three forces act on a particle situate in a fixed plane, the one of them C acting along a line vertical to the plane, the other two *a* and *b* along divergent lines in the plane; we may then quite well substitute for the two latter forces others, which give the same resultant. The first force *d*, the only one common to both systems of forces, is at the same time the only one which does not help to determine the direction and magnitude of the resultant. It is universally true that any balance of forces and any movement admits of being resolved in a thousand ways into very different combinations of particular causes. It may of course be objected that in all such cases *a*, *b*, and *d* are not so widely different from each other as to be disparate, that they still involve a common element x in spite of their differences. This x we shall be told must be reckoned as belonging to the common C, and then $C+x$ will always be the true cause of the like effect E. It may be answered that such an objection though true is yet irrelevant, for it amounts to no more than a restatement of what in the abstract is a truism, viz. that like *consequents* always have like *grounds*. In this connexion however we are dealing not with the abstract but with the concrete, and are concerned to know the guise in which these like grounds of like consequences appear in the actual observation, and we found just now that the like elements or attributes in two causes are not always the vehicle of these like grounds. On the contrary these like grounds are in fact often concealed in the combination of *prima facie* unlike elements, attributes, or conditions. These ambiguities then must be got rid of by means of collateral experiments. We must know whether C alone is able to produce or sustain E; if it is, then of course it does not necessarily follow that a and b are without effect, but they are anyhow elements in the cause, which we could do without, inasmuch as we then get the case $(C - a = E)$ and its consequences as above considered. We must know furthermore if a and b alone produce E or no; if they do, then agreeably to the same first case C is not necessarily inoperative, though it will be no more than a contributing cause of E, which might be dispensed with. If neither the one nor the other is the case, then $C+a$, $C+b$, $C+d$ are pairs of mutually indispensable contributing causes of E, and it is now time, by new combinations of our perceptions or by varying the experiments, to find out what is the common element x in a, b, and d, and perhaps also what is the particular element c in C, which together constitute the true and sufficient cause $c+x$ of the identical effect E.

263. By means of the inferences which we have thus far passed in review, we shall not always be able to determine even the proximate and sufficient causes of an effect, much less to find out the sort of causal tie, which holds the two together. To do both is our end and aim and we shall come nearer to reaching it, if we can observe the *changes of quantity* on the part of the effects, which attend changes on the part of the causes. There is scarcely any sort of effect, which does not admit of some quantitative change or other. Even such effects as do not directly display a more or a less, may be made to do so indirectly. Thus a state of equilibrium cannot be more or less equilibrium, but it may oppose a greater or less resistance to any attempts made to destroy it, or the force needed to maintain it may vary. As before, I group together the simplest cases we can observe by way of example.

1. The case ($mE = mC$). Let us represent to ourselves once more the pure case, which we before denoted by BF and may now denote by CE. This formula means that C is the whole cause and nothing else than the whole cause of E, E the whole effect and nothing but the effect of C. Assuming then that both terms admit of direct quantitative determination, we regard it as a self-evident principle that like differences between two values of C will find a response in like differences between corresponding values of E, C and E thus standing in simple direct proportion to one another. Then mE will be $= mC$. This formula is no mathematical equation but a logical symbol and presupposes that the effect no less than the cause is capable of being measured by a standard of its own suited to its nature and permissible in its case. It asserts that if this is so the unit of the effect E is contained in any effect whatever exactly the same number of times as the unit of the cause C is contained in the cause which operates to produce that effect. This relation however is self-evident only in cases where a number m of particular causes C produce, each by itself, the same effect E, and where all we do is to add up the sum of these separate effects, which will then be proportional to the sum of the causes. Suppose we pay away the same amount C of money on m different occasions, and each time for the same amount of goods E, then assuming that prices remain stationary, the total bought will be mE when the total spent is mC. Let us take another example. Suppose m to be equal but separate impacts which act on the same number of different elements and give to each of them the velocity E, then the sum of all the velocities produced will be $m.E$, or the amount of the motion generated will be $m.E$, if we regard the number of elements as the index of the mass. It is otherwise if the several causes and their effects are actually bound up with one another. A lump sum mC will buy more goods than would the same sum in m separate purchases. Here there intervene complicated commercial

considerations, which enhance its value in the eyes of the seller; in the abstract it remains true that each C is no more than the condition and adequate ground of a single E; this is the only consequent which in the abstract the ground justifies, it is only in the real effect that it is modified by those accessory causes. In the same way an impulse C may give a body the velocity E, but mC if it acts on the body all at once is not unlikely to shatter it instead of moving it forward. mC always remains the rational ground of the velocity mE, but the result is modified by other circumstances consisting in the texture of the body. There is only one condition under which it is self-evident that we can expect the cause mC to be followed by its due effect, the motion mE, viz. that we may regard a material element as the mere substratum of motion, destitute of any native power of reaction of its own. We may put it in a general way thus. In applying our principle we suppose the m fold cause to be equal to m particular causes C, and assume that there are no circumstances of any sort present, which would compel a single element in this sum to take more or less or other effect than if it were present alone and the rest of the terms not there. The m fold cause will then produce the m fold effect, and conversely in cases where our observations reveal this relation approximately we may be pretty sure that we have before us a pure case CE, which is identical in the sense specified with a pure causal relation BF.

2. The case $(E = \mathfrak{C})$. It is often the case that a cause C acts on the same object t times, t being understood to mean either the number of times this action regarded as momentary is repeated, or the number of time units, in each of which the continuous force C produces a certain degree of effect. Now if this force is of such a kind as to allow the object exposed to its influence to remain identically the same, the same effect would take place afresh in the object every fresh time we let the same cause operate on it. Thus after the cause had operated t times

or after the time t had elapsed there ought to be present in the body t times as much effect, provided that is that agreeably to the law of persistence every earlier given effect is preserved and not annulled by any counteracting force. This is the case with motion in space, in the case of which we presuppose that the causes producing motion either do not change the object moved or only bring about in it inner states, which throughout exercise no counteracting influence upon its assumption of new motions e. If by the effect E we understand the velocity generated, E will always $= e.t$ and depend on the time. Now for an opposite case. A constant cause C acts continuously on an object during a certain time t, during the whole of which time the object maintains an uniform state E, always equal to the constant C. Such a case cannot be a pure one; besides C there must be contributing causes or conditions Z, which cancel the influence of the law of persistency and render it impossible for the particular impulses to accumulate, and thus would leave the effect E constant and independent of the time. One more example. A cold body grows warm under the rays of the sun, and is then found to maintain a constant temperature for any length of time during which it is further exposed to the same rays. The mere incidence of the rays cannot have caused this phenomenon; it is only accountable for on the hypothesis of a companion cause, namely the radiation which proceeds from the heated body: when it has once reached a certain temperature relative to its surroundings it is obliged by the law of radiation to give out in its turn just so much heat as it continues to receive.

3. The case $(dE = \dfrac{m}{E} dC)$. There is really no case except that of simple movement through space in which we can assume that the effect produced in the object a will not in any way prejudice the effect immediately to follow. In general this a is changed by the first operation

into a: and this fact, that the object that receives the effect does not remain the same, constitutes a variable concomitant condition Z, which associates with each fresh impulse of the cause C effects of which each is more different from the first than that which it succeeds. Let us first assume that the change of a into α is of such a kind as to tend to thwart the next operation of the cause, in the same way as an already compressed body offers resistance to any fresh compression, as the mutual approximation of its elements increases the repulsions operative between them. The measure of this resistance cannot be a constant quantity independent of all the agencies, which here co-operate. It must on the one hand be proportional to the specific intensity of the inner repulsions, to which the resistance is due and which are different for different bodies; on the other hand it must be proportional to the amount of compression already effected, since it is this which by bringing the elements closer to one another in the manner described intensifies their mutual repulsions. In the former of these two conditions we get a constant coefficient for the influence which the cause C may still exert, a coefficient which depends on the nature of the object a; the other condition compels the amount of such a subsequent influence to stand in inverse ratio to the amount of the result E already attained to, and this last amount itself continues to depend in case of two different causes C and C_n on their respective amounts. Now natural causes are never quite instantaneous in their action. We can analyse every C into a number of dC, which are successive, though for the rest their distribution in time is arbitrary. Each of these fractions dC of the cause would if it acted singly produce a corresponding and constant fraction of the effect $dE = m \cdot dC$, but inasmuch as each of them acts on an object which is already modified by the action of its predecessor, the effect dE is altered for each of them. It therefore makes no difference whether we regard C and C_n as two different causes or as two different values, at which one and the same growing cause C has stopped in its growth or is for the purpose of our analysis supposed to have stopped. If we then signify by $E = f(C_n)$ the result already produced by n successive dC, we obtain for the effect dE which will result from the addition of yet another dC the following: $dE = \dfrac{m}{E} \cdot dC$. Among pure quantitative functions it is the logarithm C, which shows this mode of growth, and so we come upon logarithmic expressions in calculating operations which by their own results create obstacles to their own repetition proportional to those results.

4. The case $(dE = mE\,dC)$. We have just seen that a cause cannot when repeated have its effect diminished merely because it is not acting for the first time. Just as little can its effect be increased by the mere fact that it has already acted several times. Both effects are ascribed to habituation: we say 'practice makes perfect,' and also 'habit hardens.' An increase in the effect produced obliges us, no less than a decrease, to assume a contributing cause Z; this Z consists in such a modification of the object a influenced by the cause into α as facilitates every subsequent operation of that cause by continually opposing to it less and less resistance. Thus the first blow shakes a stone in such a way that the second blow has only to intensify the vibrations already going on within it in order to overcome the cohesion of its parts. If nothing else enters into the calculation we must for reasons of the same sort as in the above case reckon the magnitude of the effect produced as at any moment proportional to the aggregate result or to the integral of the earlier effects. In the case of pure quantitative functions of C it is the exponential function e^c, which[1] possesses this peculiar

---

[1] [There is here an unavoidable ambiguity of notation. e which was before the symbol for *effect*, here stands for the base of Napierian logarithms.]

property of a differential quotient equal to the integral itself. Thus we shall often meet with applications of this formula as well as of the other in mathematical expressions of the forms which natural effects assume.

5. The case ($dE = m . \sin C$). In no one of the cases which we have thus far examined do we get effects, which alternately increase and decrease at the same time that their causes go on steadily increasing. Whenever therefore E periodically alternates from increase to decrease, while C changes in one uniform direction, there must exist besides C one or more companion causes Z, the relations of which to C are either in themselves variable or are so deranged because it happens that they operate together that the effects of all now accumulate upon and now cancel each other, and so pass through maxima and minima from the one to the other of these reciprocal attitudes. We can conceive of the combinations possible in this case being infinitely numerous; the formula I have used is no more than a very inadequate symbolical expression of these possibilities.

CHAPTER VIII.

The Discovery of Laws.

264. IN the relations between causes and effects examined in the previous chapter lie the clues by which we are guided in instituting fresh experiments or seeking for fresh observations in order to exclude the possibility, which still remains, that different causes may produce the same effect. The general import of this procedure is always the same: from the impure observations SP or CE we have to discover the pure case $\Sigma\Pi$ or BF, by eliminating from the observation all that has nothing to do with the causal nexus before us. I see no reason to analyse this general precept any further into a number of separate methods. It is much more worth our while to point out that in elementary algebra we have already an instructive type of the very various modes of operation by which we may reach this end. We have given us equations which jointly determine the relations of two or more unknown quantities; these equations we transform in all sorts of ways by adding on new quantities, by subtracting others, by multiplication and division of the whole; and are thus at last able to compare the equations immediately with one another, and adapt them to the elimination of particular unknown quantities. The present problem is to be solved in a similar way, now by a timely addition of fresh conditions, whose influence we can calculate; now by a suspension, equally calculable in effect, of given conditions; or again by altering the relative position of the co-operating cause; or, lastly, by modifying our own attitude towards the material we have to observe. I will not stop to decide whether we shall ever be able to reach by such means a pure case BF; but even supposing we were so lucky as to have discovered the exact cause C of the exact effect E, we should yet in no case have completely satisfied our curiosity, save in the case of historical enquiry. For the only conclusion we could draw from this pure case CE would be that whenever the same C really recurred the same E must attend it. But the practical needs of life, no less than the interests of science, urge upon us the further question: how will E change into E^1 when C passes over into C^1, or what shape will an effect E have to assume when the place of the C observed is taken by another C^1, of which we can state exactly how it differs from C? In a word, we desire not only to be certain that there really is a connexion between C and E, but to know the *law* according to which that connexion comes about and varies.

265. The term *law* has different meanings as we use it in connexion with different circles of human interests. Its logical meaning however never varies. Stated in its complete logical form a law is always a *universal hypothetical judgment*, which states that whenever C is or holds good, E is or holds good, and that, whenever C undergoes a definite change into C^1 through a variation of itself dC, E also becomes E^1 through a definite variation of itself dE which depends on dC. A law is hypothetical, because it is never meant to be a mere enumeration of what happens; its sole function is to determine what should or must happen when certain conditions are given. All laws are thus hypothetical in their import, and those which refer to permanently given or permanently presupposed conditions are no exception to the rule; they only seem to be so because they are not stated in the form of an hypothesis. Thus we enunciate the following in a categorical form as a law of nature: all ponderable elements attract one another inversely as the square of their distances from each other. Here we merely state the fact that in the case of such elements a particular condition is adequate to produce this consequence; this condition is perpetually fulfilled and consists in their simultaneous presence in the same world. Again the constitution of a state categorically maps out the relations which hold between the various groups of its members, but always under the tacit proviso that so long as the state exists at all, these fixed ordinances shall be constantly maintained and renewed as generation succeeds to generation.

But besides being hypothetical—that it is as a matter of course—every law is also universal, and must on that account be as strictly distinguished from a mere universal matter-of-fact as from a decree made for a particular case. Kepler's law that all planets move in ellipses round the sun, which is fixed at one of the foci, is originally no law at all, but the mere expression of a fact. It gets the name of law, thanks to the accessory idea (which is perfectly justified) that all planets owe their movement to a common ground, and that we may therefore assume that the proposition will continue to hold good no longer as a mere proposition, but as an actual law for bodies which are still beyond our ken, provided always that they show themselves to be planets by revolving round the sun. A law which gives powers of expropriation for the purpose of laying down a particular line of railway is logically considered a decree or mandate; but inasmuch as the mandate is not arbitrarily given but is based on a general law, which pronounces expropriation under certain conditions to be always legitimate, it may fairly itself assume the more pretentious name. It is implied in the idea of a law that it should pay such regard to variations or differences in the condition and consequent, only the idea cannot always be realised. The certainty that two bodies attract each other is in itself a fact which needs to be further determined; natural science does not see in it a law until it can assign the particular ratio in which the attractive force varies in its amount in dependence on differences and variations in the mass and distance of the bodies, or on some other condition of variable magnitude.

It is the same with moral and judicial laws also. A commandment so universal as that which enjoins love of our neighbours may fairly, as an expression of the deepest motive which can govern us, possess a higher value than can any law, yet in its form it lacks the precision of a law; for it is neither clear *prima facie* what result should follow from such love, nor in actual life can the commandment be fulfilled, without the love which it prescribes—whatever it may consist in—having a definite degree of liveliness, or without its force flowing along a channel in one case along which it does not flow in another. The general formula we have quoted gives no hint whatever as to what this channel shall be. Judicial laws, on the other hand, are based on the distributive *suum cuique* in its widest significance. Whether they prescribe actions or fix penalties, the predicate they attach to every case of the recurrence of what they bring under the general notion of any legal relation is not intended to be incapable of modification. Differences in quantity between various cases have a real significance in the eye of the law: it is only the defectiveness of our standards for determining those differences, which compels us in practice to be content with roughly graduating the scale of legal consequences, when we would far rather make it exactly proportionate to the individual differences on which those consequences depend. It would seem that none but purely negative laws and moral prohibitions ignore any such graduation of ground and consequent. I leave it to the reader however to judge, whether in a theoretical sphere negative judgments are to be regarded as laws at all, and not rather as contrapositions, in which for merely logical purposes we have changed the positive assertion of a law into the negation of its opposite. In any case by putting it in the form of a universal negative, we lose a part of the truth, viz. the measure of the distance by which each case is separated from the predicate, which is simply denied of them all As regards moral prohibitions, it is true that we do not find in them as such any reference to such a gradation or adjustment of penalty to guilt, nevertheless in passing judgment on a breach of them, we always make such reference. They prohibit beforehand any appropriation of another's property, but the commission of such an act is according to its particular nature subjected to very various degrees of disapprobation and punishment.

266. There is a difference of intention between a *law* and a *rule*, which may in most cases be easily seized, though it cannot be maintained in all. In practical life a law determines a state which is to be brought about by an activity or mode of conduct, and which is essential to the fulfilment of the ends of the political or social community; the rule supervenes as a practical ordinance, and since there are many possible courses of conduct, all in themselves equally contributory to the realisation of that state, the rule helps us partly to select the most advantageous of those courses, partly to secure, if only by fixing a definite mode of procedure, the requisite uniformity and harmony between individual performances. In theoretical investigations of reality, we mean by a law the expression of the peculiar inward relation which exists between two facts and constitutes the ground at once of their conjunction and of the manner of this conjunction; and in every simple case there is but *one* law. The rule, on the other hand, prescribes a number of logical or mathematical operations of thought, by which we are so to combine our perceptions as to arrive at conclusions, which in their turn tally with reality, and there may be several such rules all equally sound for one and the same case. Thus it is only for the law that we claim an objective truth. The rule is merely subjective, and sums up the various adjustments of our thought, by which, starting

from the standpoint we occupy over against things, we so far master their connexion as to be able to calculate and predict the consequences flowing from given facts of reality, and divine aright their antecedent grounds and causes. These operations of thought which the rule prescribes need not take the same path as the development of things themselves. They need not necessarily move a *principio ad principiatum*; instead of the conditions on which a thing really depends they may employ trustworthy signs or symptoms. They must never indeed lose all connexion with the reality, but they are free to make use of any roundabout method, which our attitude towards things necessitates, and to transform the inner relations of things as they like. This difference in intention between a law and a rule is no doubt a wide one, yet in making it we are hardly ever quite unbeset by doubts, least of all where we are concerned with the investigation of reality. It is clear at the outset that not a few of the methods of procedure at present in vogue are mere rules; but more than that, it remains an open question whether any one of the laws, which we believe ourselves to have discovered, really deserves the name in the special sense explained above. We are accustomed to use the name where we have reached very simple and universal propositions about the actual conjunction of phenomena. Thus we regard it not as a rule, but as a law of nature, that the force of gravitation diminishes according to the square of the distance; yet the inner nexus between the terms of this proposition is still undiscovered, and we do not know how it is that the quantity of space, which intervenes between two bodies, can cause their reciprocal effect to vary as it does. Ultimately, therefore, even this law is a mere rule, which teaches us how to calculate from given data of distance and mass the variations of their effects; it does not exhibit the inner connexion of these effects with their conditions. We shall have occasion to recur later on to this question. At present it is enough to notice that in the considerations which immediately follow we shall look on the law as no more than the simplest rule which conjecture has to guide it in getting at the genuine nature of things.

267. Thus far we suppose that the means specified have enabled us to discover as accurately as possible the pure causal connexion between C and E. We also suppose our experiments or observations to have supplied us with a number of pairs of values of this cause and its corresponding effect, these values being quantitatively determined and forming a double series. It is anticipating somewhat, yet we may suitably preface our attempt to determine the universal law of such a double series by a consideration of the various causes, which may produce a divergence between the quantitative relations which we find and the true relations of things which we are in quest of. In the first place let it be borne in mind that what we observe is not the things themselves, but the impressions, which things make upon us. We will not at present attempt to settle whether the impression produced in our consciousness *can* ever be like the things and their relations which produce it. One thing however is clear on the face of it, and that is, that it is not obliged to be like them, but may change with every change in the disposition of the recipient subject. Hence a doubt as to how far we can conclude from the subjective excitements produced in us by an assumed external world to the objective nature of this reality, and this doubt affects the whole realm of our knowledge. We will not go into it at present, but are content to understand by such truth or correctness of our observations, as we at present aspire to, their universal validity for all human observers, who are normally constituted and placed under similar conditions. If it is asked how we can be sure that any particular observation possesses such universality, we can only answer that practically the ultimate decision in every case rests with the overwhelming majority who agree in their views, as opposed to the minority who disagree. If anything appears to me different from what it appears to everyone else under exactly similar conditions, there must be some error in my individual observation, an error which will vary and may be set right by repeating the observation, if it can be traced to mere momentary inattention, but which becomes a permanent, and in a narrower sense *personal error*, when the anomalous organisation of the individual's senses is to blame for it. How widespread is such defectiveness of sensible apprehension in regard to the qualitative content of sensation, is shown by the way people will differ in their judgments as to the resemblance and contrast of colors, or the harmony and dissonance of tones. Such disagreements, however, are equally noticeable where it is a quantity which has to be estimated. For all practical determinations of quantities given in reality ultimately rest on the accuracy of our sensible impressions, and all that artificial methods and instruments of measurement can do is to transform what is too big or too small, the one by splitting it up, the other by somehow magnifying it, in such a way as to bring both within the sphere of more moderate intermediate quantities, of whose equality or inequality we can judge with sufficient accuracy by help of our sensible faculties alone. And really it is to such a simple judgment as this last that all our measurements are reducible. Nature does not endow us with a power of specifying offhand how great is the difference between two unequal quantities of space, or time, or intensity; we only acquire such a power by long practice, and then very imperfectly. All that we are directly sensible of is that two quantities of the same kind are on the whole equal or unequal; the amount of their difference is measured in an indirect way by finding out how many definite and equal units of quantity taken together exactly make up that difference. We say that a line b is bigger than a line a, because to begin with it contains a length *equal* to a, while perception reveals to us a further residue d, which that a does not contain. The size of d is only to be found by employing a standard of length, and it is found the more accurately the smaller the units, which we can distinctly observe by our senses, and which added all together produce a length *equal* to d. But even if we use a microscopical standard we must admit that everything ultimately depends on the certainty with which sense-perception shews us that the extremity of the d to be measured exactly coincides with the extremity of one of these infinitesimal units of measurement. When intervals of time are equal we recognise them pretty accurately as being so in virtue of our feeling of the equality of one beat with another; but we can only measure unequal intervals against each other by dividing them into beats or equal recurring units; nothing but the immediate sensible impression, however, informs us of the equality of these units themselves. And when we use clockwork to mark the recurrence of these units with audible ticks, the accuracy with which it does this still rests ultimately on the certainty and precision of the visual impressions, which helped us to set out the spatial dimensions of the works and their parts in such a way, that their movement shall in fact give out those signals at equal intervals. Lastly, if this expedient is to serve to fix the times, on the expiration of which certain phenomena only observable by other senses, as by the eye, occur, nothing but the immediate impression can tell us that a phenomenon of this other kind exactly coincides in time with this audible signal, and it is just here as we know that our judgment is for physiological reasons not so acute as we could wish it to be—on the contrary, it needs the previous correction of our personal error.

In conclusion, I will but briefly mention, what is familiar to every one, the relativity of all our determinations of measure. There is nothing absolute except the numerals by the help of which we count the recurrences and specify the number of units found. The units themselves can only be determined relatively to each other, and there is no sense in asking how big anything is unless we measure it by a presupposed standard. To find those units, that is, to determine them in such a way that they may be fixed, useful, and unambiguous, is itself a problem, which the art of observation has to solve. It is enough at present to remark, that in unchangeable natural bodies we have a means of determining units of length, while we have exact periodic astronomical appearances whereby to determine units of time; and if it is the intensity of moving forces that we have to measure, we can sometimes observe how they balance each other, sometimes what velocities they generate. As yet however we are without means of arriving at observable units of measurement for the strength of sensations, feelings, and desires.

268. Supposing that this primary defect, the personal error, has been remedied, what we observe may still fall very far short of the truth, owing to the position, which either individually or as men generally we occupy towards things themselves. We could illustrate this from other than spatial phenomena, still it is they which enable us most readily to appreciate the frequency with which the same process or the same object yields very different images according to the point of view of the spectator. I think I may hazard the assertion that every regular event gives a regular projection of itself for any point of view we like to take, but the rules by which we reason from one such phase of the object to another are framed in such a way as to favor one point of view more than another, and on that account it is often exceedingly difficult to go back from the event as *projected* to the event which *produces the projection*. A circular movement will only appear circular to a spectator, whose standpoint is somewhere in the line drawn through the centre of the circle at right angles to its plane; to an eye situated anywhere outside this axis and this plane it will appear an oval; while if one views it from any point in the plane of the circle but outside its circumference, it will appear as an oscillation in a straight line. The synthesis of the times traversed by the moving point and the loci corresponding to the times will form a separate series for each point of view, and each such series will be regular in its formation, though one of them will have much more value than another as an indication of what really takes place. Now if this was all that met our observation and if we had not already got a stock of other experiences in regard to what is true in reality and of usual occurrence, we should have no reason to desire any other rule than that, say, which in our example, expresses the rectilinear oscillation. But in nature we are seldom left without secondary features, which force themselves simultaneously on our observation and lead us first to doubt and then to correct our first impressions. That we observe that circular movement means not that we think or represent it mentally but that we *see* it, and we only see it if rays of light are reflected from it on our eyes. Hence it follows that changes in the apparent size and illumination of the body must accompany its movement for every observer who is placed outside the axis. Only a person who takes his standpoint in that axis itself can fail to notice these variations and so feel no impulse to seek an explanation of them. Now let us place ourselves in the very plane of the circle, the body will then, as it travels from one extremity *a* of its apparently rectilinear path towards the middle of the same, wax in size and brightness, while after passing the middle it will wane in both respects till it reaches *b*; if it then recedes from *b* to *a* this decrease in bulk and brightness continues at first, reaches its minimum at mid-path, while from these onwards to *a* the body waxes afresh. If one takes it that all these appearances are real, one has many questions to answer. Why does the body reverse the direction in which it is moving when it reaches the extremities of its path, and why does its velocity increase as it approaches the middle and decrease as it approaches the ends? Either there is something in that middle point the effect of which is to draw the body towards it, or there must be present and at work in the prolongations of its path equal and opposed forces urging it in that direction. But why, if that be so, should it pass through both the minimum and the maximum of its size and brightness at the same middle point and yet the force or forces remain uniform? The easiest conjecture to make would be that the two appearances were merely coincident; quite apart it might be said from its movement along its path the body is subject to periodic increases and decreases of bulk, which however are merely functions of the time not of the place. Still as at any time t it must be in some place or other it may at the moment of its greatest bulk just as well be in the middle of its path as anywhere else, and as its bulk requires in order to reach its minimum the time t, which it takes to accomplish a half oscillation, this minimum too must take place just as the body occupies this same middle point.

But who would credit such an explanation as that? In the rest of nature such periodic enlargements are altogether unheard of, while changes, such as we have described, in the apparent size and brightness of bodies are quite familiar; we know that bodies are liable to them according as they alter their distance from our eye. Relying on such analogies then we shall try to grasp or apprehend the fact observed as the projection of other and truer facts. We notice no withdrawal of the body between the loci of the maximum and minimum, on the contrary both coincide with each other in the middle of the path. Moreover the ways by which it goes and returns appear coincident at every point. Taking all these considerations together we are obliged to suppose that the true path is a plane closed-up curve, one of the diameters of which must lie along our line of sight at the centre of its apparent path. By comparing the particular apparent loci occupied at successive moments of time we shall further discover whether the true path is a circle, an ellipse, an oval, or what. The mere mention of the name of Copernicus will be enough to make the reader understand how the accumulation of insoluble difficulties in the facts as observed impels us to transform our views of nature, and how much at once becomes clear when we grasp what is sensibly given as a mere projection of a reality beyond our observation. In order to that however we must already be in possession of a store of universal truths as well as of earlier experiences of facts; pure logical precepts may stimulate but cannot conduct us to the goal.

269. We must now go back a step. Before we try to interpret the observed facts in the manner specified, we must be in possession of the actual laws, which we think of reducing by means of such interpretation to a form at once simpler and more in correspondence with the real course of things. Nothing is given to help us in the discovery of these laws beyond the series of values displayed by the causes and their corresponding effects. Now even if we assume that these numbers before us are perfectly correct as a statement of what we succeeded in observing, still the transition from this series of isolated terms to the universal law of its formation is always a *jump* on the part of thought. How do we know that such and such a law is the only one valid for the series and true? There is no process of demonstration by which we can find such a law, none by which it could be shown to be what it claims to be. We can never do more than guess at the law and then by the help of innumerable secondary considerations heighten the probability of its being the true one. It is of importance to be quite clear on this point. If we have to start with a limited number, say n terms of a numerical series given in the order in which they succeed one another in the series, it will be easy to find a simple general formula, exactly corresponding to these given n terms and expressing their general term; but even then this formula need not necessarily be the only possible one: it may at least be apprehended in different ways. For example, let the given

terms be 1, 3, 5, 7, 9; then if 1 denotes the place in the series occupied by the first of the given terms, $2n-1$ will exactly express the general term. But if we think the general term in exactly this manner it will hardly correspond to a real physical relation, of which it is meant to serve as the regular expression. The same given series may however be thought as an arithmetical progression with the initial term 1 and the difference 2, and besides that as the series of differences got by subtracting the square of a whole number from the square of the one following it in the numerical series. Both readings of the series may be expressed by the same general term, both determine every term of *this* series, but the genesis of each term is conceived differently in the one case and in the other, and this difference of manner is of importance, because it allows of our making different assumptions in regard to the physical relations of the phenomena expressed by this series.

Thus without going any further we here have unsolved doubts in plenty. But this is not all. The presuppositions we make in this case are not at all the same as what we make in the case of observations; a general term found in the manner just described holds exactly for only the n terms, from which it has been generalised. Not so with the laws which must be generalised from observations; we require these to hold good no less for the values of the causes and effects which we have not observed than for those which we have. We can of course interpolate terms in a given series; that is, we can calculate missing links in such a way that they will fit into a series agreeably to a law of its formation, which we have beforehand abstracted from the given terms, and which often proves to be not a little complex. But then we assume that the particular law developed from the given terms holds equally good for terms not given,—an assumption which is always permissible when we are merely concerned with the completion of a *conceivable* series, but which is altogether inadmissible when the question is whether this conceivable series itself corresponds to a something *real* even where this correspondence has not been observed. Thus before we demand that a law, which we have somehow got out of the given terms, should be extended to terms not given, we must have reasons, which justify our pursuing such a method of interpolation at all. We may illustrate this by a very simple example. Let us figure to ourselves the values of C as so many abcissae x, each larger than the last by Δx, and the values of E as so many ordinates y. Now if the given series gives the same value $y = B$ for all values $m \Delta x$ of x, it may of course be the case that the equation would hold good for all the unobserved ordinates, which correspond to fractions of a Δx. In that case the line joining the extremities of all the ordinates is a straight line and parallel to the axis in which the abscissae are taken. Still this does not follow as of course. Take any two Δx we like, the ordinate y between their extremities may have every possible value, and the curve which unites the various co-ordinates y may describe every conceivable path. It may be real or imaginary, straight or crooked, y may pass through one or several maxima or minima, even through infinity, and all these indeterminable paths may be as different as you please in the interval of one Δx from what they are in that of another. From such considerations as these we may derive a minor rule for selecting observations, like that we have noticed above for imperfect inductions. The rule in question forbids us to form the series of pairs of values in such a way that C progresses according to a regular law, and none but the particular values of E are permitted to appear, which correspond to these symmetrical values of C. If we do so the chances are that we shall only get a series of singular values, of maxima or minima, or fixed values of E, which periodically recur, and which either give us no insight or suggest false surmises as to the intermediate course of the curve. A regular advance of C by equal increments no doubt helps us to guess the universal law of the series; but if we wish to confirm this guess we must make the increments of C change as unsymmetrically and irregularly as possible. To put it quite simply, a man who never observes a place of public resort but once in every seven days and that on a Sunday afternoon, has no right to suppose because it is crowded then, that it is as crowded on a week-day. A man who never looks at the moon but through a chink which only allows him to see it at its full height, cannot guess the path it pursues through the heavens for the rest of its time. If on the other hand we find that the values which y assumes for intermediate values of x, taken at random from between the values already considered, adapt themselves to the law derived from these latter, we have for the first time some justification for interpolating all the other y's in conformity with this law. Strict logic would not admit even this to be a complete justification; so long as it is impossible to observe *all* the successive values of C and all the corresponding effects E, so long we remain in doubt whether the law which holds good in the cases observed would hold in those not observed.

This doubt is narrowed in practice by collateral considerations based not on general principles of logic, but on our actual knowledge, which as a rule is enough for the purpose,—of the matter under investigation. If for instance we are investigating the way in which a particular natural force acts, we know for certain that E cannot be infinite for any finite value of C; and we shall know enough of the peculiar character of the force in question to be able to judge whether it is possible for its effects to increase steadily, or to oscillate periodically, or to sink to zero for particular values of C; lastly we shall know if they are likely to accumulate undiminished by the lapse of time, or whether we must assume that some counterforce is constantly annulling wholly or partially the results generated. It is these assumptions, which are grounded in fact, which justify our transferring the law for the pairs of values we have actually observed to values not observed, and of doing so with a strong probability of being right. There is still another expedient in cases, where there is no restriction to the number of possible expedients. By means of autographic arrangements attached to the apparatus in which the effects of the force are rendered visible, we can compel the force to register of itself the results which it produces at each moment of its continuous working. By help of such mechanical means our observations, which would otherwise be always limited in number, are so infinitely extended that they follow each other without any break, and the visible curve thus generated allows us to form as safe a judgment as can possibly be based on observation in regard to the continued or intermittent nature of the effect, the uniformity, retardation, or acceleration of its rate and its periodical or non-periodical increase. It is always of course open to those who are given to logical hyper-criticism to object that every curve drawn consists ultimately of a series of point-like deposits of pigment and that these only appear as a continuous line to the naked eye, which interpolates whether we like it or no. After all, we may be told, you have only got a number of particular perceptions and these do not allow you to infer the nature of effects, which found no pigment available to register themselves by and which therefore correspond to the gaps between the colored points, which make up the curve. Let us leave such objections to answer themselves; all I wish to do is to accentuate the truth that the discovery of an universal law is always a guess on the part of the imagination, made possible by a knowledge of facts. This knowledge is recalled to our memory by the resemblance of the given case to analogous earlier cases, and thus offers itself as an explanation. But a demonstrative method, or a method which involves no logical jumps, a sure logical receipt for arriving at the true universal law of a series of events, does not exist.

270. If we return to our series of values in order to see how far the problem in hand is successfully solved, we are confronted by numerous cases in which it emphatically is not. Among such are all those statistical calculations, which view a result E, which really depends on the cooperation of several conditions, by sole reference to the influence of a single one of these conditions, and then attempt to find an universal law in regard to the relations of the two. Thus it is attempted to estimate a man's present expectation of life by sole reference to the age he has already reached. This self-contradictoriness of the problem at once shows itself; if a variable quantity E is a function of C, x, y, and z, we cannot express it as a mere function of C alone, entirely neglecting x, y, z, which ought to enter into the true expression as part of the collateral conditions. Nor in fact would a man ever make such an attempt unless, once more, he had experience which taught him to put some trust in it. However much the procedure may lack precision from a theoretical point of view, he still knows that as a matter of fact something comes of it, though not quite what he wishes; and conversely it is the absence of all result in other cases, which induces him to abstain from similar attempts. What result we do usually arrive at in such cases is based on the following considerations. Among the conditions on which the continuance of a man's life depends, that which in estimating it we regard as the most important is beyond doubt the age C, which he has already attained; for inseparably bound up with that age is a modification of his bodily system, which continues slowly to run its course and is ultimately sufficient of itself, even though all other conditions remain favorable, to make death inevitable. During long periods of one's life however the action of C changes slowly and inconsiderably, while in other sections of one's life it increases very quickly and significantly; hence it follows that the same outward conditions have an uniform influence on the body during one period of life, and during another an equally uniform but uniformly different influence. It is upon this interaction of the present stock of vitality and circumstances that a man's capacity of further life really depends, and so we may suppose that between certain fixed ages the expectation of life decreases according to one tolerably constant law, between certain other limited ages according to a different but equally constant law; we cannot however conceive of an universal law which should determine the expectation of life universally for the whole of life, and so for any age a man may have reached. In such investigations therefore partial laws or formulas are usually laid down, which are only meant to hold each of them for values of C which lie between two fixed limits, and to help us to estimate the corresponding values of E. Theoretical significance these formulae have none; they are merely practical short cuts or synoptical expressions of how things take place in the gross; if they are very simple and yet exact enough for our purpose, they aid our calculations; if they are, to start with, of a complicated nature it is at best empty affectation to lay them down at all; in such cases it is more useful to go back to the original form of a table containing in its simplest form the mass of observed facts, from which they were derived.

271. But matters may be less unfavorable, and we may be able to reckon on the presence of a universal law capable of being expressed by the help of two centres of relation C and E. The question then arises, which we are to choose of the many laws that may with equal truth or with equal approximation to the truth be supposed to underlie the series of pairs of values presented us. In raising this question we make assumptions slightly different from those we have hitherto made. The numerical terms of our series will not repre-

sent the observable facts with such complete accuracy as we supposed before; they will contain inaccuracies, but we are for the present content to believe that these are small, and that they are not all on one side, but exceed the truth about as often as they fall short of it. Accepting these conditions a doubt arises whether the particular formula, which fits in most accurately with the given values, is to be regarded at all as the law we want. The pure case BF will hardly fall within our observation quite unalloyed; the result which the condition B would by itself alone involve will be somewhat altered by the simultaneous co-operation of other causes which we can never wholly eliminate, and this matter of fact, impure already, will be still further modified for the worse by the slight flaws which are inseparable from our observation. Thus the data from which we start involve what we want along with disturbing elements which we do not want; a formula, which was exactly adjusted to those data, would be a copy of this mixed matter of fact, but not a law for the pure case, which we sought to separate from its alloy of accidental and irrelevant circumstances. This consideration forms the general ground upon which we permit ourselves if at all to neglect the slight divergences, which still remain between the given values and a law approximately covering them; we then put down these differences as due to *unknown* disturbing causes. Cases however may arise, in which a law completely answers to the given values and must yet be regarded as not the true one, or anyhow as less true than another, which answers less closely to them; this will be the case when there are *known* disturbing causes, which must necessarily act, but of which we find no hint given in the former law. Let us assume that two bodies a and b revolve together on different planes and at different distances round a third c, which steadily attracts both; and that it strictly follows from our observations, that the two bodies describe two similar regular ellipses: then either the observation itself must be pronounced defective, or the elliptical orbit cannot be regarded as the law of these movements in the desired sense. For if we only admit first the attraction between c and a and between c and b and admit of none between a and b, *a fortiori* however if we do admit there to be attraction between these two, the path, which a would describe, were b not present, must be modified when b is present together with it. Either therefore the real paths of the two bodies, when they are moving together, diverge from a true ellipse, in which case our observations are inaccurate and fail to reveal to us these slight divergences; or the ellipse is the actual path of either body, in which case the path prescribed by law is some other one, which they would traverse, except for these disturbances. For after all in such investigations as these our aim is not merely to get an universal expression or copy of the facts as they result from the application of an universal law to the definite conditions of a special case; what we do want is rather such a general statement of the law as will allow us, just because these special circumstances are excluded, to judge of the results which would follow, though the collateral circumstances were changed, from the same or similar main conditions. In such cases then as this we shall be inclined to doubt the truth of an assumed law, when it fits in with a faultless and all too striking exactness to the given observations. If it be asked what other law should be held to be a truer one, we answer that that can only be conjectured according as the disturbances we disregarded can be estimated on other grounds. The doubt raised in us however may induce us to combine our observations in a new way, or to institute experiments which may throw light on the matter.

272. In case there are several laws, which all come about equally near to fitting the data before us, we are accustomed conformably to the above to prefer the simpler and to see in simplicity as it were a guarantee of truth. Against this

view, which raises the *simplex sigillum veri* into a universal principle, logic must enter a no less universal protest. If what we have to do is to calculate a special case by the light of a general law, the simpler formula is of course to be preferred, because it is *more convenient*; but from a more general point of view its simplicity is no test of its truth or probability. We must carefully consider what we may generally expect in the particular field, which we would explore. If it is clear that in that field a result E depends on divers independent determining elements, then a *simple law* expressive of their connexion is of course not impossible, but extremely unlikely. Properly the first feeling we should have on finding such a law would be one of distrust in its validity; we should believe we had taken things too easily in our observations or in our reasonings and had left out of sight some of the essential conditions; we shall only be satisfied if a searching investigation shows that these neglected conditions really always cancel one another's influence in such a way as to justify our excluding any reference to them in the universal law. Say we have found from mere observation that a body starting from the surface of a sphere under the attraction of the centre of the sphere always reaches a certain other concentric surface with the same final velocity, no matter along what path it passes from the one surface to the other; such a remarkable discovery as this we could only credit on one condition, namely if it were shown that this remarkable compensation of different collateral conditions really takes and must take place in the case.

We are easily deceived in similar cases, when the result found is not so paradoxical as the above. The formula $T = \pi \sqrt{\dfrac{l}{g}}$ seems to unite all the determining elements, upon which the time of a pendulum's swing depends, for a superficial observation does not give any effect to the angle of vibration. A more exact theory however shows that this simple expression is only approximative and that the true law is far more complicated. A certain speculative principle which we may come across later on leads us to suppose beforehand that in nature there exists a variety of compensatory arrangements, in virtue of which certain types of resulting events are maintained in perpetual conformity with the same simple law, no matter how different the medium, through which in particular cases these types are realised. Nevertheless one should only count upon the presence of such arrangements, where observation beyond doubt reveals them; on the other hand, where we have no means of thus forecasting the limits, within which the result of imperfectly known conditions must confine itself, the supposition of simple laws and the predilection for them remains an error only to be guarded against by a thorough exploration of all essential details of the given object of investigation. The present state of natural science does not perhaps make these warnings so necessary as they were a score of years ago, when there was a strong tendency to explain such complex phenomena as organic life by very simple, but no less inadequate principles. Of course it is very different when the object with which we are dealing belongs to a class of phenomena, which we cannot regard as changeable products of a number of independent causes, but rather as themselves manifestations of those fundamental forces, whose constant action under all sorts of secondary conditions makes up the complex tissue of physical processes. For these cases which do in fact realise approximately or completely the type of the presupposed pure case BF, we certainly must regard the simplicity of the law as a sign of its probable validity; yet not for the somewhat aesthetic reason that simplicity is in all cases a characteristic of truth, but because for these pure cases only one of the simple forms of regular coherence—already noticed (§ 263)—between cause and effect is in fact *conceivable*.

273. The reader will have noticed how much importance attaches to already acquired knowledge for the discovery of new laws, and how we even went so far as to appeal to all manner of previous considerations and accessory thoughts, through which alone the immediate data of sense come to have a precise meaning. The usual way of stating the necessity we are thus under is to say that we need *hypotheses*, in order to make use of the results of observation. In fact we may be inclined to apply this term hypothesis to several of the modes of thought, of which we have already availed ourselves. Thus we may say it was to make an hypothesis to infer back as we did from a periodical increase and decrease of an effect while the cause constantly increases to a shifting of the relative positions of the active elements associated in the cause. I think fit however in the interests of logic to define terms differently and to distinguish between *postulates*, *hypotheses*, and *fictions*. The regressive inference just mentioned is a postulate, that is, it expresses the conditions which must be set up, or the ground of explanation which must be given by some reality, whether thing, force, or event, before we can think the phenomenon in the form in which it is presented to us; it thus requires or postulates the presence of something that can account for the given effect. The postulate is not therefore an assumption which we can indifferently make or leave alone, or discard for another; rather it is an absolutely necessary assumption, without which the content of the observation with which we are dealing would contradict the laws of our thought. Nor is it at all necessary that the postulate should be so indefinite in respect of its content as it might appear to be, judging by the way in which I have just described it; on the contrary, what must be there, or have been there, or be accomplished in order that we may conceive the given phenomenon as really happening may be something altogether definite. What *is* left indefinite is the answer to be given to an essentially different question, namely, the question who or what that is, which by its concrete nature introduces exactly those conditions, which according to the postulate must needs be fulfilled in order that the given appearance may be possible. If a body of known mass moves in a known curvilinear path with a known velocity, we can assign with perfect accuracy the sum of the conditions, i.e. of the resultants B, B^1... which must act upon the body at every moment if it is to move in this way. All that remains indefinite is the source from which B and B^1 come, whether they are both of them simple impacts of simple forces or themselves the resultants of several joint forces, whether in short they are effects of forces or communications of already existing movements. It is clearly an abuse of language at once to apply the term hypothesis to all such demands of thought. If someone merely tells us that this curvilinear path requires forces of a certain intensity and direction to divert the motion from the tangent just so much in every moment, we should answer him in some such way as this: you teach us nothing which we did not know before, you merely repeat the conditions, which it was evident from a bare analysis of the given appearance must be supplied by *any* theory, which could be brought forward in explanation of the facts.

But we mean something else by an hypothesis; we mean by it a conjecture, which seeks to fill up the postulate thus abstractly stated by specifying the concrete causes, forces, or processes, out of which the given phenomenon really arose in this particular case, while in other cases may be the same postulate is to be satisfied by utterly different though equivalent combinations of forces or active elements. Thus we may fix at once two characteristics of the hypothesis. Firstly it is far from being an empty surmise, which comes into our heads without any reason at all: it always rests on a postulate, which we must accept, and is designed to explain the contradictions or lacunae, which make the given appearance *prima facie* unthinkable.

These it explains by assuming a secret inner organisation of real things and processes, in which these contradictions vanish, while at the same time it becomes conceivable how and why the said contradictions unavoidably arise for us in the outward appearance, which alone we can observe. The second characteristic of an hypothesis is closely connected with the former: every hypothesis is meant to be an account of a fact, and is no mere figure of thought or means of envisaging the object. A person who sets up an hypothesis believes he has extended the series of real facts which he can observe by a happy divination of facts not less real though falling outside the range of his observation. In such a case there is no need for the facts thus divined to be simple and ultimate facts; they in their turn may give rise to researches going still further back into the grounds of their possibility; it is enough for the hypothesis if the facts it *supposes* can be conceived as really existing, though we reserve for another time the question how they come into existence. Students of Optics found (to put it briefly) that observed facts make it necessary to postulate that rays of light act in the same moment in a different manner on their right side and on their left, and that this action itself alternates incessantly with the time, and that therefore there must be some cause capable of bringing about just this phenomenon. The physical hypothesis was that this postulate would be satisfied by transverse vibrations on the part of atoms of ether. What may be the source of these transverse vibrations, which form so indispensable a preliminary in the explanation of the phenomena, remains a question for the future to solve; in any case however it involves no contradiction, which would prevent our conceiving it as a process which actually takes place.

We have still to explain what we mean by *fictions*. These are assumptions made by us with full consciousness of the impossibility of the thing assumed, whether it be because it is self-contradictory or because for other than intrinsic reasons it cannot pass muster as a constituent of reality. Fictions are of use when there is no proposition T, under which a given case M can be logically subsumed as a case of its application, whereas there is a proposition T^1, from the actual applications of which M is only distinguished by a definite difference d. We then class M under T^1, draw therefrom the conclusions we want and correct them later on by adding on such modifications δ, as are rendered necessary by the distinction d, which still remains. The finding of the circumference of the circle by inclusion of it between an outer and an inner polygon may be regarded as merely a method of limitation, unless we like to consider the conception of the length of a curve as in itself a sort of fiction; but anyhow the formula $ds^2 = dx^2 + dy^2$ is certainly a fiction, if the symbol $=$ signifies real equality and not the mere approximation thereto. As long as ds is a real arc, so long the equation is false; but as soon as ds loses all quantity all the terms become nought and the equation loses all meaning. It leads however to an infinite approximation to the true value, as by gradually diminishing ds we gradually diminish the error committed and by so doing render the sum or the integral of ds ultimately independent of it. It is hardly requisite to remark upon the extraordinary importance of such modes of procedure for the intellectual process of discovery; but we also encounter them in other branches of knowledge, and the lawyers' custom of turning to the most nearly allied maxim of law T^1, when there is no special rule under which a particular case may be brought, is from a logical point of view to be classed as a fiction, though we generally apply the name only to cases of a peculiar kind. Jurisprudence must of course be left to shape its own nomenclature; still I cannot believe that what used to be regarded as a fiction was not something more than a mere transfer determined by a fresh act of legislation of all a man's legal rights and obligations to a subject, who *per se* stood in no relation to these. I think it depended on something further, and in the case of the Roman adoption the assumption of the father's name who adopted seems to me to prove that, as a psychological fact, an attempt was made to begin with to regard a relationship which could not be established in reality as yet after all established, while the corresponding sum of rights and duties was determined as the result and on the basis of this function.

274. So important are the results which we expect from hypothesis that we cannot blame the attempt so often made to subject to some sort of discipline the free course of the discoverer's imagination from which alone hypotheses can flow. But we must observe that though most of the rules laid down are truly excellent so far as they can be carried out, yet we must not regard a particular hypothesis as illegitimate because it disregards them; if we do we seriously curtail the utility of hypothesis. Let us illustrate our meaning. It is alleged in the first place that the hypothesis must satisfy the postulate, on which it is based, not by a fictitious representation, but by assigning a reality, and that it should therefore make assumption only of what may be thought as fact, not of what is inherently self-contradictory. This is obvious enough; still we go too far, if we require that the content of an hypothesis should always carry with it the possibility of being directly refuted by subsequent observation. We may look on this requirement as constituting an ideal, and it certainly is a very useful rule to observe, for it teaches us, where we can, to construct our hypothesis in such a manner, that its falsity, if it be false, transpires at once instead of being for ever proof against direct refutation by reason of its content being wholly inaccessible to observation. Still we should have to sacrifice many useful assumptions, if we pressed this demand in all cases. The teaching that the points of light, so conspicuous in the heavens at night, are bodies of vast size, only very remote from us, is at the bottom only an hypothesis, by means of which we try to understand the otherwise inexplicable daily and yearly motions of these lights. However false this assumption may be, it is clear that no future advance of science can ever directly refute it; we must therefore abide content if our hypotheses are thinkable and useful, if they are capable of explaining all interconnected appearances, even such as were still unknown when we constructed them, if that is to say they are indirectly confirmed by the agreement of all that can be deduced from them in thought with the actual progress of experience. But if we would be so fortunate as to find an hypothesis, which will not lack this subsequent confirmation, we must not simply assume anything that can be barely conceived as real; we must only assume that, which besides being thinkable conforms so to speak to the universal customs of reality, or to the special local customs which prevail in that department of phenomena to which the object we are investigating belongs. We do proceed so in all fields of enquiry. For instance, if in the text of a legal enactment a particular phrase only admits of an ambiguous deduction being made in regard to a given case, we do not interpret it in an arbitrary fashion by simply allowing our wits to play freely on it; we go back to the *ratio legis* on which the formula is based, and by the light of that seek to interpret the phrase in a manner suitable to the particular case. It is the same in the natural sciences; there too a successful hypothesis is always due to the attention paid to analogies noticeable in the material world at large or in particular departments thereof. Nothing but the analogy of fluids and of the atmosphere could have originally suggested the hypothesis of the continuous filling of space by matter; there was nothing in solid bodies to suggest the idea, for most of them are not only divisible into parts but are composed of a number of actual parts. In the case of such bodies the notion of the continuity of matter was only applicable in regard to their minute parts, and so it became a scientific truth that they consisted of discrete atoms, each of which could just fill its own small space continuously and no more. Now when it was found that solid bodies became fluid and fluid ones solid, and that even gases assume solid and liquid shapes under certain conditions, the atomistic theory was fully justified from that point of view; it only transferred what was actually true of one part of the body or of certain forms of it, to other bodies or other forms, in the case of which the same state could not as a matter of fact be demonstrated to be real, though it could be shown to be possible, inasmuch as upon this assumption the appearances presented by them remained perfectly conceivable. As soon as it is found that certain groups of phenomena are readily explained on the supposition that nature habitually acts in such and such a way, fresh discoveries are made every day, because people at once try how far other facts may be referred to the same principle. Such was the case with the undulatory theory. On the surface of water, in strings, on resonant surfaces, waves could be directly seen and their shape rendered visible in particular cases by artificial means; there was no apparent reason for supposing these movements to be confined to certain materials and there was accordingly much to be said in favour of the hypothesis, which sought to explain on the same principle first the propagation of sound by the air, next the movement of the luminiferous ether, and lastly the phenomena of heat.

Similarly, in the organic world, people stumbled at a few points on a division of labour of which they had never dreamed; where before very different functions had been attributed to the same substratum, each of these functions was shown to have a special organ of its own, which did not do service for any other function. It was then suggested hypothetically that the same thing went on in regard to the nerves organic to the different sensations of colour and sound; whether the truth of the matter has been reached is still open to doubt, but from the point of view of logic there can be no doubt that the hypothesis is justified.

Again, movements are often observed in plants, even contractile movements; still it does not appear that these are due to the contractions of living contractile tissues as are the movements of an animal's body; consequently, plausible as this hypothesis is in itself, it is not advanced in this case, because *prima facie* it does not seem to agree with the habits of nature in this region; on the other hand it is worth while enquiring whether this semblance is not a fallacious one.

275. There is yet another condition which a hypothesis must fulfil. It should be exactly adjusted to the postulate which it is framed to meet, and not contain either more or less than it must contain if it is to answer to the demands of the postulate. Hence a rule which must be carefully observed in constructing hypotheses. When we have to account for something which happens, we must not look vaguely about as if for inspiration; we must before anything else rigorously analyse what is given, and so lay down the exact postulate which the hypothesis must satisfy. When we have done so we may neglect for the moment the secondary features, of which we know from other sources that they can easily be treated as mere accessories, when we come to define in a more concrete manner any hypothesis which can come under discussion; but all essential elements of the problem, all, that is, which are not themselves mere consequences of other elements, must be accurately observed, for it is entirely from the way in which they are conjoined that we have to conjecture the most suitable form of the hypothesis we shall choose. We must then make a survey of our world, to see if it contains any elements, causes, forces, or combinations of forces of such a kind as to satisfy the postulate laid down; after the fullest survey of these and guided at once by a practical and theoretical motive we shall make choice of those which fulfil the specified requirements in the simplest manner and in the most complete accord with the ruling analogies of the particular department in question.

For example, a body is found covered with wounds; our first concern will be to settle whether the wounds must have been inflicted while the man was still alive or after he was dead; we then try to estimate the magnitude, mode, and direction of the forces, which could have caused the wounds. Having thus ascertained the conditions we found a postulate on them, and enquire whether this postulate is satisfied by assuming a mere natural force to have acted or only by presupposing a weapon to have been wilfully employed. This enquiry may be said to settle the *form* of the hypothesis, e.g. we may have to make the assumption that murder was committed, after which we proceed to detect the agent not by the help of ill-founded fancies, but by asking ourselves what persons there are of whom the deed might be expected, partly because their relations to the murdered man would have supplied a motive, partly because there is nothing in their characters to prevent our suspecting them without direct evidence. We have no space to give in all the necessary detail an example, which would illustrate the extreme care which in judicial investigation is taken to satisfy every part of the postulate; a conviction founded on it is not regarded as a safe one, unless it accounts for every single circumstance, which because it is a violation of the ordinary course of things would require to be specially accounted for even if we were not dealing with a case of felony. In such a case a man is forced to be circumspect by the vastness of the issues at stake; his judgment is rendered keener by the thought, and he reasons with far greater accuracy than he would in conducting many a philosophical speculation, in which much worse errors are condoned because they can do no one any harm. We find plenty of people who without seriously examining some phenomenon which strikes them as strange put it down to what they call the fluid of animal-magnetism, and this without specifying the circumstances which need to be explained. They talk in a vague and general way of this fluid being emitted and immitted, forgetting that such barren generalities are perfectly useless as explanations of the kind, quantity, and sequence of the phenomena for which they are supposed to account. Natural science is not so liable to go wrong in this way because it must state its problems with so much mathematical precision even to render them intelligible.

276. I shall presently have to speak of individual facts, in treating of which the important point is not so much the simplicity of the hypothesis framed with a view to their comprehension as the completeness with which the hypothesis covers all that is contained in the facts. Experience teaches us in how many roundabout ways an event is sometimes brought about in a particular case, whereas in other cases it may arise from several simpler causes. But at present we are not concerned with individual facts; we are still trying to discover the matter-of-fact which is the common basis of a whole class of frequently recurring events; and here in deference to a sort of principle of 'the least cause' we must prefer the simpler hypothesis to the more complicated: not because simplicity in itself is any guarantee of truth, but because if we go out of our way to assume any datum whatever, which is not indispensable in order to the production of the thing, we make an utterly void supposition overstepping the given postulate and therefore unjustifiable in point of method. But our procedure may be logically correct without being endorsed by reality. Suppose we have selected our hypothesis and are trying to deduce from it the original appearance, we may find that our deductions do not agree with the data, either because our analysis of the latter was defective, or because fresh observations, which were impossible before, have brought out new aspects of the thing. In that case the hypothesis must needs be amended. This may be done in two ways. The hypothesis contains elements, which in themselves admit of being modified, and we determine these in a more suitable manner, so that as grounds for the deduction of the given fact they are no longer either too wide or too narrow but just adequate. The other way is to add on fresh subsidiary hypotheses in regard to a few of its leading features. In advocating this mode of procedure just here I am at issue with a much-advocated theory which regards such a grafting of fresh hypotheses upon old ones as a sufficient proof of the inadmissibility of the latter, and insists that we ought to replace them at once by simpler ones. We do not really act upon any such theory either in everyday life or in science. We do not pull a house down and build it up anew just to get rid of a flaw, which a slight modification of its construction would remedy; we do not at once devise a brand new constitution when a few provisions of the old one begin to be oppressive; and widespread as is unfortunately the tendency to ride principles to death, the opportune adjustment of necessary changes to what is permanently good in old institutions has always been considered the true art of statesmanship. And if we look at the way in which the body of science has grown up historically we see that it too is very willing to essay new points of view under old and incommodious forms, if only not to lose any of the truths which have once been won through those forms. I do not mean to say that science should or will rest content with such methods; we all trust that the result of all our painful investigations may prove a simple and thoroughly consistent whole; but until we have arrived at that result we must not be deterred by the oddly complex and patch-work garb, in which our views must needs be clothed, if we are careful to adjust them to each freshly known or better known feature of our object by means of subsidiary hypotheses tacked on to our earlier assumptions in regard to it. This is the only way in which we can hope to reach the simple and plain result we seek. The more carefully we now proceed the more surely may we expect that in the course of our procedure (just as in any intricate calculation, which must yield a simple result in a foreseen manner) our manifold assumptions will spontaneously reduce themselves to simpler and more universal ones, so that in spite of all the circuitous reasonings employed a net result will remain with us, which is not only simple and synoptical, but completely covers every part of our postulate. In conclusion all will admit that a lucky gift of insight may make us able to do without all these roundabout methods; but logic cannot impart inspiration; the only method it can teach is what we have cited :—we must curb our impatience and steadily go on transforming a hypothesis once essayed, until we educe from its inappropriate transitional forms a simple shape of it, which satisfies both our requirements and those of the object. We must not be in a hurry to lay down before our labour is finished principles good for nothing but parade, or we shall be misled into making light of problems, into neglecting inconvenient peculiarities, into acquiescence in views which in a rough and coarse manner reflect the large outlines of a thing, but are quite inadequate to account for its particular features.

277. A nice point remains to be noticed. Nothing can seem more imperatively necessary than that a hypothesis, which is meant as a conjecture of something which really is or happens, must before all things allege nothing but what is in itself *possible*: and of course it must assume nothing which is ascertained to be impossible : but still there is a doubt as to where the possibility which is still admissible begins and ends. I have tried to solve the doubt by carefully choosing my words; I have said that the hypothesis may legitimately involve anything that can be mentally represented as given matter-of-fact, but nothing else, and I really believe not only that this is all we should require but that we may admit so much as this to be possible without coming into conflict with the idea of the hypothesis. The hypothesis intends to conjecture a fact, but it is also content that this fact should when conjectured just exist in the way in which facts really observed so often exist: viz. that while we can conceive it or picture it we cannot explain the manner in which it may possibly come to be. Nothing can warrant our assuming by way of hypothesis a circle, which is at the same time a triangle; it is beyond the constructive power of our fancy to frame a mental image of such a figure, nor could it ever present itself to our senses as a given matter of fact. On the other hand we may assume the existence of invisibly small yet extended atoms of unchangeable shape and size; there is no contradiction in the notion of them, which would prevent our conceiving them as possible objects of perception, were our senses rendered more acute by artificial means. There is no reason why we should not look on the existence of such atoms as real, and suppose that though they are inaccessible to our unaided senses they are yet the basis of the phenomena which we can observe. We may probably have to modify this idea, when we try to think it out and examine its possibility as an element in the system of nature; but still there is no need to do so, till we have availed ourselves of it as a preliminary principle and found it of permanent use in accounting for particular phenomena. In the same way the theory of transverse undulations of a luminiferous ether answers, we saw, the requirements laid down by a postulate of observation, and such undulations can no doubt be conceived as really taking place, though no light has yet been thrown on their physical origin. The entire supposition of an infinitely extended homogeneous or isotropic ether is indispensable so far as we can see to our theory of the propagation of light, but it belongs to the same class of ideas; we can picture it clearly enough, but we cannot in the least see how so uniform a distribution of interacting elements is possible as a mechanical result. Those who admire the logical methods of natural science occasionally deceive themselves, when they represent the whole structure of our cognitions as resting on absolutely sure foundations; we are rather like men who are tubbing a well with masonry; like them we build from above downwards and so are we obliged to assume a substructure of hypothetical facts, which we trust will be sufficiently firmly upheld for a time by the unanalysed ground at the bottom to support our superstructure, until we can carry our knowledge a step deeper down and replace the hypothetical basis of our knowledge by a basis of facts, and then go through the whole process over again. It must be admitted that at this rate we leave a doubt as to where hypotheses and fictions, laws and rules respectively begin and end; I have hinted at this idea before and I shall recur to it again.

CHAPTER IX.

Determination of Individual Facts.

278. WE cannot be certain about a matter of fact unless we have ourselves directly perceived it; and even then only on the supposition that our interpretation of the sensible impression, which is all that is originally given, is correct. We interpret this by combining it in the form of a judgment into a whole of interconnected parts. When our information comes to us through others, we can only be sure that our information is trustworthy when we can rely on the witnesses or reporters. There may be much to recommend and justify the confidence we repose in them, but nothing can ever demonstrate its necessity. Again we habitually argue back from given facts to facts not given, but only attested by the former as their causes. Every such inference is liable to be wrong, because although every consequent must have a ground and a single ground adequate to produce it, still there may have been several different but equivalent matters of fact, all equally entitled to be called the cause—because each of them involved the ground—of the given effect. Again we frequently argue forwards from observed circumstances or events to a future or contemporaneous fact, which however withdraws itself from our observation. There is an uncertainty about all such inferences, because every condition may in the actual course of nature meet with a counter condition, which though it never annuls the consequences of the other, yet hinders them from actually assuming the particular form in which, except for that hindrance, they would have manifested themselves. It follows that wherever anything is outside the range of immediate perception, we are in our judgments of reality limited to probabilities, and have to look about for means by which to raise these probabilities as nearly up to the level of certainty as is sufficient for our purpose.

279. In thinking about such matters we are swayed by two very general and somewhat antagonistic principles. In the first place there is no such thing as a train of events, causally related and belonging to one another, which runs its course by itself in a world of its own; on the contrary, every such series of events goes on in one and the same world at one and the same time with numberless others. It always therefore seems utterly unlikely that any cause should unfold without a hitch the whole endless series of effects, which would have flowed from it if it could have acted alone upon the component parts of the world. A conviction that such is the case colours our daily life and conversation; it finds expression in the old warning not to moor one's ship by a single anchor, nor one's life by a single hope. If we are anxious to bring about a particular result we take a variety of precautions, each of which will effect what we want; if one miscarries, another will reach it; if they all come to nothing through the operation of external disturbing causes, we shall be able to console ourselves with the conviction that such a conspiracy of chance as would prevent a single one of the many causes on which we relied from producing the desired effect was quite as improbable as that they should one and all have succeeded. In the same way we distrust a historian who deduces mighty revolutions from mere trifles, or the doctrinaire who because some tendency really had a decisive influence in an earlier epoch, pretends to see in all the details of the history of centuries just its reactions and no more. The former loses sight of the innumerable collateral conditions, in virtue of which alone so trifling an event

could even seem to be fraught with such vast consequences; nor do the reasonings of the other carry conviction with them; mankind is a collection of many heads, which for ever teem with unconnected and incalculable impulses. We cannot believe that these have been wholly without influence in determining the course of history, especially when conjoined with the influences of nature, which follow an arbitrary order or disorder of their own. We are æsthetically dissatisfied with any poetry which sets before us a human character which is unswervingly self-consistent in all its actions, great and small; such a character lacks the air of being a genuine creation of reality, because no trifling irrationalities of behaviour are ascribed to it, no venial but wayward likes or dislikes: such a mere personification of an abstract quality is wearisome in fiction, while in life, if such a man could live, he would be so repulsive that we should hardly feel towards so impersonal a being the moral obligations, which are only intelligible between persons. No less incredible would a story be in which all the endeavours and resolves of a thoughtful man were brought to nought by a constant recurrence of adverse accidents. Were such a work meant seriously it would shock us, and we could only endure it as a bit of comedy which awoke in us the soothing reflexion that the whole sphere of action was an insignificant one, as well as a happy disbelief in the reality of what was being tricked out before us as a possibility. Even music seems, not untrue indeed, but insipid and unmeaning, if the flow of its melody can be too easily discerned beforehand. It must not make the simple forward movement which answers to its initial strain; it must reveal its living elasticity by the suddenness of the turns which it seems constrained to make by obstacles, which encounter and thwart it. Lastly we distrust any practical project which instead of co-ordinating side by side, paratactically, to use a phrase of syntax, independent conditions of success, lets them depend hypotactically on a web of mutually conditioning presuppositions. Such schemes only provoke ill-success; for in multiplying the parts of the structure we only multiply the points of contact with hostile influences, and by making one depend on another perpetuate the effects of a check once received.

280. The second of the two principles mentioned is suggested by the fact, that although we can imagine several different groups of equivalent causes agreeing in the attribute of producing one particular effect, still each of these groups will have in addition to the common effect other and peculiar accessory effects of its own which will differentiate it from the rest. Now what we look upon as a single matter of fact is very often a complex whole composed of manifold effects all gathered into one. The different combinations of causes then adequate to produce just this complex effect will be very few, so much so that may-be only one of the many combinations we are accustomed to meet with in our experience will be really adequate. So long therefore as a given matter-of-fact is only known to us in its large outlines we are accustomed to suppose very various causes in order to account for it; as soon however as the finer side traits which characterise it come to be known, our choice of causes narrows itself considerably, till at last we find that there are very few facts, of which we can make hypothesis, which will satisfy all the requirements of the postulate founded on these data. Among these facts we then select that one in particular which at once is the simplest and presupposes the least number of mutually independent and co-operating elements. Nor is the above principle a ruling thought in science only; it governs the most various considerations: a whole chain say of simple facts is set before us in evidence, which taken in connexion with each other may be conveniently explained if we assume that a particular deed was committed; from such a hypothesis we can, we will suppose, deduce everything in the facts except those slight accessory circumstances, which depend on accidental conditions and really give to each particular commission of a deed a peculiar complexion of its own, which it shares with none other. The defendant will ascribe each link in this chain of incriminating evidence to a separate cause compatible with his innocence, and will try to explain away the conjunction of them all as due to a mere unfortunate coincidence; but the persons trying him will turn their attention exclusively to the assumption which explains them all in their connexion with each other, and are hardly likely to listen to his forced pleadings. Just in the same way a patient often consoles himself by referring each of the several symptoms of his malady to a trifling cause of its own; but he does not for all that deceive the physician, who by his diagnosis pitilessly exposes the serious complaint, which at once renders the concurrence of all these accidents conceivable.

I hardly need add that these obvious principles of judgment only suffice to recommend one preliminary conjecture in preference to another; where we have important issues to decide we must never forget that what is improbable is still possible. It is not enough therefore merely to follow out to its conclusions the particular assumption which the evidence before us forces upon us as the most natural. For it even to come near to deserving belief, it is not enough that all the evidence should of itself converge in favour of it; we must have carefully tested the less likely suppositions which the nature of the matter admits of, and have found that they leave just as many lacunae and contradictions in the facts to be explained as does the former. Besides this we must take care as far as possible to argue only from positive evidence; negative evidence is ambiguous: whether it alleges the omission of an action, or the absence of a state, it can only be used to prove a matter-of-fact when what it denies may be regarded as being necessary under any other presupposition. All that follows from a denial of anything is just the denial in turn of what we cannot think without virtually affirming the thing denied. Lastly in deciding a question the mere quantity of evidence matters little—what matters is the quantity of independent evidences. And in this connexion we must be on our guard against a common form of error in reasoning. We may be right in punishing a fault once, but when its inevitable consequences crop up again and again the inclination we feel to chastise the offender over again for each of these in turn is wrong : in the same way the probability of a conjecture is unfairly exaggerated for us, when after the mark which first led us to make it, the consequences necessarily involved in the possession of that mark gradually disclose themselves ; no doubt they agree with our conjecture, but we cannot use them to strengthen it. In conclusion, the observance of all these rules, of whose application it would be much more interesting to give examples than to formulate them in this dry logical manner, is compatible with much error ; still we must not underrate their real value on that account. One practical maxim we may draw from the consideration of all these imperfections : where we must act, whether we would or no, and where we can never rise in our calculations to the level of certainty, there we may confidently trust to probabilities ; where on the other hand we are not obliged to act at all, or at any rate not obliged to do anything extreme and irrevocable, the proper course is not to regard our personal convictions, which rest on mere probabilities, as sufficient warrant for carrying out our belief in action.

281. Where we have matters-of-fact given us, with whose inner coherence we are in a measure acquainted, and would estimate more accurately the probabilities based on such coherence, we trench on a field which spreads beyond the scope of the general precepts of logic, and in it we must rely only upon our actual knowledge of the particular case. In regard to future events, however,—and I shall consider no others in what follows—we often find ourselves differently placed. Of a number of mutually exclusive alternatives we may know that one or the other must happen; but not know of any ground for preferring one to the rest; nevertheless practical needs may force us to make choice of one, and to base our actions on the supposition that it will happen. Under such circumstances we can only regard all equally possible cases as equally probable in reality. There is no other rule by which we can be guided in our judgments. Now we disclaim all knowledge of the circumstances which condition the real issue, so that when we talk of equally possible cases we can only mean those particular cases which are co-ordinated as equivalent species in the compass of an universal case; that is to say, if we enumerate the special forms, which the genus can assume, we get a disjunctive judgment of the form: if the condition B^* is fulfilled, one of the kinds $f^1, f^2, f^3 \ldots$ of the universal consequent F^* will occur to the exclusion of the rest. Which of all these different consequents will in fact occur, depends in all cases on the special form b^1, or b^2, or $b^3 \ldots$, in which that universal condition is fulfilled. If we knew this particular form of B, say b^3, we should be able to deduce for certain the corresponding value f^3 of the consequent, as suming at least that we had discovered the law by which B and F are connected together. For our present purpose, however, we suppose that we are ignorant of the special shape which B will assume if it does really occur; it follows of course that, if B be realised, some one or other of the consequents $f^1, f^2, f^3 \ldots$ must follow; but from our point of view they all remain equally possible, inasmuch as the only condition, so far as we know, of their being any of them realised, is the validity of B *in general*, and that holds equally good for all and favours none in particular. Let us assume for the present that the universal condition B can, if it assumes all the variations compatible with its nature, produce n, say six different consequents $f^1, f^2 \ldots f^6$, then

* ['Bedingung' and 'Folge,' the initial letters of the English words not being convenient symbols.]

the general condition B must be realised in n, i.e. six different ways, for each of the equally possible and mutually exclusive consequents to be *able* to realise itself. Thus we see that, assuming what is equally possible to be equally real, the chance that a particular case will occur admits of being mathematically determined; for each of these f has an equal share in the prospect of being realised in a particular case, with the others which are equally entitled with it to be real; but the sum of all these probabilities must be a constant quantity independent of their number, for it must denote the certainty that some one or another of the particular consequents f, however many they be,—that is to say that F generally—must occur in each individual case so soon as the general condition B is realised in any one of its forms. This certainty is equally absolute for every B and every F, and only in relation to it do the respective chances of the several cases admit of being quantitatively determined; consequently there is no reason for, or advantage in assuming the constant in question to have any other value than unity; the chance of any one particular case of the n co-ordinated cases f thus becomes $= \dfrac{1}{n}$, and the sum of the n chances $= \dfrac{n \cdot 1}{n} = 1$, or in other words 1 is the exponent of certainty. Thus far I have used the expression 'co-ordinated cases' without explaining it; I do so now in order to prevent misunderstanding: a co-ordinated case is a case which answers to one and only one of the mutually exclusive values b^1, b^2, .. of the condition B, and these rival values may occur in reality; it does not answer to a more general form B^1 of this condition, which can never exist in reality, because it embraces several of the particular values b^1, b^2 ..; it follows that each of these f's is also an elementary and particular form of the consequent, without in turn itself comprising other species which can exist apart by themselves, and of which it is merely the general expression. For example we may if we choose give the disjunctive judgment the form: if B holds good, then either f^1 or F^m holds good, by F^m being understood all the m or $n-1$ consequents f, which are not f^1; in such a statement f^1 and F^m are not co-ordinate terms; the chances of f^1 indeed remain $\frac{1}{n}$, but the chance of F^m is the sum of the chances of all the elementary cases which in thought we unite under this formula, and so it $= \frac{n-1}{n}$.

Now it often happens that we are led to institute an enquiry by the interest which attaches for us to some property which the different cases comprised under F^m have in common, and for that reason we separate them from the rest and denote them by a common name as *one* case, to which we oppose the rest. If we would then formulate the probability of this collective case F^m, we may say it is equal to the proportion, which the number of elementary cases combined in it bears to the aggregate sum of all possible cases; or we may state it more accurately, taking account of the connexion of the whole matter, thus: the probability of F^m is equal to the ratio, in which the number of the variations of B, which may issue in a case of the kind F^m, stands to the entire sum of all possible variations of B; in a simpler and more general form still: the probability of F^m is equal to the ratio which the number of chances favourable to it bears to the sum of all thinkable chances, $= \frac{m}{n}$. This fraction is what we understand by the mathematical probability of a future event, and is not at the bottom essentially different from, but only more accurately determined than the probability of common parlance. For usually we say vaguely a thing is probable without specifying the degree of probability which attaches to it; of two events that one is pronounced absolutely probable, whose mathematical probability is the greatest or at any rate usually if wrongly regarded as greatest, the other event only appearing improbable in comparison with it. In treating of chances mathematically we do not ordinarily talk of a thing being improbable, but if we did we could only mean that which is relatively less probable.

282. From small beginnings, which seemed at first to be useless except to satisfy scientific curiosity, the calculus of chances has developed in the hands of the greatest mathematicians into an extensive body of doctrine, bearing fruit in the most diverse fields of scientific research, besides throwing light on many practical questions, the grand logical achievement in fact, which the modern spirit of discovery has to set over against the wonderful but fruitless theories of antiquity. In this form it has outgrown the limits of this treatise, and though every detail of it would always be more entitled to a place in a system of logic than those useless syllogistic subtleties, which in deference to our extravagant love of classical literature we have to be always repeating, still I am forced to confine myself to the enumeration of the simple logical thoughts, which are merely preliminary to calculations into which we cannot at present go any deeper. But in doing so I am conscious that a gap is left, and must point out that this gap needs to be filled, though I do not attempt to fill it myself.

1. In the first place we must make it clear to ourselves what we mean by the probability, which we have just learned to measure in the simplest cases mathematically. It does not imply any positive assertion on our part touching the real future occurrence of the event, to which we attribute it; it does not express any objective property or nature belonging to the event, but denotes throughout what is purely subjective, viz. the degree of confidence, which we may reasonably accord to the future occurrence of a particular case, when all that we have given us to go upon in forming

our judgment is the number of cases possible under the particular given conditions and not any actual ground carrying with it the necessity of one of them to the exclusion of the rest. Let, in accordance with § 281, the probability that a particular side of the die will face upwards after the throw $= 1/6$, the probability that one of the five other sides will fall upwards $= 5/6$; then all that these two numbers signify is this, that *before* the throw the trust we may reasonably repose in the occurrence of the first case must stand to our trust in that of the second in the ratio $1 : 5$; they contain no positive prediction that the one or the other will occur, or that on repeating the throw the one will occur more frequently than the other. We postpone the question, how far such an inference from the calculated probability to the real event is permissible.

2. If two mutually independent variable conditions B and B^1 may lead to n and n^1 different cases respectively, the chance that a particular case in the one series will coincide with a particular case in the other is equal to the product of the chances, which each of the two has in its own series, i.e. to the product of $\frac{m}{n} \cdot \frac{m^1}{n^1}$, where m and m^1 respectively signify the number of favourable chances belonging to each in virtue of the constitution of its condition B or B^1. If two dice are thrown, the side which the one shows uppermost has nothing to do with the side which the other shows uppermost; but each die has 6 sides, each of which may fall uppermost, and each of these may with equal possibility coincide with any one of the six sides of the other; there are thus 36 possible cases and the probability of each single one of them is $1/36 = 1/6 \cdot 1/6$. If however we look upon it as making no difference, which of the two similar dice shows the one and which the other of two different numbers of points, the probability of any two in particular concurring $= 2 \cdot 1/36 = 1/18$; for if we throw but one die or the die B there is of course but a single chance

of any particular side falling uppermost, but if we throw two dice, that is in case of the combination $B+B^1$, there are always two chances in favour of any two differently marked sides falling uppermost together. On the other hand the probability that two similarly marked faces will fall uppermost together must still remain $= 1/36$, for there is only one combination which can produce a particular doublet. Lastly, if our object be to throw both dice together and get a particular number of points between the two, the sum 7 has most probability $= 1/6 = 6/36$, for it has 6 favourable chances in the combinations $6+1$, $5+2$, $3+4$, each of which occurs twice; the smallest probability, viz. $1/36$ attaches to the sums 2 and 12, each of which can only be produced in one way.

Again, suppose we put in an urn B 17 black and 3 white balls, in a second urn B^1 6 black and 4 white balls, and then ask what chance there is of drawing two white balls, one from each urn; it is evident that in this case as in the last what the one hand grasps is quite independent of what the other hand has grasped; but the probability of drawing a white ball out of the first urn is $m = 3$ favourable chances out of 20, the probability of drawing a white from the second urn is $m^1 = 4$ out of 10. Now there are 10 balls in B^1, and we may draw a white ball from B with any one of them; also there are four whites among these ten; consequently the chance of one of these four being drawn along with whatever we draw from the other urn would be $4/10$; but as the chance of our drawing a white ball from that other urn was only $3/20$, the chance of our drawing two whites together one from each urn will $= \dfrac{m}{n} \cdot \dfrac{m^1}{n^1} = 3/20 \cdot 4/10 = 3/50$.

We should get another result if we gathered all the balls into one vessel and drew twice out of it, taking care however to restore the ball first drawn before we drew a second. The result of the second draw would then as in the above case be independent of that of the first; for each draw the probability of a white ball being drawn would $= \frac{7}{30}$, so that the probability of two whites being drawn in succession would $= \frac{7}{30} \cdot \frac{7}{30} = \frac{49}{900}$, that is to say would be less than in the first case. The difference of the two results may seem strangely great, as without calculating it one would hardly suppose there was any essential difference between the two modes of proceeding; there is however, inasmuch as it is harder or easier to draw one of the white balls just according as there are more or fewer black balls mixed with them. The chance, $\frac{7}{30}$, of drawing a white out of the whole collection of balls amounts no doubt to $\frac{14}{9}$ of the chance, viz. $\frac{3}{20}$ that there is of drawing a white out of the urn which contains 20 balls; for the same reason however it amounts to only $\frac{7}{12}$ of the other chance $\frac{4}{10}$, which is the chance of drawing another white from the other urn, which contains 10 in all. Consequently the chance of drawing two whites by the second method is only $\frac{14}{9} \cdot \frac{7}{12}$ or $\frac{49}{54}$ of the chance of obtaining the same result by the first method; we have in fact $\frac{49}{54} \cdot \frac{6}{100} = \frac{49}{900}$. It is better to be quite clear on this point, so I will take a still simpler example. Let us assume that the urn B contains but one white and no black balls, while B^1 contains one white and one black; then if we draw from B we are certain of one white ball, whose probability therefore $= 1$; and we may draw either a white or a black from B^1, with either of which it may concur; thus the chance of either of these cases, one of which consists in two whites following one another is $\frac{1}{2} = 1 \cdot \frac{1}{2}$. Such is the result got by the first method, that of dividing the balls in separate urns. By the second method however, which consists in putting them all in one urn, we are certain of nothing; for the first as for the second draw the chance of a white is the same $= \frac{2}{3}$, and that of two whites in succession $= \frac{4}{9}$, that is to say smaller than it is upon the first method.

3. Suppose the variations of a condition B produce a series of cases of the kind f, but the actual occurrence of

one of these cases modifies the condition B^1 which leads to consequences of the kind f^1; the chance that a particular case of the series f will coincide with a particular case of the series f^1 is equal to the product of the independent chance of f into that of f^1 as modified by the occurrence of the former. We get such a case by slightly modifying the last example. If we put back the first ball drawn into the urn, which contains 30 balls, we leave the second draw independent of the first; but if we do not restore it, the urn will only contain 6 white out of 29 balls; the chance of still drawing a white becomes $6/29$ and that of alighting on two in succession $= 7/30 \cdot 6/29$, and is only about 0.88 of the chance which there was of drawing two successive whites, when the ball first drawn was put back into the urn. This was to be expected, as the number of white balls is now proportionately less than that of the black, among which they must be sought. Under this head fall many of the problems to which the calculus of probability may be applied, and great care must be taken to discriminate them from the former class. We very often have to do with events, whose chance of recurring in the future depends on the number of cases, in which on previous occasions either they themselves or others standing in a definite relation to them, have been realised; and it is not always easy by analysing this interdependence to ascertain the influence, which the occurrence of one case exercises in conditioning the probability of the one to be next expected.

I have no space to illustrate this by examples, but shall give an instance of a different sort. An eye-witness imparts something he has seen to someone, who in turn imparts the information to a third person. Now we know from experience that the further news travels in this manner the more distorted it becomes, and accordingly it has been proposed to ascertain what degree of trust may be reasonably reposed in a statement in proportion to the number of people concerned in its transmission to us. I do not believe that any amount of calculation will really help us to answer the question. To begin with, it is not quite plain what we are driving at. An allegation is either right or wrong; but if wrong it deviates more or less from the truth; and we might assign to it a greater or less degree of credibility according as it deviates more or less, supposing it to be possible to measure against one another the different amounts of these deviations. But this we shall seldom be able to do; each term of a judgment, expressing an original observation, can be taken apart and falsified in a way peculiar to itself and when falsified can be variously combined with other terms; the aggregate of errors thus arising cannot be regarded as constituting a series of terms, which we can compare together, and we should thus have no available standard by which to estimate the objective credibility of the statement as handed down. But after all this is not what we really want; we want to ascertain the particular degree of trust which may be based on our knowledge of a single condition, which we have stated, viz. of the number of times a bit of intelligence has been handed on from person to person before it reaches us. But here the objection at once occurs that this condition of transmission does not in itself contain anything that could at all justify us in predicting a gradual falsification of the statement transmitted. When, as in the above example, we have drawn a white ball and removed it from the vessel, which has in it 30 balls, 7 of them white, we know that the conditions of a fresh draw are changed and we know exactly by how much; on the other hand if we restore the ball we are equally certain that the conditions are the same as before, that the second draw is a *res integra* so to speak and its chances the same as those of the first. It is to the latter not to the former case that the problem now before us corresponds; the mere fact of transmission, taken in itself, cannot cause me to transmit something else than I have heard; so far as the mere transmission goes there would be not a mere probability but an actual certainty that the last hearer will accurately receive the original statement. Thus the falsification of a statement depends not on the number of times it has been passed on but on the size and sort of errors made in it each time it has been passed on; consequently our knowledge of the number of times it has passed from mouth to mouth will only help us to estimate its trustworthiness, if the size of the various errors be either constant or a regular function of that number. There is not the least ground for assuming any such thing; we see it to be quite the reverse if we really reflect on the very various cases which may occur. The eye-witness A may or may not have wished to communicate aright what he has rightly observed; his hearer B has or has not understood him aright, or he may have understood him and yet desire to hand it on himself in a distorted form; a third person C, who intended to distort afresh what he already misunderstood, may chance to hit upon the actual truth in what he communicates. If we consider all these possible conditions we see clearly that the trustworthiness of a communication in no way depends in any regular manner merely on the number of times it has passed from mouth to mouth. We disregard these conditions because we are ignorant of them; but if we had the power of knowing them all the question would answer itself and we should not need to calculate it at all. All we can do in the matter therefore is to make utterly arbitrary assumptions in regard to all these conditions, which would be tantamount to bringing the whole thing down to the level of arithmetical examples, which had no bearing on or application to real events. Such would be the following sort of calculation: say that we hear and in turn report anything with such accuracy as to deduct one tenth of its credibility; then after the 20th repetition of the statement its credibility would only be $0.9^{20} = 0.1216$, only a little more than $1/7$ of what it was originally. Here all is arbitrary assumption; it is arbitrary to assume that the credibility diminishes in geometrical progression, instead of arithmetical; the latter is quite as conceivable. No less arbitrary is it to suppose at all, that the exponent or difference of term from term must be equal; the result too which we thus reach has no meaning; it might perhaps be true of frivolous street-gossip, but as regards serious historical traditions it is a gross exaggeration of the rate at which their untrustworthiness increases.

4. Given certain facts we have to conjecture their true causes; we must calculate the probability with which the given effects would follow from the various possible causes, and select that cause as the true one on presupposition of which the facts would most naturally follow. I draw four times in succession from a bag, and draw from it 3 white and 1 black ball, restoring the ball each time, and the question is asked what number of balls of each sort must the bag most probably have contained in order to give this result. In order to answer the question we must know the whole number of balls in the bag, in order that we may be able to state the number of conceivable combinations capable of causing the given result. Suppose there were 4 altogether. Now to account for the result at all there must be at least 1 white and 1 black; how many more of each kind remains indefinite; there are 3 possible combinations, which we can assume: 3 whites + 1 black, 2 whites + 2 black, 1 white + 3 black. For these 3 combinations the chances of drawing a white are respectively $\frac{3}{4}$, $\frac{2}{4}$, $\frac{1}{4}$, of drawing a black $\frac{1}{4}$, $\frac{2}{4}$, $\frac{3}{4}$; the joint chances however of drawing in 4 successive draws 3 whites and 1 black become on these various assumptions $\frac{27}{256}$, $\frac{16}{256}$, $\frac{3}{256}$; consequently the first assumption, that 3 whites and 1 black ball were in the bag, is the most likely; at the same time the fractions got give the particular probability which each of the other two possesses. A very simple consideration confirms this solution. Had the bag had in it but a single white, according to the third hypothesis, we must in 4 draws have grasped it 3 times, while we only once grasped a black ball

out of three which offered themselves,—a supposition obviously less probable than four draws in which each ball has its turn. It may be noticed that this calculation of course presupposes that the different causes, which we can assume in order to account for the given facts, in themselves possess equal probability; this was the case here so far as any distribution of the two colours among the 4 balls was in itself quite as possible as any other; where the probabilities of the causes are not equal, due account must be taken of the same in our calculations.

5. When we see the same result repeat itself under the same general condition B we are led to expect it to occur again if B recurs. The chance of its really doing so admits of being calculated. A bag has in it two balls and it is found that so often as we draw we always get balls of one colour, say white, so that the colour of the other ball remains unknown to us. Hence we expect to get a white upon drawing a third time, supposing ourselves to have drawn twice. How shall we measure the probability of our expectation? One ball must be white, so that there are only two possibilities, either the other is black or both are white. Now two whites have already been drawn in two draws, and the probability that this which has happened would happen becomes on the first assumption $1/4$, on the second $= 1$; consequently the odds in favour of the rival assumptions stand to each other as $1 : 4$ and as their sum must be $= 1$, the first must be put $= 1/5$, the other $= 4/5$. In case we make a third draw the odds in favour of the white are $1/2$ on the first assumption and 1 on the second; the sum of the favourable chances presented by both assumptions taken together is thus $1/5 \cdot 1/2 + 4/5 \cdot 1 = 9/10$. In this case the actual event had occurred and we only knew and calculated the *a priori* chance which it had of occurring under two rival presuppositions as to its conditions; but even where we have not this knowledge, we may draw an inference as to the chance that an event will recur from the

number of times we have actually observed it occur. Suppose we are quite ignorant of its conditions and grounds and only know that an event E has once occurred under certain conditions, say at some critical moment of time t, it may at first sight seem as if the chance of its occurring a second time under the same conditions was exactly as great as its chance of not occurring at all. But this is a miscalculation; were it true the observed fact of its having once occurred would be ignored in our calculation, and as the same reflexion might be fairly made after the event had occurred for the mth time, we might find ourselves in the absurd position of maintaining that the fact of an event having occurred even an infinite number of times did not make its occurrence next time any more likely than it would have been, if it had never yet occurred at all. This however would be evidently paradoxical; for every fresh repetition of an event is a fresh and additional testimony to the continuance of the unknown causes on which it depends, and so strengthens the probability of its occurring again. Our conclusion therefore in regard to the first case must be this; that E will not occur is in itself just as likely as that it will; but for the existence of causes which bring about E we have the testimony of this one observed case of its occurrence; for the existence of causes which prevent E we have nothing but the bare possibility. We consequently have two reasons for expecting E to recur, where we have only one for expecting it not to, as the two chances stand to one another in the ratio $2:1$, while their sum must $=1$, the chance that E will recur $= \frac{2}{3}$. In general therefore, if an event E or a particular cyclical course of like events E has been observed m times without any exception, the probability that E will happen again in the same way is $= \frac{m+1}{m+2}$; in this fraction the denominator represents the sum of conceivable cases, since after m real cases have occurred there are always two additional cases, which we can think of as occurring, viz. the repetition or non-repetition of E; the numerator as usual denotes the number of favourable chances. I think this simple deduction of the formula will satisfy the reader; it is to me as convincing as the more obscure analysis, by which it is usually obtained. One sees that as m increases the fraction approaches nearer and nearer to unity, and so it becomes more and more nearly certain that E will recur. The example usually adduced is that as the alternation of day with night has been now historically attested for 5000 years, the probability of the same alternation recurring to-day $= 1,826,214 : 1,826,215$; that is one may bet $1,826,214$ to 1 on its occurring again. Now if it is true of calculations of probability in general that they do not express what will actually occur in the future, but only the degree of subjective confidence, which we repose in their occurrence; it is in a certain sense doubly true of these cases, as we clearly feel when m is a very small number. For then the assumption from which we start is that the number m of cases in which E has been observed to occur testifies with a certainty proportional to the magnitude of m to the *continuance* on the next occasion of the causes favourable to E: and this assumption is itself but a probability, the strength of which is somewhat arbitrary, and of which we only know that it increases with the increase of m. Properly therefore the formula would not directly measure the probability that E will recur, but the probability of this probability, which comes to this, that not only the value to be assigned to the probability, but also our confidence in this value approaches nearer and nearer to certainty as m indefinitely increases.

6. A future event may be fraught with good or evil for us, and it is usually a sense of these consequences to ourselves which impels us to gauge the strength of our confidence in its happening. We shall shape our motives and actions according to its strength, and these will therefore depend doubly on the likelihood of the event E and on the com-

parative amount of the advantage we hope to derive from it. If we multiply the probability of E into the amount of attendant advantage we get what we term *mathematical expectation*, which thus admits of being precisely determined. Let a game be so arranged that the player gets two thalers if on the first toss he throws heads and five thalers if he throws first tails then heads. The probability of the former case is $= 1/2$, its expectation $= 1/2 \cdot 2$; the probability of the second case is $= 1/4$, its expectation $= 1/4 \cdot 5$; lastly the aggregate expectation of winnings when play begins can only be the sum $9/4$ of these two expectations; for though the two lucky cases exclude one another according to the arrangement, yet the expectation of winning must clearly be greater when both the two prizes are offered than when only one, and the expectation of the one must be exactly left over, if the expectation of the other is reduced to nothing by the gradual diminution of the prize assigned to it. The same reasoning would apply, if it were agreed that the player should receive two thalers if he threw heads the first time, and then another five in case tails followed. The two winning cases are then compatible with each other, but here too all that can be won is either two or seven thalers, and the chance of winning either is $1/4$. In this case then as in the former $9/4$ of a thaler represents the aggregate expectation of the player and the utmost he can reasonably stake upon it. Suppose again that of different events E, E^1, E^2, which we may expect, some are fraught with evil, others with good consequences to us; in that case it is easy to see that the aggregate expectation which we may entertain, if by our own actions we are willing to risk their happening, must equal the difference between the sum of the mathematical expectations of the favourable events and the sum of the expectations of the unfavourable ones. If this difference be a negative quantity it expresses the magnitude of the risk we run or, more correctly speaking, the magnitude of the anxiety we should feel. This principle is wide and important in its applications; by means of it we are not only able to determine what bets and games of chance are fair and equitable —a sort of calculation we could as well do without as we can do without its object—but it also assists us in arranging the most serious public and private business, such as the management of finances, the undertakings of trade and the organisation of all sorts of insurance companies.

7. This is the place to mention one other idea. Even the mathematical expectation of an event does not determine its value for us irrespectively of our own condition before it occurs; in judging of its real value for us we must take this condition into account. A moment's joy to the miserable or a trifling gift to the poor is of greater value than a fresh triumph to the fortunate or splendid winnings to the rich. No doubt as a matter of fact one that has much is wont to desire so much the more, but in this respect logic takes the point of view of equity, according to which it ought not to be so: in assuming as a self-evident principle that the *relative* value of an advantage bears an inverse ratio to the advantages of the position to which it is added, it expresses the standard according to which a man seems to be justified in desiring to improve his condition, when the good things available for this improvement have also to satisfy the wants of others. This general law does not admit of being mathematically applied, unless all the advantages of a situation and all the good things requisite in order to better it admit of being mathematically compared; it is therefore chiefly of use in regard to the increase of a capital, which can be expressed in money. Let V be a capital which we have already got, and z the addition which it is to receive: then this increase of V may always be regarded as the sum of an infinite number of smaller increments each of the size dz; the relative value however of each subsequent $(n+1)^{\text{th}}$ augmentation by a dz is in inverse proportion to the size of V as already enhanced by the preceding increments, that is to $V + n\,dz$, and would

thus $=\dfrac{k \cdot dz}{V + n\,dz}$. In this formula k is a specific coefficient, which differs with the different sorts of cumulative advantage, but is constant for all z of the same kind and does not admit of further determination in the abstract; and as it forms a common factor in all values which we can compare we omit it in what follows. The relative value of the aggregate increase by z is then the integral of this expression, in which we must replace $n\,dz$ by values of z ranging from o up to z: it is therefore

$$= \log(V + z) - \log V.$$

In accordance with this formula we should find that for a capital $V = 1000$ the relative values of the increase when $z = 1000$, $= 2000$, $= 3000$, $= 4000$, are approximately 1, 1.6, 2, 2.3: that is to say, they grow very much more slowly than do the increments themselves. For the different capitals $V = 1000$, $= 2000$, $= 3000$, $= 4000$, the relative values of the increase, when each is augmented by $z = 1000$, are approximately 0.301, 0.176, 0.125, 0.097. When we have thus calculated the relative values of the advantages which some event will bring us, we may multiply them by the chance there is of their ever being attained which we will call m: by this means we get $m \log\left(\dfrac{V+z}{V}\right)$ for our *moral expectation* of them, i.e. the mathematical expectation of these advantages reduced to their relative values; and this is what in all sorts of enterprises determines the amount of risk we may prudently incur in view of some prospective advantage. We have assumed the factor m to be constant however high z is; it may be so, but it may also be a function of z or of $V + z$, in which case of course it is to be included under the integral sign and brought into the integration. In point of fact there are many sorts of undertakings in which while the first success is hard to win, subsequent successes become easier and easier, or in which the possibility of further success diminishes with the increase of what has been won. Lastly the formulae do not help us to measure all that one may wish to measure. By treating z only as the sum of dz, without taking account of the time t which it takes to achieve the summation, they neglect the distinction between gradual and sudden improvements. The real, actual, or physical values of the two *may* be the same, but their psychical effect, or, to put it simply, the pleasure they occasion, may be different, and this after all enters as a factor into the idea of the comparative value of an advantage. Let us assume first that the extent to which a particular satisfaction admits of being further enhanced $= \dfrac{1}{V}$, if V represents the degree of satisfaction of the same sort to which one has already attained; and secondly that the increase in the satisfaction generated remains proportional to the size z of the sudden increase in the advantage; then $\dfrac{z}{V}$ will measure the pleasure due to the accession of z. But it is easy to see that these are not the only conceivable assumptions; it might even possibly be found that the eventual enjoyment is also a function of m, i.e. of the chance that z will occur: we might perhaps be more deeply affected on winning a satisfaction, of which we had almost despaired, than on winning one of even greater comparative value that was more probable.

283. The last observation just touched upon problems which have not as yet been brought within the range of calculation, though there is nothing to prevent their being so brought, if an advance in psychological knowledge should ever afford us starting-points from which to grapple with them. Other problems there are to which it is but an idle play of words to try to apply the calculus of chances. For although this method of inference does start from our ignorance of the special grounds, which condition a particular event, still it makes certain presuppositions, which we cannot neglect. In the first place it presupposes the truths logical and mathematical, of which we must make use in order to be able to calculate at all. The truth of special laws, limited in their action to a group of facts, the non-existence of which is just as conceivable as is their existence, may, as we shall presently see, be proved by means of calculation; but from what basis could one legitimately start to show the law of identity or the doctrine of disjunctive judgments to be more or less probable? The very simplest determination of any probability presupposes a disjunction of all possible cases to be given, that each of these cases is identical with itself and not the same as any other, and that each of them is exclusive of the rest. It follows that before we set about to prove an event, or a state, or a series of events to be probable, we must have presupposed the particular content in question to be part and parcel of a world, in which universal laws demarcate what is true from what is untrue, what is possible from what is impossible, what may easily occur from what may not.

But the calculus of probabilities is subject to other limitations besides these. The object, which its problems concern, must be regarded by it as not merely thinkable in the abstract; it must also presuppose the presence of conditions, which necessitate the realisation of one of the disjoined cases to the exclusion of the rest; to use the language of its formulae there must always be a certainty $= 1$, which is the sum of all the probabilities of the particular cases, which we can think of. This was noticeable in our examples throughout. *If* a die has been thrown or *if* two have been, we can determine the respective chance of any of the particular cases which may result; but unless we specify how many dice are to fall and how many times in succession, it is quite impossible to determine the scope of the disjoined possibilities and the unity by reference to which the chances of each are to be severally measured. It follows that we can only calculate such events as depend on one another within a regularly ordered world; ultimate facts, which contain an independent absolute being of their own, we cannot calculate. It would be mere senseless play of wit to reason thus: prior to all existence there is the same chance of the existence of something as of nothing; but one or the other must take place; therefore the chance of something existing is $=1/2$: but this something would necessarily be either one or many; consequently the chance of there being many elements is $1/4$, and the chance of there being one is $1/4$: lastly assuming that there are n elements, they may be all alike, or some different, or all different; the case of these being all alike would be but one of the m cases which would thus arise, and consequently its probability is $= \dfrac{1}{4m}$. Prior to all existence, we must observe, there can exist no ingenious spirit to institute such a calculation of what will be; could we conceive however of such a spirit as existing outside the world and speculating as to whether it is likely to come into existence or no, still that nothing would involve no condition of any sort, which would necessitate a real settlement of the alternative presented in thought between being and not being, so that the end of the whole matter would still be nothing. But suppose the alternative to have been somehow settled in favour of being, this being could not possibly be something, which were merely thinkable *in abstracto*; it must be capable of existing and can only be some determinate being, which excludes all other thinkable being. Such determinate being would from the very beginning have a certainty of its own $= 1$, while the probability of all other kinds of being would be not exactly $= 0$, so much as an idea without any assignable meaning. It would be different if we wished to determine the probability of these ultimate facts from given data: on the assumption that all reality is bound together by law, these given data would (not as the ground of their reality, but as the source of our knowledge of them) constitute a condition which would compel us to assume the one or other form of those ultimate facts to the exclusion of the rest.

284. There is one other point we shall do well to bear in mind. In probability we have after all no more than a measure of the confidence we may legitimately place in the occurrence of an event, *before* it has occurred. *After* it has occurred however what was previously its greater or less probability does not continue to attach to it as a permanent property, from which we may regressively draw some other conclusion in regard to the causes of its being realised than just this that they have actually come about. We are victims of all sorts of illusions on this point. For example an event E occurs, which on previous calculation was very unlikely to occur as compared with a whole class of cases, which for the convenience of thought we gather into one and collectively oppose to it as a second rival case non-E; in such a case we are apt to imagine that not only a special and peculiar but a *higher* cause was necessary in order to bring about E. To take a common instance: some object is of little significance, almost unknown and seldom spoken of. We stumble on its name once, after which it meets our eye again and again in conversation, in books, in periodicals; here is a coincidence, the chance of which, if calculated beforehand, was infinitely small and we call it a very strange incident. But a moment's reflexion will convince us that there is very little strangeness about it; how infinitely more numerous are the cases in which the incident does not turn up than those in which it does! How many names just catch our ear once without ever being repeated in such a way that their repetition strikes us as odd! To put what I mean in a perfectly general way, let us suppose there to exist some condition B or some group B of different but co-operant conditions; these according to the different and in the abstract equally possible variable attitudes, which they can assume towards each other, would bring about a number n of different results E; the probability of each individual E is then $= \frac{1}{n}$ and by consequence the same as that of every other *determinate* E, but, if n be infinitely great, infinitely small as compared with the probability that *any* one indifferently of all the remaining $n-1$ events will happen, which we collectively oppose to it. But the latter, the collective probability has another significance than the former—the individual, for all the $n-1$ events cannot be realised, but only one of them to the exclusion of the rest.

A famous instance will illustrate the extent to which we may be led astray by such false comparison of things, which are essentially different. The planetary system, according to Laplace, and so far as he knew it, consists of 11 planets and 18 satellites; we are acquainted with the revolutions of the sun, of 10 of the planets, of the moons of Jupiter, of Saturn's ring and of one of his satellites; the rotations of these bodies together with their revolutions form a group of 43 movements in the same direction; would we assume that this uniformity is all a matter of chance, we find on calculating it that the probability of such an assumption being true is something less than unity divided by four billions. I have no doubt that fresh advances in astronomical science will leave this number substantially correct, but what follows? Simply that the particular cause or grouping of causes adequate to produce this state of things is or has been real. It does not follow that this grouping of causes itself requires any other cause than just that so-called chance, by which we mean no more than that the mutual relations of several realities, which we presume to form a group, may without contradiction be combined in an infinite number of ways. Out of all these four billions of possible cases never more than a single one can be realised, and no matter which of them it be, we shall feel just the same surprise at its happening in particular as we should have at any other of the four billions, had *it* happened. The case would be utterly different, if all those other dispositions of events really formed a single second case, capable of being realised as such; in that case its chance, denoted by four billions, would have at least admitted of being directly compared with the probability of the other case, i.e. with unity, although even then the sort of conclusion would not have been justified but only rendered more attractive. No doubt a plausible attempt may be made to justify the reduction of the whole number of cases to a single pair of alternatives; nothing, it may be said, but this given disposition of all masses and motions could secure the stability of the planetary system and the continuance of its movements; no one of the million other arrangements would have served to produce this state of equilibrium. We concede all this, but might it not be also pleaded in favour of each of the other arrangements, that it too had in store for the planetary system a particular destiny of its own, that on presupposition of it alone among the many millions of possible presuppositions could that peculiar destiny be fulfilled, so that if the uniqueness of the result constitutes a claim to a higher origin each of these rival dispositions may with equal right prefer such a claim? It would seem then as if it was not the unique result as such, but the unique result which was better than its fellows, which finally prevailed. But why should superiority in itself constitute improbability? And after all *would* this case which ultimately prevailed be better than others? No doubt as things are our blood is ever fresh and new, yet at the expense of for ever circulating in the same forms; but is it really and without qualification a finer thing that it should circulate as it does than that it should not? The perpetual repetition of these forms may no doubt appear very grand to us to-day, to-morrow may it not strike us as rather tedious? Would it not be a finer thing if the planetary system were not in such stable equilibrium, if all its relations were for ever changing, so that vegetation and natural beauty, animals and man should develope in ever new and interesting forms and history be really the history of a progress, of a manifest advance, instead of the chronicle of a cycle of ever-recurring events? And to conclude, inasmuch as the heavens are infinite, may not all the millions of differently ordered systems be actually realised therein? With us the system of equilibrium, at unknown distances the rest? And then surely our own system would only possess such reality as its probability entitles us to claim for it, it would be but one among millions.

285. Thus far we viewed the calculation of chances as a mere means of ascertaining accurately the confidence we may repose in the occurrence of future events. There now arises a natural desire to know how far these previous calculations are as a rule confirmed by the actual course of events. The answer usually made is that the more numerous the cases, which make an event F possible, the more closely does the number of times it actually occurs tend to coincide with the number calculated. We can only get an answer that is at all trustworthy by means of experiments of the simplest kind, in which care is taken to restore after each mth experiment the group B of conditions, upon which each particular case F depends, in such a way as to leave the composition of B exactly the same after as before that experiment, differenced only by the variations, whose influence on the net result of the series of experiments it is the very object of our enquiry to ascertain; taking care at the same time to prevent the entrance of any alien cause not implied in the idea of such variation, whether that cause consists in external circumstances or in a change of the object of the experiment or in unfair intervention, on the part of the person experimenting. These conditions are fulfilled in experiments made with dice. We calculate beforehand that, if two dice are thrown once, the chance of getting a particular combination of points, e.g. $5 \cdot 6 = \frac{1}{18} = 0.056$, which for a thousand throws would be 56; if now we make trial of these 1000 throws one after another, and find, as in fact has been found to be the case, that the specified combination occurs 50 times, we see that this number already approximates pretty clearly to the number calculated; yet more when in 10,000 throws it rises to 570. Each single throw in such a case depends, if we leave out of account the uniform or changing resistance of the air, on the following conditions: on the velocity with which and the angle at which the die impinges on the receiving plate, upon the position of its sides and corners at the moment of impact, upon its own elasticity and on that of the plate. We may regard the last of these conditions as constant, for as we should expect from a calculation of its probability, the die will extremely seldom touch the same point of the plate, so that the elasticity of the point of impact will not change to any appreciable extent, if it was the same to begin with for all points of the plate. If, however, we would still regard it as variable, it may be included, just as well as the slight and gradual changes in the shape and elasticity of the die, among the variations of the conditions, the effect of which is being investigated; for since the two changes do not depend on each other, but may co-operate, they do not when taken together favour one particular throw more than another, but favour now one now another indifferently. The first-named condition, the velocity and direction of the die, depends of course on the movement of the hand that casts it; but were one even disposed to favour a particular throw by this means, one could hardly do so effectually; for *after* we have obtained a particular throw, we neither retain a clear recollection of the group of muscular feelings, which accompanied it, nor are we able to reproduce the exact movements, on which those feelings depended, so as to exactly copy the throw; and the least deviation would have the effect of favouring some other combination of points than what we wished to throw. These very changes therefore of our movements are among the legitimate variations of the conditions of the result we are investigating.

The same advantages are presented by a rotating drum, into which m white and p black balls are introduced and into which each time we have drawn we re-introduce the ball drawn before drawing again. If we then turn the drum we do not of course restore exactly the same position to the balls, which they had before we drew, but still we only produce one of the variations of this position, with the influence of which we wish to become acquainted. If we distinguish the whole condition B, upon which the event F in each separate case depends, into a constant and a variable element, we may say that in the first case the shape of the die forms the constant element as does the number of black and white balls in the second, while the variable element consists in the first case of the velocity and direction of the die, in the second case of the relative positions of the balls and the direction given to the hand in drawing. If we actually make the second experiment the result obtained is similar; the greater the number of draws the more nearly does the ratio between the numbers of the white and black balls drawn approach to the ratio between the numbers m and p, in which they were present in the drum.

286. Theoretical considerations have been based on the results of these experiments, which I cannot persuade myself are correct. A vicious circle is involved in all attempts to show that the results mentioned occur always with an *intelligible necessity*. In the first place one cannot argue from m series of experiments, in which we have really obtained it, to its being obtained in every $(m+1)^{\text{th}}$ series, so long as the unknown variations of the conditions, which have there produced the said result and would produce it here, are *individually* subject to no rule whatever. For the idea that they will at least *on the whole* continue to compensate themselves in the same way here as there—and it is only on this condition that the attempted universalisation of the observed results would be permissible—this idea, I say, has no *objective* validity, nor is it to be deduced from anything we already know to be real; it is indeed simply a way of expressing our subjective and almost tautological maxim, that that is most likely to occur in reality, which previous calculation shows to be most likely. Provided, that is to say, no uniform cause gives the preference to one of the possible cases of the kind F over another, we must ascribe the same chance of being realised to all cases, which in their idea are co-ordinate or equally possible; in which case all that is meant by saying that some particular fact or event is to be expected as most probable is just this, that in a great number of experiments the *actual* number of times a case F occurs is equal to the *calculated* number. If this expectation is verified in m series of experiments, that has *actually* occurred m times, which *before* the occurrence was the most probable: but it does not therefore become a demonstrable necessity that it should again occur in every $(m+1)^{\text{th}}$ series of experiments; that indeed remains the most likely thing we can expect, when we are brought face to face with this new series of experiments, but it may always turn out to have been a wrong expectation.

In the second place no single series of experiments can really comprise an infinite number of experiments; it must always stop short at some finite number, however large it be. Thus it can never be a real fact of observation, that the number of *actual* realisations of F approximates *without limit* to the *calculated* number as n increases: it is always an inference from the facts. Now assuming that in n experiments we reach a point at which the two numbers coincide or that they have so nearly coincided that their difference need not be considered, it would be a very arbitrary procedure to break off the series just at this point. It is obvious that the law of such equality or approximation comes true if we continue the series till it comes true and *no longer*. But what if we prolong the series? Possibly the theoretical and the real results will converge still more; possibly again each additional round of n experiments will have the same or nearly the same result as the first had, and the difference d will not be sensibly diminished by prolonging the series: and to these possibilities we may add any other less regular succession as *also* possible. Only these different suppositions have not the same amount of probability; so long as we consistently avoid presupposing any constant cause, which in a series of experiments to be made might give one case F a preponderance over others, our most probable assumption is merely, that as n goes on increasing the number of observed realisations of F will continually approximate to the number of them calculated beforehand. If in a large though limited number n of experiments this expectation is *not* verified, a constant or uniform condition *may* be chargeable with the result, though it *may* also be due to the combination on no principle of variable conditions. As often however as our expectations are verified by what really occurs, we are presented with a *fact*, at which we cannot feel any surprise just because it was beforehand not improbable, but still a fact of which we can just as little prove that it was necessary as we can prove of the verification of any mathematical chance that it was necessary. In the experiment with the drum and balls an uniform proportion gradually revealed itself between the numbers of the differently coloured balls drawn; I cannot believe that this uniformity is really *explicable*, if that means anything more than probable. The distinction made between the constant and the variable or accidental causes which jointly produce an effect is a very true and significant one, but this is not in my opinion the place to appeal to it. It is argued that however irregular the successive arrangements of the balls may be, there still remains one constant element, namely the unchanging proportion of white to black balls; this in a great number of draws *must* make itself felt by producing some constant effect: for there is no reason to suppose that just where the hand alights balls of one colour will be found oftener than in proportion to their relative number: if such were found to be the case, we must, it is argued, break with our supposition and assume some constant collateral cause which favours that colour. Against this view it may be objected that the constant causes spoken of could not make themselves felt by merely being there, but only so far as they act. In the experiments with dice the shape of the die and the position of its centre of gravity were such constant causes and both took effect in each single case. In virtue of the former the die could only fall on six sides and not on a seventh, in virtue of the latter it could not help falling on one of its sides instead of coming to rest on one of its angles or corners; on which of its sides it should fall, however, was just what these constant causes did not determine. It is the same with the experiments with balls in a drum; two of the conditions are constant; firstly the colours are only white and black, so that no blue or red ball can be drawn; secondly their numbers m and p are constant, though the relative numbers of the few balls which come within reach of the hand each time it draws are none the less to be classed as variable elements in the condition; hence it follows that this constant condition, the ratio $m:p$, does not take effect, though it actually exists. I do not therefore see the necessity of assuming—what contradicts our pre-supposition—a constant collateral cause to account for the apparent anomaly of a different proportion of balls being drawn to what is in the urn. On the contrary all that is needed to produce such a result is that the positions of the balls should be changed on no principle, and such irregular change is just what we presuppose and try to bring about by turning the drum. Such change of their positions renders possible every and any combination of the balls, makes it possible even that all the balls of one colour should be missed and even that this exclusion of one colour should be repeated over and over again in successive experiments, everything being designedly so arranged that each $(m+1)^{th}$ experiment is entirely independent of the mth. All that can be said against this is that it is the reverse of probable; all that is probable is that the number of times a ball of a particular colour is grasped will tally with the number of balls of that colour which there are in the urn. But this too is no more than a probability; if it be nearly verified by experience we have got a fact, not inexplicable, inasmuch as we see quite well how easily the causes which contribute to that result may come together, but not explicable in the sense that one could demonstrate both that and how they *must* thus coincide in the long run of cases, whereas, when the cases are few in number, there is no must about it.

287. In the foregoing examples we were cognisant of the nature of the constant causes as well as of the extent to which those which were not constant might vary; hence we could in anticipation of experience make assumptions as to how often an event they conditioned would occur, and find our assumptions verified by experience. We now turn to events of which we know neither the constant nor the variable causes, but which we observe to occur over and over again. What conclusions can we draw from the regularity with which they occur? Here we know neither how many are the cases, which are barely possible, nor how many chances in favour of the event in question there may be among them. The only distinction we make is between the occurrence or non-occurrence of E, regarding as cases, in which its occurrence is possible, all those which realise the particular centres of relation, which being given make E intelligible, and comparing with the numbers of these the number of cases in which it is realised. The constant and variable causes on which blindness depends are hidden

from us; but the number of cases in which this defect may owing to those causes occur is equal to the number of the population. If we compare with the entire number of persons belonging to one generation the total number of blind people among them and conceive of this comparison being extended over several generations, we can quite see how it would transpire, whether such a constant ratio is on the whole to be found between the two numbers, as would point to the presence of a group of constant causes favourable to blindness in the mass of men, but in the individual modified in their effects by variable causes. But this is not all; in most cases it will probably need a considerable length of time for the variable causes to realise themselves by turns in such completeness that they cancel each other's influence and allow the constant ones to assert themselves. Hence it is usual to try and discover units of time, in which the ratio of the actual to the possible cases of E becomes the same, due regard being had of course to the periodical changes to which the number of the latter are liable. Now the year happens to be the particular unit of time during which most of the variable conditions, which affect men at all generally, run through the cycle of their possible values, and so the first question to ask in investigations referring to human affairs is naturally this: within these units of time does the ratio of the actual to the conceivable cases of E remain uniform or approach to uniformity? The answer to all these questions may just as well be negative as affirmative. If an event E occurs at all frequently during a certain period of time, there must be within that period some constant cause of it, at least in the sense that some ratio exists, which to a definite extent promotes the combination of variable causes which favours E. Then as often as an unit of time recurs and the same proportion of real cases to possible ones is reproduced, so often are we warranted in the regressive inference, that that constant cause has existed. But it is not at once clear how we can argue forwards, that for the next equal interval of time the same proportion will hold good as a predetermined law. Such an assumption can only be regarded as the safest rule to go by in judging of the future, when no data are known pointing to the intervention of some change in those unknown conditions. If the rule holds good as foreseen we are justified in once more making the same regressive inference as before, and sure enough the oftener we can make it, the oftener that is the rule is confirmed by the facts, so much the stronger becomes the probability, that the group of conditions, which has remained constant over so many units of time, will remain unchanged for the future. To more than this probability however we can never attain, and so it is very unsafe to characterise the results of such observations as *laws* of what happens, or actually to speak, as we sometimes do, of laws of big numbers, as if the mere bigness of a number of compared cases must of necessity introduce a regularity in the course of a certain class of events, which has no independent foundation in the nature of those events and their conditions. A law, as we have seen, is an hypothetical judgment and enunciates the necessary validity of a consequent provided the antecedent be valid. Statistical laws must not aspire to satisfy this definition or they certainly lose their value; for they say no more than this : *if* in the next unit of time T *all* known and unknown conditions be as in the last, then will the series of all the consequences, consequently also the sum total of E, be the same. Of course it will, for if we suppose the past to take place over again, it will wear just the same aspect as it wore then. Those who talk about statistical laws no doubt do not mean to be guilty of tautology; on the contrary they mean to state their antecedent clause categorically, that is, to assert that such an identity of all conditions will take place; it is obvious however that such an assertion can never be certain, but only probable. Such propositions therefore are not laws, but *analogies*, which extend a proportion, which has held good in n cases, to the $(n+1)^{th}$, not proving but only assuming that between n and $n+1$ there is no change in the conditions on which their validity depends.

288. Among events, which in their frequent recurrence depend at once on constant and on variable conditions, may be properly classed our own *observations*, by which I mean the simplest kind of observation, viz. the measurement of a quantity given in an act of perception. Here thé constant cause consists in the true value of this quantity, for this under entirely similar conditions would always have the same effect on our susceptibility. The variable causes are the external circumstances and the changes in our psychical state, which modify that effect in different ways on different occasions of its repetition. To elicit from the different measurements thus obtained, the true value of the thing measured, would be impossible if we ascribed to the measurements made every conceivable degree of inaccuracy: that would mean that we thought we might substitute for the values found any others we liked as more correct, and that would be stultifying the very idea of a measurement. We therefore presuppose that knowledge, aptitude, and attention have combined to make the measurements fairly trustworthy and only leave a chance of error very small compared with the magnitudes themselves which have to be measured. Now suppose we wish to determine some single unknown quantity A, at first every isolated measurement we have of it must pass muster as a true determination of A; for even if we had doubts of its accuracy we do not know how far or in what direction to rectify it and have no grounds to go upon. On the other hand though the quantity A can only be one and the same, observation may give us different values for it; we have then no absolute ground for trusting one value more than another, and as we must now suppose all our observations to be more or less erroneous, we are most probably right in fixing its true quantity at a value, whose assumption involves the least sum of errors in the measured values. The arithmetical mean M, i.e. the sum of all the measured values divided by the number of measurements, is thus to be regarded as the most probable value of A. The difference between this mean M and the true value A is the residuary error, which, so long as we have no other accessory conditions by which to determine A, cannot be got rid of, but only reduced by multiplying the number of equally careful observations.

On the other hand if we have repeatedly measured different quantities ABC, and are still furnished with other conditions, which the values thus obtained must satisfy, it may be that the different arithmetical means, which would individually give the most probable values of ABC, will not collectively satisfy these accessory conditions, and so stand in need of rectification. For example, we may have repeatedly measured the three angles of a triangle and found that the sum of the mean values thus obtained amount to $180° + d°$; this $d°$ being incompatible with the nature of a triangle will point to an error in the result, which must have arisen out of errors in the measurements and can only be got rid of by altering the values found. But the reduction required may be distributed in very various ways among the three measured angles; and the question arises, what sized error may be most probably ascribed to the measurement of each angle. This suggests an enquiry based on principles, which if not demonstrable *a priori* are at any rate very probable and in harmony with experience,—an enquiry into the relative probability of the occurrence of errors in our observations generally. In the idea of a careful observation as such there is nothing to imply error at all. The chance therefore of our having hit on the truth is always greater than the chance of our having fallen into any particular error. Similarly it is involved in the presuppositions, on which the eliciting of true values from observations always depends, that the chance of large errors is less than that of small ones, and the chance of positive errors exactly equal to the chance of negative errors of the same size. This suggests one way of picturing the problem. Let a straight line be chosen as the axis of abscissae, take in it any starting-point to correspond to a total absence of error, and from this point let there be divided off in opposite directions abscissae $\pm a$, $\pm \beta$, $\pm \gamma$, in ascending order of magnitude. At the point of no error or zero-point draw to the line an ordinate of any length, symbolical of the chance of there being no error: this will be the longest of all the ordinates, and all the others, drawn at the points $\pm a$, $\pm \beta$ . . will diminish in length symmetrically on both sides of it according as the errors symbolised by $a\beta\gamma$, the respective chances of which they denote, increase in size. But experience at the same time teaches us that the chance of errors does not simply decrease in the same proportion as their size increases. So long as the errors are trifling the chance of them decreases less rapidly than their size increases, but the greater they are the faster does their decrease in probability outstrip their increase in size. Hence the line joining the upper extremities of all the ordinates cannot be formed of two straight lines, meeting over the zero-point and symmetrically approaching the axis of abscissae on both sides, in such a way as to form a triangle with a segment of the axis. On the contrary the line in question is a curve, the vertex of which lies above the zero-point and which branches out therefrom in two symmetrical limbs, which are concave towards the axis of abscissae. The course of the curve is thus easily followed in the neighbourhood of its vertex, it is not so easy to follow as it approaches the axis. We may regard errors of any size as possible, errors of even infinite size; these too will have their degree of probability, infinitesimal though it be; in consequence each limb of the curve must ultimately become convex toward the axis of abscissae and approach it asymptotically. But we need not take into account such infinitely large errors; we may consider that in careful observation, errors which transgress by the whole amount of the value to be measured, do not occur at all; the curve will then remain concave and cut the axis at two points.

I cannot here go into the lengthy investigations which have been instituted with a view to determine more exactly the most probable form of these curves, their equation and from that the chance that an individual error will occur. Still I should like to give my reader some idea of the means to this end ultimately employed in such speculations, though I will not follow them more closely than my purpose requires. I will at once drop out of sight the tracts of the curve which approach the axis of abscissae; we are only concerned to ascertain the chance of such errors as we must expect to fall into even in careful observations, and accordingly we shall only consider a short arc of the line, which lies on either side of the apex. We have seen that this line cannot be a straight line; the next simplest thing to assume is that its equation is of the second degree. The symmetrical values of the ordinates on this side and that of the zero-point are possible on such an assumption, accordingly we make it and choose from among the sections of the cone, which however all lend themselves to the experiment,—the circle. Let the longest ordinate r, drawn at the zero-point of the abscissae, denote at once the true value of the quantity to be measured and the magnitude of the probability that this true measurement has been obtained in our observations. Let the abscissae $\pm a$, $\pm \beta$, $\pm \gamma$ denote the size of the errors by which the different measurements diverge from the true value r; for the present we think of these as expressed in parts of this true value, so that $\pm a \pm \beta \ldots$ are for $r = 1$ proper fractions of unity, while if we take $r = r$ they must be replaced by $\pm r a$, $\pm r \beta \ldots$; finally the ordinate y which corresponds to each abscissa denotes the chance there is of that particular error in measurement being made, which deviates from the true r by the size of this abscissa: if then we assume that the equation of the circle holds for the curve in question, y is $=\sqrt{1-x^2}$, where x is the general expression for the changing values α, β, γ. Now we saw that the chance that different and mutually independent events will concur is measured by the product of their respective chances. Bearing this in mind we shall see that where, as here, we are directly compelled to assume a number of errors in our measurements, because these do not harmonise with an ulterior condition, and where, moreover, various combinations of errors may be assumed, which would all satisfy this condition, that combination of errors is the most likely and should be assumed, which allows to the product of the individual chances of error the highest value. Now this product consists of nothing but factors of the form $r\sqrt{1-x^2}$ and it clearly reaches the highest value, when all the several factors take on at the same time the highest values compatible with the conditions of the problem. This happens, when in all factors at once the subtractive elements —here the sum $\alpha^2+\beta^2+\gamma^2$—are reduced to a minimum. This minimum value presupposes, as one easily finds out, that the sum of the errors $\alpha+\beta+\gamma\ldots=0$; and this can only be the case, when these first powers of the errors have different signs, and must be the case when the arithmetical mean of the observations to which they belong, is taken to be the true value r of the quantity to be measured. We thus find that this obvious and in simple cases satisfactory principle falls within the lines of the process of determining r by means of the sum of the squares of the errors. Now suppose we have made m observations of a quantity and have derived different arithmetical means from them, by crediting them each with this or that error and correcting it accordingly; our method seeks to determine that particular mean which comes nearest to the truth, inasmuch as it rests on the most probable combination of such corrections.

In the above we have not tried to exhaust the subject, we have only just approached it in such a way as to give a general idea of what is meant by this method of the *least squares* and of how it came to be called by that name. Our brief exposition will not serve as a basis for a number of more delicate solutions, in regard to which as well as in regard to the introduction of the calculus the reader must be referred to the classical exposition of Gauss and to the text-books which found upon that exposition. It must be borne in mind that the validity of the method always depends on certain very probable though not strictly demonstrable presuppositions; for its full and adequate substantiation we must look to the results to which, especially in astronomy, it has led.

CHAPTER X.

Of Elections and Voting.

289. ELECTIONS and voting are processes of framing judgments; judgments, that is, whose validity we mean to create by our own decision, and not merely to acknowledge. The logical calculus has taken account of these processes in various ways. It has been asked what expectation of a just verdict, or of a proper decision, or of a wise election, can be based upon different forms of procedure; but, as questions like these can never be answered apart from special and arbitrary presuppositions of a psychological kind, I shall here exclude them, and confine myself to the enquiry into the means of attaining what is formally the object of all voting, namely, a decision that shall express as completely as possible the collective will of the voters, independently of the degree of wisdom that may guide the several wills which go to compose it.

In common life such a collective will takes the shape of public opinion; and the matter which it affirms or rejects has been gradually defined by the countless reciprocal influences of all who have the power of manifesting inclination or aversion. But a logical treatment presupposes that the matter in question is already put into shape as a definite proposal V or a series of proposals V, W, Z; that the expression of will takes place by simple acceptance or rejection of what is so put forward; and finally that there is a definite and limited number S of equal votes, to which and to no others it belongs to establish the collective will.

290. To take the simplest case: if there is a single proposal V put forward, and a decision absolutely must be arrived at, the only possible ground of determination is an Absolute Majority. It is the only result which cannot help occurring either for or against V; supposing the case of equality of votes to be provided for by some fixed agreement as to a casting vote, or as to giving the preference to the affirmative or to the negative conclusion. But there are great limitations on regarding an absolute majority as the true expression of what could rightly be called the collective will of the voters. The several votes are themselves no exhaustive expression of the several wills; being restricted to 'Yes' or 'No' they have no means of distinguishing a decided will for or against from mere acceptance or non-resistance. This constant defect in all voting can only be remedied by previous Discussion. This allows fitting expression to different intensities of affirmation or rejection, and gives scope for the influence of personal authority, which has to lose its power in the actual and formal voting in which the votes must be counted and not weighed. It is for the individual's sense of propriety to decide how far in the subsequent giving of the votes account is to be taken of the division of feeling for and against, which after discussion is at least known to all. Other conventional rules, such as the requirement of a two-thirds' majority, diminish this evil without removing it; the only unambiguous result would be unanimity, but neither it nor the two-thirds' majority can be required without endangering the certainty of coming to a decision. So these two regulations are only appropriate where there are other weighty reasons for giving to the conservative preference for the existing state which is known, an advantage over the impulse to innovations whose result is unknown.

291. No general reason can be found in Logic for departing from an equal value for all participating votes; but in actual life there have been both fair and unfair reasons constantly operative to attach different weights to the votes, so as to give an advantage whether to greater wisdom, or to the more important or the more specially menaced interest, or to claims to peculiar preference which had some historical origin. It is sometimes done by simply counting the single vote of the preferred person as equal to several votes; sometimes by breaking up the totality of voters into a number of groups in each of which a separate vote is taken, and substituting the majority of the majorities which arise in this voting for the absolute majority of the total number; sometimes by having recourse to indirect voting, in which each of the groups transfers its right to a delegate and leaves the decision to the majority of these nominees.

The first case requires no separate consideration; the last withdraws itself from all logical treatment in cases where the deputy so commissioned has to vote independently himself, and not to represent a decision already taken by his electors. For the certainty with which the result in that case corresponds to the collective will depends upon the doubtful reliability of the electors' judgment in estimating the agreement between their deputy's sentiments and their own. On the other hand, the second case, that of division into groups which are to vote separately, has the following determinable peculiarities.

1. If we take the total number S of the votes as $= 2m \cdot 2n$, one of these factors indicating the number of groups made, and the other the number of votes in each group, then $(m+1)(n+1)$ will be the number of votes in the absolute majority of the several absolute majorities which result within these groups. And this value remains the same if we substitute for one or both of such even factors the odd numbers next above $(2m+1)(2n+1)$. Suppose M on the other hand to be the simple absolute majority of the total number of voters S when voting without subdivision, we may easily convince ourselves that

$(m+1)(n+1)$ is less than M for all uneven S which are greater than 7 and for all even S which are greater than 12, and so in all cases that need be considered with reference to voting. Thus it is always possible by a suitable subdivision of S to bring about a decision resting on the *minority* of the total number of voters; and it may be asked which modes of division are the most adapted for making this winning minority as small as possible. A precise answer to the question would be far more lengthy than the matter deserves; for in application we shall always have to be satisfied with an approximation, because our precise estimate would be made useless by any trifling accident that prevented a vote from being given on which we had reckoned. So I content myself with what follows.

2. If we consider S as the product of two even or of two uneven factors, and thus either
$$= 2m \cdot 2n \text{ or } = (2m+1)(2n+1),$$
if we replace m in the formula for the winning minority by an expression in terms of n and S, and if we differentiate with respect to n, we obtain as condition of a minimum $2n$ or $2n+1 = \sqrt{S}$ which gives the other factor $s = \sqrt{S}$, and therefore $m = n$.

If we take S as product of an even and an uneven factor, $= 2m(2n+1)$, we obtain in the same way, as a condition of a minimum that the even factor $= \sqrt{2S}$, which gives the uneven $= \sqrt{\tfrac{1}{2}S}$. The manner of their deduction prevents either of the formulae from applying precisely in these cases where both the number of votes and that of groups can only increase by entire units, and not continuously; in particular, their application cannot be regular for small numbers of whose amount a unit is a considerable fraction; and lastly, the advantage of odd numbers over even, as the winning minority for $(2m+1)(2n+1)$ is not larger than that for $2m \cdot 2n$, will also be detrimental to the influence of these rules. Still, for high values of S, as unity, or the difference between odd and even, forms a progressively smaller fraction of their amount, these two formulae really give the two least values of the required minorities. They are obtained by separating S into two factors either as nearly as possible equal to each other and to the square root of S, or one of them as exactly as possible double the other. Thus 225 considered as 15.15 and as 9.25 gives the two least minorities 64 and 65, but as 5.45 and 3.75 the larger ones 69 and 76; 11025 as 105.105 and as 147.75 the least minorities 2809 and 2812, while on the other hand as 175.63 and as 9.1225 it gives the larger numbers 2992 and 3065; and finally 20,000 breaks up to best advantage as 200.100 and as 125.160, with the minorities 5151 and 5103. In the case of small numbers the influences of the different conditions cross each other very markedly; 36 taken as 6.6 gives the minority 16, but even as 4.9 gives the smaller minority 15 because of the favourable influence of the odd factor; the most advantageous subdivision is 3.12 giving 14 as the minority; for in this the even factor 12 comes nearer to the square root of $2S=72$ (which is greater than 8) than does the even factor 4 in the division 4.9. On the other hand 81, being the square of an uneven factor, has no subdivision more favourable than 9.9 giving 25 for the minority; the other into 3.27 is too remote from both conditions. For 144 one minimum 49 is obtained out of 12.12, the other 45 out of 9.16.

3. In the first of the most favourable cases, that of equal factors, the winning minority, expressed in terms of S, $=(1+\frac{1}{2}\sqrt{S})^2$; in the second, that in which one factor is double the other, it =

$$(1+\tfrac{1}{2}\sqrt{2S})(1+\tfrac{1}{2}\sqrt{\tfrac{1}{2}S}).$$

Both expressions approximate to the value $\frac{1}{4}S$ (only the second does so more slowly) as S becomes greater, but remain always greater than that fraction as long as S does not become infinite. Thus the winning minority has a lower limit, and can never, by the most advantageous subdivision, be reduced to a quarter of the total number of votes.

4. Finally, S may be a prime number, which in any case can only be made divisible if increased or diminished by a single unit at least: i.e. for the present purpose, by giving to one of the groups a single vote more or less than the others have. A choice is therefore inevitable, and may be exercised as we please; beyond a doubt it is equally justifiable to consider 67 as $66+1$ and as $68-1$, making in the first case 5 classes of 11 votes and 1 of 12, in the second 3 classes of 17 and 1 of 16; if it is required for the sake of fairness that the majorities which make up the winning minority shall always include those of the more numerous classes, we shall obtain in the first case $3.6+1.7=25$, in the second $3.9=27$. When once this path is open, it is followed even where there is no need; and then the inequality of groups is readily put up with as long as it remains within reasonable limits; and it further diminishes the winning minorities very considerably. Thus we obtain for $64=6.9+1.10$ the minority $3.5+1.6=21$ (even if we make a rule of requiring the majority of the larger group to be in it) while 8.8 only gave the greater minority 25. We all know that this resource has been abundantly employed from Servius Tullius downwards to a very unfair extent, which must look for its justification not to Logic, but to politics.

292. When we come to choosing between different proposals V, W, Z, Logic as such would make requirements that diverge from the usages observed in practice. If a number of persons desire to unite in a collective determination such as to produce the greatest general satisfaction, they ought not to obtain the result as an inevitable consequence of a summation of declarations of will, none of which takes account of any of the others. A rational will must attach importance to not giving its decision without knowledge and consideration of the other voters' inclinations or aversions, opposed to its own; especially as the necessity of finally declaring itself in a bare Yes or No leaves

no means of finding expression for the different intensities of its volition and so of securing for it neither more nor less than the just measure of effect. Previous discussion, to which I referred above, cannot entirely satisfy this requirement; for if everyone wanted to declare himself completely, the discussion would turn into voting, only without the precision of form which makes the ascertainment of the final result easy and certain. So an attempt must be made to effect by the actual mode of voting as nearly as possible what discussion aims at doing.

If we consider V, W, Z, as three persons, one of whom is to be elected, we may adopt the following procedure. A preliminary vote upon all three candidates at once would show what degree of approval each of them meets with, compared to the others. If no one of them obtained an absolute majority of the votes, the relative majority could not be taken as decisive except in elections of very small moment; but it has an importance which may be seen in everyday life. The candidate who has the most votes compared with the others attracts attention and often gains the other votes as well; but just as often his prominence arouses antagonism, and compels his opponents to combine in support of a rival. Hence it is the general rule to require an absolute majority; it gives the only security that the sum of negative votes must be less than that of affirmatives, and that therefore the will of the majority has been hit upon; and this is the *ultima ratio* which must always give the final decision when opinions remain unreconcilable and yet a collective resolution is indispensable.

But further; if an absolute majority has been obtained[1] for one of the candidates, say for V, still it is neither essential, nor right in itself, to accept this at once as the decision. This preliminary voting only showed the number of voters who preferred or postponed each of the candidates to the others; the degree of such preference was left

[1] [I.e. in the preliminary vote.]

undefined, and so also was the feeling of each voter to the candidate whom he has not named. To bring this to light a second and tripartite vote would be required; being a vote of Yes or No upon each of the candidates separately so as to give each elector the possibility of directly recording his vote against any particular candidate, while before he could only express it by preferring another to him. If we suppose that in the first voting V obtained 11 votes out of 20, W 5, and Z 4, then, excluding incomprehensible inconsistency on the electors' part, every candidate will retain in the second process the votes of those who preferred him to the other two in the first, but the remaining votes may be very variously divided. It is possible that V may now meet with a decided opposition of 9 votes, while Z who was only preferred by 4 may find no opposition at all and win 16 votes more; and W may get 10 of the 15 which he had not before.

To obtain a final result out of this it must be considered that the votes obtained in these different votings are of unequal value. Those of the first process showed how many voters thought a candidate the best, and though their approval may have been very different in degree still we may regard all these *preference* votes as homogeneous and attach the same weight m to all of them. For the best that anyone can say of a candidate with reference to the election as such, is that he is for him; whether he respects him more or less apart from this is indifferent, for every election can only aim at the best result under the given conditions, and at not the best absolutely; any one who is for V or W under the given conditions is for him altogether. The same assumption holds of the negative votes in the second voting; anyone who has the opportunity of pronouncing directly on V or W by Yes or No, and votes against both, is absolutely against them, and has accomplished his will completely, as regards this election, if the vote of rejection is carried; no matter how thoroughly he may hate or despise V or W in other ways. So all the unfavourable votes may be considered as homogeneous and assigned the same weight q. But those favourable votes which are only obtained in the second voting are obviously of less value than those which were obtained in the first; they are only permissive, while the others were preference votes; and this difference, which marks a middle grade between voting for and voting against, is of course of importance for the election in hand. Still, what weight a permissive vote ought to have compared with a vote of preference, is a question which the voter who gave it could probably not answer with precision; besides, his acquiescence would not indicate the same degree of approval for every candidate to whom he gave it, but a greater, perhaps, for W than for Z. Therefore, though it at once involves a serious failure of accuracy, yet the only possible attempt to make a general estimate even approximately of the difference of the permissive votes from the preferential is to assign to all votes of the former class a common value p, which must be a proper fraction of m, and the amount of which can only be fixed by convention. On these assumptions the votes would be calculated in the above example as follows: for V, $11\,m - 9\,p$, for W, $5\,m + 10\,p - 5\,q$, for Z, $4\,m + 16\,p$; and so finally, if we arbitrarily take $m = q$ (giving the preferential vote equal weight with the vote of rejection) and $p = \dfrac{m}{2}$ (giving the permissive half the weight of the preferential), the result would be only 2 votes for V, on the other hand 5 for W and lastly 12 for Z, in marked contrast to the result of the first voting.

Various circumstances combine to make these logical requirements unrealisable in practice. In the first place, on grounds of social propriety, we should desire to avoid voting against persons altogether. Next, even if it were admitted, there would be great reason to doubt whether the second voting would be carried out with the requisite impartiality, even supposing it to take place before the first. Those who were determined to give their votes of preference to V would probably not admit even to themselves that they could be content with W or Z, and their 11 votes would appear in the permissive voting too as so many votes against W and against Z as well. And lastly there would in every case be the same preliminary question what was best to aim at with a view to the matter in hand, whether the completest satisfaction of the majority or the greatest average satisfaction of all; and this would have to be determined before the ratio of weight between affirmative and negative votes could be fixed. It need not necessarily be equality; on the contrary, there may be cases in which a single unfavourable vote may fairly balance more than a single favourable one, and the decision would have to be obtained not so much by the greatest number of votes for a candidate, as by the lowest number of votes against him. It clearly makes a difference whether the matter in hand is the decision of some gravely responsible business, say an election to some office of political importance, or whether it is the organisation of amusements in common, perhaps the election of the president of some social gathering. In the latter case it would be absurd to make 9 members out of 20 discontented in order to give 11 others complete satisfaction; but in the former it may be reasonable to satisfy the majority of decided wills completely, rather than light upon a choice that only met with the lukewarm approval of all. But it is just in the second case, where the method described would give the most desirable result, that the inadmissibility of negative votes makes its application difficult; in the first, where its result might be less desirable, its application would be less difficult, for in this case the votes of rejection would be a less serious slight, as they might possibly be directed against the views represented by a candidate and not against him personally.

293. There is another mode, a sort of process of elimination, that may answer our wishes when an election has to be made out of a very large number of candidates; as when a constituency has to name some one out of its own number. It is usual in these cases to take a first vote by way of fixing upon some three names which are the first to attract the electors' attention before minor considerations come in to restrict it, and at present therefore appear the most desirable to each of the voters. It is possible in this process to attach distinctions to the order in which each elector names or writes his three candidates; and to put the one mentioned first above the others; but I assume for simplicity's sake, that the order of naming is quite indifferent. Then it is conceivable, though very improbable, that the same three candidates, V, W, Z, may receive all the votes; if this occurs, it becomes impossible for a final decision to be obtained by election, for a fresh vote could not give a majority for any of the three unless some voters retracted their previous decision without any ground in circumstances for doing so. In this and all similar cases the only remaining possibility is either the lot, or the decision of some external will, e.g. that of a higher authority.

On the other hand, if V and no one else obtains a vote from every voter, his election is decided beyond a doubt, whatever number of votes W and Z may have obtained; for then there are no concealed votes of rejection which nothing but want of opportunity has hindered from being recorded. But supposing V to have only obtained an absolute majority, W and Z considerable minorities, and the rest of the votes to have been scattered, then it becomes possible that there are such votes. So, considering our observations above, we cannot hold it quite justifiable to break off the election at this point and regard V as elected; it is better to take a fresh vote for W against Z, so that actually voting against W may be avoided by voting for Z, and *vice versa*. One of the two must obtain a larger or smaller absolute majority. Supposing W is successful, a third vote as between him and V will give a final decision. Of course this final voting will be wholly superfluous if the absolute majority which was in favour of V on the first vote maintains itself unaltered; but a reasonable motive for a change of feeling may have been furnished by the result of the second voting. If in it the votes for W and for Z are nearly equal, it would prove either that V's opponents are not united, or that no other choice meets with more uniform agreement than that of V, and this would give the previous majority a reason for persisting in their conviction. If on the other hand W got all the votes, the majority in question might think this a good reason for going over in the last vote to the minority, already considerable, in favour of W, in order to produce a result which should have no decided opponents. Many more modifications are conceivable; I will not follow them out, for the discussion threatens to be longer than its importance warrants; moreover it is at least doubtful whether such a process of elimination is really more flattering than open rejection. And finally, V, who is elected, may decline the post. This alters the conditions with reference to which the votes were given so completely, that it becomes necessary to repeat the whole process of election, or perhaps to make an independent selection of Y, as a third candidate besides W and Z.

294. If V, W, and Z, are not persons, but legislative proposals, there is no reason for shunning the direct negative vote; and it might be demanded on logical grounds that a vote of Yes or No should be taken on each of the measures proposed, but that the obtaining of an absolute majority by one should be no bar to voting on the others. The decision would then depend either on the largest of the majorities or on a fresh vote which would be final. This procedure would cause those whose opinion had gained a considerable number of votes, to adhere to it in the final voting; but any who found theirs in a hopeless minority would have time to attach themselves in the final vote to the opinion which they liked next best to their own and which might have a chance of gaining the deciding majority by their accession. Still, there is here too the same psychological reason which I mentioned before, against this procedure; any one who decidedly preferred a proposal V would not declare freely that W or Z would also be tolerable to him, but would be tempted to reject them both. Therefore as it is the traditional rule that the adoption of one proposal *ipso facto* shelves all posterior ones, the order in which VWZ are put to the vote acquires great importance as affecting the choice made. I concur with Trendelenburg's statement[1] of the wish that may be felt on logical grounds respecting this arrangement, the most difficult problem of parliamentary tact; viz. that the adherents of every opinion should have an opportunity of emphasising it with all the weight they can command; of negativing what they want to reject directly, not indirectly by the acceptance of something else which has only their partial approval; of affirming what they wish immediately and exclusively, not by the rejection of something else of which they disapprove only in part; and finally, that it should be possible for everyone to begin by defending and recommending what he thinks best of all, and only to retire upon his second or third best after the first has failed. But whether the universal accomplishment of this postulate for everyone entitled to vote and in respect of every proposal before a meeting is not as a whole frustrated by a fundamental contradiction; whether, therefore, it is conceivable that everyone's sentiments should be gratified by just those proposals being broken up on the parts of which he thinks differently, and just those united which he wants to see accepted or rejected together, demands no investigation. It is quite clear that in each case the solution of the problem can only be approached by an acumen developed in long and uniform practice, after entering thoroughly into the subject-matter under discussion. The procedure to be observed can only

[1] ['Ueber die Methode der Abstimmungen,' Berlin, 1850.]

be learned or taught by help of definite instances, not by universal symbols representing possible cases, and only in practice; general rules can give very little help.

295. It may happen to begin with that the proposals in question VWZ do not compose the complete disjunction between the members of which there is a choice, but that there is a fourth member consisting of the rejection of one and all of them; i.e. that speaking generally a new resolution is as such unnecessary, and it is possible to maintain the *status quo*. There are two reasons that may lead to the choice of this alternative; either the desire to protect that particular *status quo* on principle against all innovation, or the absence of an acceptable proposal among those put forward, though on grounds of principle there is no opposition to a reform. It is important to provide expression for the distinction between these two dispositions. The mere rejection of all individual proposals successively does not provide it; this only proves that the change which would have been acceptable has not been proposed; but it should be possible to reject generally and as such the invitation to change which all the proposals have in common. This is effected by the motion to pass to the order of the day, that is, therefore, that the whole of the proposals in question should be excluded from being debated or voted on, and so their common element should be negatived in a correspondingly general form. Where anyone's will is in favour of such a negative it is his parliamentary duty to contribute to a full expression of the state of opinion by making this motion, and not to content himself with throwing out all separate proposals, until it has been rejected. Even where there is only a single proposal instead of several, the motion of the order of the day may be in place; its meaning then is to reject not this particular proposal as such, but the general intention out of which it has arisen and others might arise. Thus the order of the day when voted without a statement of grounds, may act as an expression of contempt for a proposal that is legally or morally disgraceful, or as a refusal to entertain one that is extraneous, and beyond the competence of the voters, or finally as a riddance of a dangerous proposal the mere discussion of which it is the interest of the commonwealth to avoid. Or such acts of rejection may be mitigated by a motived order of the day, which recognises in its statement of grounds what there is in the proposed measure that is just in itself, but denies the propriety of introducing and debating it at that particular moment.

296. If two proposals V and W are so related to each other by way of subordination that W is an 'ameliorative motion' or amendment that aims at modifying the purport of the substantive motion V by addition, omission, or alteration, then it is logically speaking a correct usage to take a provisional vote on the amendment before the final vote on the substantive motion. For no decision on this latter can rationally be solicited from the voters till its wording is completely and unequivocally settled; certainly not while its details are open to subsequent modifications the acceptance or rejection of which if it could have been foreknown might well have succeeded in totally reversing the favourable or unfavourable impressions which had been prematurely recorded. The vote on the amendment W serves to fix unequivocally the purport which the substantive motion V has when put to the vote; therefore the rejection of V annuls the previous adoption of the amendment, which was only provisional.

If there are several mutually exclusive amendments W and Z to a substantive motion V, or several accessory proposals about the special modifications necessary to applying V in practice (as often happens when details of quantity remain to be fixed), the safest course would be to vote separately on all such proposals and let the decision go by the greatest majority. Only if, according to the usual practice, the acceptance of one by an absolute majority is to exclude all the others from being voted on, the order of putting them to the vote becomes important, and the obvious advice is to arrange the proposals so that the two least divergent shall always be next each other. This is the practice under a rather different form in both kinds of auction, that by bidding and that by offering[1], and in these cases people actually calculate, and quite fairly, on the uncertainty in which each person who bids must be about the degree of the others' desire. For as the bid or its acceptance[1] by the buyer are alike voluntary, the customer is merely declaring what value the object has for him according to his own estimate and no right of his is attacked by the open competition of others or by his ignorance of the absence of any eager desires but his own. Offering seems, speaking generally, in favour of the seller, for it compels the buyer to take the object at the highest price which he thinks he can afford to give, though he would give less if he could foresee the absence of competition; bidding is in favour of the buyer because if there is such absence it is available to him; if not, at least he has only to advance on the last bid, and his time for decision is not excessively curtailed. This is a procedure in which an individual tries by a contest with others to secure a legitimate personal advantage; so its analogy is not in spirit very appropriate to the efforts of a multitude to bring to pass by common action a resolution advantageous to the common weal. Still, in form, they must take pattern from the procedure of 'offering,' only, as a rule, it will be rare to find proposals that can be so simply arranged in a quantitatively graduated series; most commonly $WZ\ldots$ will differ in purport so as to be hard to classify. In that case they must be arranged according to their anticipated degree of conformity to the general will; those that are furthest removed from the *status quo*, that demand the most extraordinary and ample mea-

[1] [I. e. in a 'Dutch auction,' where the auctioneer offers successively lower prices, and the first customer who accepts is the buyer.]

sures, and therefore have little probability of success, would have a claim to be put to the vote first; in order that, if, contrary to expectation, they were destined to turn out in conformity with the general will, the expression of that will might not have been made impossible by starting from a more likely proposal which might easily unite all the votes with premature resignation based on that erroneous estimate itself. After the rejection of such extreme proposals we might pass, as in the mathematical method of limitation, to the mean terms of the series which are more likely in themselves; with the aim of procuring the final decision in favour of the proposal which involved the least possible deviation from general satisfaction. But all these rules are ultimately inadequate; for instance, where the business is to decide upon a composite whole whose different parts can only be discussed by degrees, it must always be impossible while the special deliberations are still proceeding to discover all the inconsistencies, inconsecutivenesses, and contradictions which would arise from the ultimate conjunction of all the details of the plan, perhaps variously modified. In such cases, as in the case of amendments, the special deliberations should be treated as no more than preliminary, and an assembly should reserve to itself the power, by a vote on a second reading or by some final vote, to annihilate the monster which its united efforts have brought into existence. Lastly, it is true that the formal aim of all voting, to arrive at a collective will, would involve in the first place the establishment of a decision Z such as to give all members of the society the greatest attainable average satisfaction M, considering the lesser satisfaction of one as compensated by the greater satisfaction of another. At the same time it is also to be desired that in order to the performance of the obligation arising from the acceptance of Z an equal compliance M were to be reckoned upon in all members. I have explained why the former end cannot be attained in perfection. The latter on the other hand is of course a desire unrealisable by logical means; only this may be deduced as a logical rule which the nature of ethical ends makes necessary to their realisation, that here (for Logic can require it nowhere else) we should subordinate our personal conviction to the general opinion when different from our own.

BOOK III.

ON KNOWLEDGE (METHODOLOGY).

INTRODUCTION.

In the enquiry instituted in the last book as to the means by which we are enabled to arrange the manifold content presented to our minds under those ideal forms of apprehension and connexion with which we became acquainted in the previous book upon Pure Logic, nothing was said as to the general question of logical methods with which a theory of the nature of thought ordinarily concludes. In passing over the subject in that place I conceive that I was guilty of no unpardonable omission, nor was it mere caprice which led me to reserve that and other questions akin to it for this concluding section of my work.

297. Since the time of Aristotle philosophers have distinguished between the analytic and synthetic methods, from points of view essentially the same in all cases, regarding them as the two ultimate forms to which all methods of scientific procedure which the movement of thought follows may be reduced. In the view of antiquity any subject-matter presented for scientific investigation was to be submitted to a process of dissection which should trace it to its simplest elements or to its most universal conditions. Thus the analytic method was a retrogressive operation proceeding *a principiatis ad principia*, while the principles when discovered formed as it were the blocks which the synthetic or progressive method proceeded to build up into the individual objects of experience.

The two expressions analytic and synthetic no longer precisely answer to the instincts of modern speech, and we might easily be tempted to interchange their meanings. We no longer indulge the hope that a mere dissection of the object presented can discover within it the principles of which we are in search; experience has taught us on the contrary that for the human intelligence general principles have largely to be created out of a combination and comparison of the manifold facts of experience, and they appear to us therefore when we have arrived at them, as the final outcome of a synthetic operation of thought. In the same way we are no longer disposed to limit ourselves to a point of view which regards general principles as atoms of truth, from the mere piecing together of which particular truths are derived; to us, rightly or wrongly, general principles appear rather as containing within themselves a capacity of development, and we regard the derivation of the conditioned from its conditions as consisting at least as often in an analysis of the content of the conditions as in the combination of them.

But the question of language is not worth debating further, for it is plain to begin with that neither of the two methods can be carried out, at all events in any general application, without the other. No method of analysis can arrive by the mere dissection of the particular object presented to it, at a principle or a general truth, unless at every stage it compares the result a of the last step with some general proposition T, and by endeavouring to bring it under the latter—that is to say at this point by an act of synthesis—makes sure whether a is an ultimate principle, or whether it may not involve some contradiction for the removal of which it may be necessary to continue the analysis further in one direction or another. Nor need the proposition T which has to be recognised in such a process by any means always belong to those formal logical laws whose supremacy over the *modus procedendi* of every conceivable method is acknowledged as a matter of course. On the contrary it must often, if any real advance is to be made, be a concrete proposition which Logic cannot furnish, but which it has to accept on purely extralogical grounds, and to which the results arrived at by the analysis have to be subordinated.

As little can a method of synthesis make any way without the help of analysis. Even supposing it to start with a number of elementary truths A, B, C in its hand, it could never get beyond the tautological proposition that these several truths are all true at once, unless it can go on to show how by their possessing simultaneous validity in respect of one and the same object this or that fresh consequence x or y is necessarily developed. But whether x or y will follow can only be decided after an examination of the nature of the object in question, that is to say by a return for the time being to analysis. Such an analysis can alone furnish us with the determinate minor premiss which we require to combine with the general truths with which we began, and which supply our major premiss, in order to proceed once more synthetically to a determinate conclusion.

It must be allowed that in certain departments the synthetic method has the appearance of a greater independence. Thus geometry is able to create the objects to which it desires to apply its general truths, as it goes along, and the analytic statement of the *data* which are accepted for the purpose of deducing each new proposition occupies only a small place in its demonstrations. Still in reality it cannot be wholly absent. And in the wider provinces of scientific activity which are concerned with the synthetic construction of real things, the progressive movement from principles to facts is always preceded by a retrogressive operation, consisting in a comprehensive analysis of the *data*, which is essential to determining for the synthetic procedure itself the directions in which it has to look for those minor premises with which its general principles cannot possibly dispense.

298. Thus in fact the distinction between the two methods runs up practically into the following antithesis, which has long attracted attention :—the Analytic method is essentially the method of investigation, having the discovery of truth for its object; the Synthetic that of exposition, of which the object is to exhibit a body of truths, whether obtained in one way or in another, by direct or indirect processes, in their natural and objective connexion. And by exposition I do not merely understand communication to others, a purpose for which an exhibition of the subjective process of discovery is no less necessary and no less instructive. I mean rather the framing of the results arrived at into a logical whole, in which form alone they meet the ideal requirements which the human intellect makes of any body of truth that is to be fixed and independent.

Such being the case it appeared to me hardly desirable to introduce the question of the analytic and synthetic methods among the questions of applied logic, inasmuch as neither the one nor the other affords any practical contribution towards the solution of any definite problems,—the analytic method as little as the synthetic, notwithstanding that we regard it as the type of all methods of investigation and discovery. To instruct a person to employ the analytic method is to give him no very helpful counsel; the customary general definitions of the method really contain nothing more than an indication of the direction in which the required road still has to be looked for; to find it we must turn to the special expedients of applied logic, in using which it makes very little difference whether we choose to rank them under the method of synthesis or under that of analysis. In the same manner an enquirer who has the synthetic method prescribed to him has merely got his problem stated: to the question how to solve it, in which certainly the rules of a method ought by rights to be of service to him, no very sufficient answer is afforded by the general direction to work downwards from principles to results.

299. All this is changed if we surrender a certain privilege which in the sphere of applied logic we allowed ourselves to claim, and endeavour by this surrender to give completeness to our treatment of the subject. Thus far in speaking of the forms of proof, of the search for grounds of proof, of the discovery of laws, we have left our work throughout in a certain sense incomplete. Every attempt to establish a proposition went only a few steps back, and came to a stand as soon as some other proposition was reached, which served for its foundation, and the validity of which was not proved but assumed. This procedure answers to the actual course of thought in life as well as in the sphere of the special sciences. In ordinary life our judgment of things and the conclusions we draw concerning them rest not on a single proposition T, nor yet upon a clearly defined group of homogeneous elementary truths, but on a large number of truths of a quite heterogeneous character, yet possessed of an equal certainty; here a proposition A, which once apprehended forces itself upon us as a necessity of thought, there a proposition B expressing an immediate fact of perception, and presenting itself not exactly as necessary but as incontrovertible; a third, again, C, may be a principle of unknown origin, but one which at every moment is being put to the proof and confirmed afresh; finally we have many a proposition D springing from equally unknown sources, but admitting of no such guarantee of its truth, and yet seeming to bear within it an indefeasible claim, a claim that is which we believe ourselves bound to satisfy if the conceptions by which we bind together the *data* of experience are to answer to the truth.

Any one of these various points of certainty—and in each

of them we may suppose a number of elementary convictions to be contained and compressed—is used indifferently in the living movement of thought as occasion arises, to answer any question which comes up for solution; nay even a proposition which naturally depends on some one particular assumption, we often prove from a different one, if its dependence on the former is not at once evident. In this way we are constantly shifting the bases on which our judgments rest; at one time we set out from some law which is evident to us, and determine its effects; at another by repeated observation of the effects we strengthen our belief in the law; consequences which appear to flow by an internal necessity from some acknowledged principle, are rejected for their improbability as seen from a different standpoint; now we start from A to prove a doubtful B, now B appears the more evident of the two, and we use it to establish A; the truth being that whatever possesses for us at the moment the strongest psychological certainty passes for the point of vantage from which the other more wavering beliefs are to be secured.

300. So entirely unconstrained as this in its operation scientific thought certainly is not; still the actual science which we possess, as distinguished from the ideal science, which we might wish to possess, has resemblance enough to the natural processes of ordinary reflexion. Here also we hardly meet with any enquiry into a matter of fact, which does not depend for its determination upon certain presuppositions which we adopt now as undemonstrable but certain, now again as undemonstrable and only probable, and which are regarded either as ultimate principles of the particular science before us, or as vouched for by some other science. Even within a single province of enquiry the direction in which the required proof is looked for varies. Without exactly questioning the certainty of a proposition which we have begun by regarding as the source from which others are derived, we come nevertheless to

believe that there is some other proposition which we may place at the head with still greater security, and from which we may derive our former first principle with all its consequences.

And if we review our knowledge as a whole, distributed as it is among the various sciences, we shall find no one of these complete and rounded off in itself. In each one of them we come upon formal or material principles, whose validity is admitted because they are self-evident, or because they explain certain facts, while as to their origin and connexion with each other no enquiry is made if the question appears to have no immediate bearing upon the prosecution of the science itself.

This point of view we kept before us while we were dealing with the subject of applied logic, and we saw no reason to depart from it so long as our subject was the nature of investigation. For what we commonly call Applied Logic, or more properly the exhibition of the possible modes in which Logic can be applied, presupposes the existence of a variety of cases adapted for its application, and this is only possible if the work of investigation consists in taking some given fixed point to start from, and then connecting this by rule and law with other fixed points which are also not proved, but assumed. Such is the character of all investigations in which we are accustomed actually to engage, and in this our knowledge bears resemblance to our life. What was the origin of our race in the first beginnings of history we know not, and as little can thought carry us to its far-off future; for most of us the memory of those who have gone before fades away in no very distant past, and for all alike the prospect granted of the fortunes of those who are to come after us is still more confined; yet in the midst of this darkness on either hand, there lies before us a certain space of life comparatively clear, with plain needs, pressing duties, and attainable goals; our joy in existence, and our confidence in acting upon the present, are but little impaired by the uncertainty of the beginning and the end. And so it is with our knowledge. That there is an eternal truth, or a perfect and self-closed circle of truths, we do indeed assume, but ordinary reflexion has for such a system of truth no form of expression adequate to it, nor has it any clear conception how the members of the system are related; single portions only become plain and evident to us in a manner which we are incapable of analysing to ourselves, in the course of our mind's operation as it comes in contact with reality.. In the process of investigation we resemble men engaged in a narrow inland traffic, and we endeavour to connect the uncertain and changing scenes about us, with the isolated peaks which rise upon our view out of a coherent world of truth which we cannot see.

301. But just as there arrive moments in life when the present only seems endurable or intelligible if we can catch some glimpse of its connexion with the past and with the future, so also in knowledge there are occasions when we are tempted to pass out of the petty business of ordinary scientific investigation, and reflect upon the points it starts from, and the points it aims at; to ask where they are situated, how they are connected with each other, and whether they are secure. For the principles on which the several sciences repose do not restrict themselves to an un-aggressive sway each within its own separate province. We need only point to the very different consequences in respect of the powers that shape human life which are deduced from the principles of mechanical science on the one hand, and the deliverances of conscience on the other, to see in a single emphatic example how the claims of different sources of truth may clash and conflict in dealing with a common subject-matter. But even within the field of purely theoretical science we may find inducements enough to make that which in the living processes of thought, and in the special sciences, figures as the first

principle from which all enquiry starts, itself a subject of enquiry.

This important problem philosophy in all ages has kept in view and pursued, not indeed with entire success, yet not altogether without result; and assuredly its complete solution would be also the completion of philosophy; for such solution could only consist in the establishment of a perfected system of connected truths at once ultimate and concrete, from which all the principles which direct the researches of the sciences would be derivable, which would supply the key to their precise and real significance, and define the limits of their validity. It is no such comprehensive undertaking as this, but only a modest portion of it, which will form the subject of the concluding chapters of this work. Our object is not to enquire into the content of the principles in question, but into the grounds upon which in a subjective sense their certainty for us reposes; to ask not what is the truth, but what are the marks by which we recognise it and distinguish it from error; or, if we are to keep the old terminology, it is our purpose by following a method of analysis to obtain clear ideas as to the path by which we may hope to arrive at the principles of a synthetic development.

My reason for treating this part of Logic under the head of Knowledge, the further discussion upon which we are entering will elucidate—an elucidation which the above preliminary designation of our undertaking itself certainly requires. But in giving it the name of Methodology I confess myself to be employing the term to some extent in a sense of my own. Every science develops its characteristic methods, methods fruitful in their results, which it employs in dealing with a given class of problems. But Logic regards all such methods as special artifices with which it has no concern, but which it belongs to the special sciences themselves to furnish. General methods again, such as the synthetic and analytic procedure of which I have been speaking, do indeed find a mention in Logic; but by formulating them we should only be making a somewhat barren postulate, until we are clear as to the grounds of our belief that the one has actually led us to the discovery of the truth, and that in the other we have an instrument which enables us to develope and exhibit it in detail.

It is this last-named undertaking which I desire to indicate here by the term 'method,' using it to denote not a general type of procedure which has to be applied over and over again in a thousand instances, but rather in the sense of a definite operation which thought has to go through once and for all, and of which the object is to mediate between the various sources from which various kinds of certainty appear to find their way to us, and to arrive at a knowledge of the connexion between them, and of the limits of their validity.

CHAPTER I.

On Scepticism.

302. THE human mind only becomes aware of the laws of its own activity after it has already exerted it in a great variety of ways, when it turns back by an act of reflexion and comparison upon the various forms which this activity has assumed, and makes the rules, which it has been following all the while unconsciously, an object of separate attention. The question why those laws are binding and within what limits their observance carries with it the promise of true knowledge, comes still later. It can only arise after we have had experience of errors into which we appear to have been drawn not by the neglect of those laws, but by their observance in dealing with the different subject-matters presented to our intelligence.

If then this has been the case, and if further no success has attended our scattered and occasional attempts to remove the difficulties and contradictions which have arisen, by giving a better interpretation either to that which seemed to us to be truth, or to that which we regarded as the immediate deliverance of direct perception,—then arises that mood of wide and general doubt which constitutes Scepticism.

As a transient phase of longer or shorter duration this sceptical mood has its place in the development of every serious mind; several times in the history of Philosophy it has been emphatically insisted on as the normal and necessary condition of the mind, which is called upon at the outset of the scientific life to regard all traditional knowledge as so much doubtful prejudice, which has to be submitted to test and trial. Finally it has ᾽ established itself as a permanent result in the sceptical schools of Philosophy, which have believed themselves to have attained to the conviction of the impossibility of certain knowledge. In this final form in which alone Scepticism pretends to have arrived at a definite outcome, we shall not find it so entirely free as it flatters itself to be from traditional prejudices. One thing above all however is clear; an unconditional denial of all truth this final outcome of Scepticism cannot by any possibility include, inasmuch as not the solution of doubt merely but doubt itself is only possible on the presupposition of some sort of acknowledged truths.

Whoever entertains a hope of finding a path out of the labyrinth of Scepticism to any form of certain knowledge grants this already: for he can only find that path by an investigation, and any form of investigation is possible only on the assumption at all events of formal principles of judgment by which one combination of ideas can be distinguished as true from a second as false, or from a third which is doubtful. And again he who denies that such a way out is to be found, in the very act of denial acknowledges that which he denies. When the old Sophistic taught that there was no truth, and that if there were it could not be known, and that even if it could be known still it could not be communicated, in so doing it contradicted each of the propositions enunciated. For after all it gives out its three propositions for truth, and could not therefore deny all truth; it endeavoured further to prove the soundness of its contentions, and was bound therefore in its own interest to presuppose the validity of that particular form of the apprehension of truth—mediate apprehension—the impossibility of which it would have been most especially pleasant to point out; finally it denied the possibility of communicating truth, at the very moment when on the strength of its being communicable, it was setting itself to convince men of the truth of its own tenets.

Nor can these contradictions be escaped by avoiding the form of positive assertion in the expression of the results of the doctrine, and instead of denying the validity of any asserted truth simply returning a *non liquet* to the general question equally with all particular ones. Certainly those who adopt this course, and we along with them, are at liberty to give this answer where the question concerns the proof of particular contentions from truths whose validity is acknowledged; but to maintain that the validity of all truths whatsoever is doubtful is a proposition which may indeed be expressed in words, but the words have no longer any real idea to answer to them; we could not possibly explain the meaning of that *liquet* which we are negativing, if we had not in our mind certain conditions under which we should be prepared to affirm it, that is to say if we did not presuppose some unconditionally valid truth, from which is derived our right to doubt whatever cannot be proved to be in agreement with it.

But not only is any sceptical conclusion, in whatever form maintained, impossible without this assumption, but the very fact of doubt itself is impossible also—impossible at least in the only sense in which we are here concerned with it. Uncertainty indeed there would be, not sometimes, but at least as concerns the future, always and invariably, if there were no truth to teach us to distinguish between what is necessary and what is not; but on the other hand we should never in that case have occasion to raise the doubt whether a given proposition holds as tried by this or that standard, inasmuch as it would be a matter of indifference whether it did so or not, unless the standard in question be recognised as really such, as a veritable criterion, in a word as truth.

However thorough-going then the claims of Scepticism

may be, still it can never get rid, not only of the recognition of some absolutely valid truth, but of this presupposition also, that the human mind is in possession of certain fundamental principles which enable it to affirm at all events the impossibility of proving this or that given conception to agree with the truth which the sceptic recognises.

303. To this admission the sceptical mind readily allows itself to be driven; it has it will acknowledge a profound belief that there is some absolutely valid truth; and again it will grant that necessary laws of thought rule all our enquiries and all our doubts: the question which troubles it is whether the two—the truth and the laws of thought—coincide. Just because we know that there must be truth, and therefore that there may be error, how are we to be sure that those necessary laws which exist in our mind may not belong to the side of error, and everything therefore be quite different in itself from that which by the laws of thought it necessarily appears to us?

It is clear that a scepticism such as this, which is not driven to doubt through any special cause residing in the nature of its subject-matter, but which simply looks upon the possibility of raising a doubt as ground sufficient for actually raising it, can never admit of being refuted by demonstration. For every argument which can be brought into the field against it can only rest upon the self-evidence and necessity with which it is thought, and must belong therefore to that sphere of necessities of thought as to which the old barren question can always be renewed to infinity, whether after all things may not be in reality quite otherwise than thought makes them.

This question also has in fact been raised more than once in the history of philosophy; at the beginning of the modern era by Descartes, who after convincing himself as he thought that the soul is furnished with an equipment of innate necessary Ideas, presented the question in the following vivid form:—might not an evil Demon have so constituted our nature, that all our thoughts should be necessarily false, and yet appear to ourselves clear and necessary truths? And this hypothesis he considered he could only refute by pointing to the fact that among these innate Ideas is to be found the conception of an absolutely holy and perfect God, but, he argued a finite spirit could not have constructed out of itself that which is greater than itself, the thought of the Infinite; only an actually existing holy God could have implanted this in us, and it would contradict the nature of this holy God to practise a deception upon us. There is one feature in this demonstration which is worthy of attention; the underlying thought that in the immediate assurance which we feel of the significance of the moral Idea lies the security also for the truth of our knowledge: but certainly the off-hand way in which the two are thrown together here in Descartes' conclusion will convince no one. For after all what exception can justly be taken to those religious views, which also set out from the belief in a holy God, but find it perfectly compatible with the purposes of His wisdom in the education of mankind, that He should have wholly withheld a large portion of the truth from our human knowledge? And supposing that He had denied to us not a portion of truth only but all truth, but in place of it had furnished our soul with imaginations which for it are necessities of thought, what right should we have had to call this withholding of truth and bestowal of error by the hard name of a deception, until we had first proved that our soul possessed a right to the grant of truth which God could not disregard without prejudice to His own holiness, and that the apprehension of all existence as it really is, was the necessary prerequisite for the fulfilment of those purposes which we believe that in His holiness He designs to accomplish? Such proof Descartes has neither furnished nor attempted to furnish; he abandons himself in the above line of thought with all confidence to the guidance of certain assumptions which have their limited place in determining questions within the circle of the intercourse of human beings with each other, but become mere groundless prejudice when they are applied to that most comprehensive of all questions, what is the significance of a necessary law of thought, which manifests itself in finite minds; his argument would not hinder us in fact from assuming, not indeed that a malicious Demon, but that some creative power had so fashioned us that all things should actually appear to us by a necessity of our thought otherwise than they are.

Two alternatives are open to us. First we can if we please leave any person who is disposed to assent to such a hypothesis, to himself, on the ground that we acknowledge the impossibility of refuting him, so long as his doubts are suggested not by any positive difficulty which renders them irresistible, but merely by the possibility of continually renewing them without any positive ground whatever. In the presence of this sceptical disposition we should fall back for the purposes of science upon a principle from which in the ordinary affairs of life our opponent himself cannot escape and does not shrink,—faith in reason. We should continue to regard a necessity of thought as true until through the conclusions which it itself produces it proves itself to be no such thing, and compels us to declare it a 'show of being' only, which in such case would be not entirely a vain show but an appearance standing in a definable relation to the truth with which it can no longer be identified. This attitude towards the sceptic is that which we find observed in life, for through the world's history this groundless scepticism has always reappeared from time to time, but as often as it has made its appearance men have simply turned their backs upon it.

But in science such a treatment of the question is not altogether becoming. The second alternative appears to me the more helpful one, to lay bare the essential groundlessness of this curious solicitude, which asks whether after all things may not be quite other in themselves than that which by the laws of our thought they necessarily appear. What after all is the meaning of this addition 'in themselves,' or this being in itself of something which we oppose to our necessary conceptions of the very same something and which is supposed to be different from them? We are here in fact, as we now propose to show, in presence of a prejudice springing up from the accumulated effects of experience and education, which has crept into the heart of that very Scepticism which conceives itself to have got rid of all prejudices.

304. He who begins to reflect upon the foundations and the sources of his knowledge finds himself at starting entangled in all the prejudices which have grown up in him unconsciously as his mind has developed, whether arising out of his individual experience, or accepted from others. For the first attitude of the mind can never be doubt; it begins always with entire confidence in all its perceptions. Now no one of these prejudices is more universal than the conception of an independent world of things with which we habitually contrast our own world of thoughts. Errors which meet us within this latter world we regard as trifling blemishes easily cured, in comparison with the great and dread delusion in which it may be the entire system of the world of thought is involved as judged by that other world of actual things.

The doubting question, therefore, whether things may not be in fact quite different from what they necessarily appear to us, has *prima facie* an intelligible sense only upon the assumption that human knowledge is intended to be a copy of a world of things, and in fact that truth regarding the possibility of which for man uncertainty is felt, has been most commonly defined as the agreement of our ideas with the real condition of the things which they profess to copy. The ordinary consciousness in practical life never departs from this standpoint; philosophy, on the other hand, in the course of its speculations has abandoned it not unfrequently on the strength of knowledge of which it believed itself to be already in possession. But a scepticism which in an enquiry into the possibility of knowledge professed to renounce all prejudices, was bound above all things not to retain unquestioned a definition of the truth of which it was in search, founded upon the uncriticised prejudice that there is such an external world of things. To dispute that this assumption is a prejudice is possible only for one who never raises a doubt at all, but who feels so complete a satisfaction in the direct deliverances of simple perception as to find in it at once a convincing evidence of the existence of the external world, and an infallible revelation of its nature. But he who once entertains a doubt of the truth of any perception, and at the same time holds fast as if it were a matter of course to the assumption of the existence of the fact, to which the perception ought by rights to correspond, can, to begin with, only be raising such a doubt at all, on the strength of definite convictions as to the nature of the 'fact' in question, convictions which appear to him to be necessities of Thought, and which forbid him to take the given perception as its true representation. But further, as he can no longer regard the thing itself as given him by direct perception, it follows that the obligation to retain the belief in its existence at all can in its turn only rest upon an innate necessity of thought compelling him to supplement and complete the manifold world of perception by this thought of a world not perceived, in order to bring his ideas in their totality into an inward harmony in agreement with the laws of his own thought.

A philosophical review of these questions is necessary, not indeed to establish our immediate faith in this world of actual things, but to give us scientific justification for holding to the assumption of its reality, and on this point the systems of Idealism and Realism have arrived at opposite results. To bring so comprehensive a problem to an issue is not in the least our business here; on the contrary it is our purpose to show that as a matter of arrangement the question ought not to be imported into these introductory discussions on the theory of knowledge. With this view we have to consider a single thought in two aspects; we have to remind ourselves in the first place that any decision of the question postulates the recognition of the competence of thought, secondly we have to show that nothing else but the connexion of our ideas with each other can ever be made the object of our investigations.

305. A few words will suffice for the first point. Every criticism of the entire apparatus of our faculties of knowledge P, undertaken with a view of enquiring into its agreement with the nature of things, must presuppose in order to its decision a second source of truth Q, which gives us a knowledge, free from all alloy of error, of what that nature is: for we can only compare known with known, not known with unknown. Supposing now that this Q were given us, it matters not whether in the form of a comprehensive revelation imparted originally to our soul, or as a certainty coming suddenly upon us as an answer to particular questions one by one as they present themselves, in either case how are we to compare it with the claims of P which requires us to connect our single ideas according to determinate laws?

If P and Q agree, how could we distinguish the one from the other, in order to convince ourselves that it is not only our subjective cognition P which is speaking to us, but that it has the additional confirmation of the higher objective truth Q, evidencing its agreement with the things themselves? We could not do it at all; the united utterance of the two together would be liable to precisely the same doubts and questionings as that of P by itself. If on the other hand Q told us something different from P, how should we decide between them? Even supposing that as a matter of fact Q gave us truth and P error, how else could our faith in the superior credibility of Q be arrived at, except through the greater immediate certainty which attended its utterance as compared with that of P? But this certainty is inconceivable, except on the condition of Q coinciding with that very truth which constitutes the universal law of our subjective faculty of cognition P; what contradicts this would, even if it were given us in immediate perception, be always a riddle to us, and not a revelation. If then Q and P remain opposed, what we arrive at is not a refutation of P on the strength of the higher claims of Q, but we experience an inner conflict between two utterances of that faculty of knowledge which is peculiar to our minds, a conflict which either can find no higher court to appeal to, and in that case can never be resolved, or must be settled by the discovery on the part of that faculty itself of a higher point of view within its own province from which one or other of the conflicting utterances may be corrected, and the apparent contradiction removed. We see then that to thought and its necessary laws we are as a matter of fact limited in every resort; the faith which reason entertains that truth whatever it may be is discoverable by thought, is the unavoidable postulate of all enquiry; what that truth is can be discovered only by the reflective operation of thought, continually trying and testing its single results by the standard of the universal laws of its activity.

306. It is in vain to shrink from acknowledging the circle which is here involved, for that there is no escape from it everyone after all must see. It is also superfluous, because there can never come a moment in our experience—and this is the second point we have to urge—in which the supposed mischief which our vague suspicions apprehend could possibly become known to us. All we know of the external world depends upon the ideas of it which are within us; it is so far entirely indifferent whether with Idealism we deny the existence of that world, and regard our ideas of it as alone reality, or whether we maintain with Realism the existence of things outside us which act upon our minds.

On the latter hypothesis as little as the former do the things themselves pass into our knowledge; they only awaken in us ideas, which are not Things. It is then this varied world of ideas within us, it matters not where they may have come from, which forms the sole material directly given to us, from which alone our knowledge can start. In them, and in the course which they follow as they change and connect themselves, we endeavour to discover a regular and orderly arrangement, guided in our search by those universal principles of our thought which determine for us what we are to account as order and truth, and what as involving a contradiction or a problem to the reason.

Every discovery of such a law, regulating universally and without exception any two determinate ideas[1] B and F in their conjunction with each other in our minds, is the attainment of a fragment of that which we call knowledge of Fact[2]. If we fail in our effort to discover such a constant connexion between the two, then we have a problem before us, which we always set to work to solve in the same way. First we endeavour to find some universal relation between B and what is contained in a third idea M, and between F and what is contained in a fourth idea N, and then to show that by reason of a variable relation which obtains between M and N, that between B and F cannot be expressed in the form of a simple law such as we were looking for, but only through a law of a different kind which takes account of M and N as well.

If finally we are in doubt whether a relation which we have discovered to exist between two ideas B and F in our minds, corresponds to the reality of things, this can only mean that we doubt whether whenever B and F reappear as ideas in our consciousness the relation between their contents which we have collected from only a limited number of instances, will continue to obtain universally and without exception. But if the question be once more repeated: is

[1] ['Vorstellungen.']   [2] [Sache.]

a relation between B and F as established for consciousness even by invariable experience also true in itself, such a question is only intelligible at all on one supposition, namely if the relation existing as a matter of fact in consciousness does not accord with the universal postulates of thought,— those postulates which thought constrains us to make in the case of any relation between any two objects whatever, and therefore also of those which we are endeavouring to conceive as obtaining between real existences independent of ourselves. It is not this assumed external world of the Real which comes in here between our ideas as the standard by which their truth is to be measured; the standard is always the conception of which we cannot get rid, of what such a world must be if it *does* exist, is always that is to say a thought in our own minds; this it is by which we measure the truth of other thoughts, whether they contain the evidence in themselves, or are such as to require elucidation from without.

307. It is perhaps superfluous, but it may not be without its use, to repeat this simple argument, starting from the opposite side, and to ask what it is that must happen if we are to discover a supposed piece of knowledge Z to be a delusion. Suppose we knew from our own observation that between two ideas B and F frequently recurring in our experience the relation Z does not uniformly obtain, but on the contrary varies according to the varying relations in which B is found conjoined with M, and F with N. Suppose on the other hand that another human being lived within a sphere of experience where those conditions exclusively obtain under which the relation Z between our B and F does become a necessity. It will follow that he will never have occasion to doubt the universality of that relation Z, nor will his faith in it prejudice the coherence of the rest of the world of his ideas, provided only that Z does not conflict with the universal laws of his thought. Unquestionably the assumption that Z is an absolute relation between B and F

independently of further conditions, may make it much more difficult for him to find a simple law for the relations between other constituent elements of his experience, as C and E, which he would at once discover if he was aware of the dependence of Z upon conditions which do also in fact determine the relation between C and E. But so long as he does not extend his faith in Z beyond the objects contained in the world of his ideas, he will still be in a position to systematise the objects connected in that world, however awkwardly he may have to express their connexion. We indeed who possess the experience which he lacks are aware of his error, but we can only convince him of it by taking him out of his more limited circle of experience and transplanting him into a wider. Then when he himself finds fresh conjunctions of ideas arising in his mind distinct from those which he formerly experienced, he will allow that he has been in error; still all he will have to concede will be that he was mistaken in supposing the relation Z between B and F to obtain universally; that relation still holds true when the conditions are added upon which, though unawares to him, its validity all the while depended.

And now how will it be if we place human reason as such in the position of this unfavourably situated observer, and imagine it confined to a mode of mental representation, coherent indeed in itself, but not corresponding to the real relations which obtain in a world of things external to it? How is the standing delusion, in which in that case we are all involved, to become known to us, or how will our knowledge suffer supposing it to continue? Setting aside for the moment the instruction which an angel from heaven might impart to us, what we find is this: it is certainly not the things themselves which are here making their way all of a sudden into the midst of our thoughts, and laying bare their falsity; even if the world of things running its independent course were to enter some day upon a new arrangement which diametrically contradicted the conceptions which we had previously formed of it, such contradiction could only come within our observation through the new influences awakening in us a set of ideas which we find no longer to observe those laws of combination which we had hitherto assumed to be their laws. Then we have fallen into one of those errors of the understanding to which we of course allow that we are liable; we have wrongly interpreted this variable world of ideas, that world which is the sole material that lies open to our intelligence; we recognise now that we have learnt a new lesson, and that the proposition Z does not possess the universal validity with which we had credited it; but we have learnt also that it does continue to be valid still when the conditions of that validity with which we have now become acquainted are reckoned in. And now the universal validity of Z being erroneous, so also its limited validity is true, and we come to see that inasmuch as error can only be observable by us through an inner contradiction in our world of ideas, it follows that the recognition of truth itself consists only in the discovery of laws of connexion which this ideal world is destined always to observe, to however infinite a distance we may imagine its varying course to be prolonged. Undoubtedly the discovery of these laws is an undertaking which must remain incomplete; we are not in possession of the whole truth, we are in search of it; still so often as we correct a previous belief Z at the instance of fresh experiences in our world of thought, we have not indeed reached as yet the full truth, but we have removed the errors which without such correction would have lasted on.

308. This argument, unless I am much deceived, will satisfy no one. We are left after all, it will be urged, even if all inner contradictions are removed, walled in within the all-embracing delusions of those ideas which have grown up into a solid mass within us, and never see the truth in itself, but only as it necessarily appears to us.

Now then let us call in our angel from heaven, who beholds from his purer atmosphere things as they are. What a shock we fancy it would be to us if all at once he withdrew the veil from our eyes, and we saw how entirely different things really are from what we had imagined them.

And indeed we should experience a very agreeable shock if in that moment it were revealed to us how our old ideas, with all their old meaning, by the introduction of certain simple links in the chain hitherto concealed from us, became at once perfectly intelligible, with no gap or contradiction remaining, and intelligible by the light of the old laws which had all along directed the movement of our thought. But also on this condition only. If it were an entirely new world which rose upon our view, bearing no resemblance and no relation to that in which we had lived before, we simply should not perceive that everything was different from what we thought; for what that meant to us was that everything we thought was different from what we thought it; the wholly new spectacle admitting, as it would, of no comparison with the former one, could on this ground at all events give us no shock at all, pleasurable or otherwise; it could not so much as occasion us surprise, except through a sense of contrast, that is to say by being brought into relation with our previous world of illusion. But again we who now see ought to be the same persons who before were blind. If that moment of revelation had at the same time transformed the laws of our thought, and altered the conditions under which hitherto we had distinguished truth and error, we should indeed, if our newly discovered world completely answered to these new conditions of truth, have no occasion to doubt about any particular fact in it; but what could preserve us from the grand fundamental doubt, whether this new world of ideas with all its self-consistency may not in its turn distort the true nature of reality, and things be once more quite different in themselves from that which in this new world they appear to be? Do you hope to exclude these doubts on the ground that on our own assumption it is the truth of things themselves, and nothing else, which makes up the content of our new perceptions? But to exclude the possibility of doubt, the fact that our representation of things *is* the true one would not of itself suffice. We must also possess means to arrive at a certain *knowledge* that it is the true one. Now such means we do possess in regard to particular parts of our experience; we can measure their truth by asking, are they as judged by the universal laws of our thought in harmony with the rest of that same experience? But it is impossible to test the truth of the entire world of our ideas as such by comparing it with a reality which so long as it is not an object of knowledge is for us non-existent, and if once it becomes so must be subject to the same doubts and uncertainties to which all ideas simply as such are liable.

And finally the supposed case is in itself impossible and absurd. What can be the meaning of saying that this higher intuition, perception, cognition, gives the thing in itself, as it really is? We may exalt the intelligence of more perfect beings above our own as high as we please; but so long as we desire to attach any rational meaning to it, it must always fall under some category of knowledge or direct perception, or cognition, that is to say it will never *be* the thing itself but only an aggregate of ideas *about* the thing. Nothing is simpler than to convince ourselves that every apprehending intelligence can only see things as they look to it when it perceives them, not as they look when no one perceives them; he who demands a knowledge which should be more than a perfectly connected and consistent system of ideas about the thing, a knowledge which should actually exhaust the thing itself, is no longer asking for knowledge at all, but for something entirely unintelligible. One cannot even say that he is desiring not to know but to *be* the things themselves; for in fact he would not even so reach his goal. Could he arrive at *being* in some way or another that very metal in itself, the knowledge of which in the way of ideas does not content him; well, he would *be* metal it is true, but he would be further off than ever from apprehending himself as the metal which he had become. Or supposing that a higher power gave him back his intelligence while he still remained metal, even then in his new character of intelligent metal he would still only apprehend himself in such wise as he would be represented to himself in his own ideas, not as he would be apart from such representation.

309. In dealing with these fundamental questions I ought not to be blamed for the lengthened discussion which I have permitted myself. It is true the outcome is small. We have convinced ourselves that this changing world of our ideas is the sole material given us to work upon; that truth and the knowledge of truth consist only in the laws of interconnexion which are found to obtain universally within a given set of ideas, and are confirmed as often as those ideas recur in our consciousness; that as the thoughts which lead us towards this order of truths make way, the antithesis between our ideas and the objects to which we conceive them to be directed, itself a part of that same world of ideas, necessarily arises; that the question as to the truth of this antithesis, and the value which according as we answer it will belong to our ideas, is a question of metaphysics which has no business to be mixed up with an introduction to the theory of knowledge such as the present; that in regard to this or that among our thoughts we may doubt as to the possibility of bringing it into harmony with the rest of the content of our consciousness, and that such doubts resting on definite grounds are compatible with the endeavour gradually to remove them; that on the other hand a scepticism which indulges the apprehension that everything may be in reality quite different from what it necessarily appears, sets out with a self-contradiction, because it silently takes for granted the possibility of an apprehension which does not apprehend things but is itself things, and then goes on to question whether this impossible perfection is allotted to our intelligence. Finally we see that if we set aside this inadmissible relation of the world of ideas to a foreign world of objects, there still remains a further line of enquiry open to us,—the endeavour to discover within the world of ideas itself what are the fixed points, the primary certainties, starting from which we may be enabled to bring the rest of the shifting multitude of its ideas into something like orderly connexion. I shall find and shall avail myself of various opportunities hereafter for elucidating this point of view; I go on at present to glance at the different methods of procedure which the sceptical philosophy has followed, and which have been pursued in the various departments of enquiry to which they have been applied, upon the whole with greater completeness in antiquity than in modern times, when many of its questions are no longer able to excite an active interest.

310. Sextus Empiricus has left us a *collectanea* of the tenets of Scepticism down to his own time. The Sceptic does not any more than other men deny the sensuous perceptions, the feelings of pleasure and pain, which we experience. They force themselves irresistibly upon him, and are independent of his opinion. On the other hand everything that is contrasted with these phenomena, as a noumenon, or as a thought, which itself not given in the phenomenon, seeks to bring the content of the perceptions into some inner connexion,—all this is made open to doubt, and any statement we venture from this point of view may be met with equal propriety by another which contradicts it. Nothing therefore remains for the wise man but to refrain from either affirming or denying either the one proposition or the other, and to find in this suspension of judgment that peace of mind which so long as he considers it his duty to decide

between two conflicting hypotheses, he must necessarily seek in vain.

But when Scepticism, not content with representing an abstention from any affirmation as the condition of mind actually found in its adherents, undertakes to prove it on logical grounds to be the only legitimate attitude of the mind, it becomes at the very outset false to itself, presupposing as it does at all events at this point the truth of those logical laws of thought by which alone it can establish the cogency of its own reasonings. And not only so but in its efforts to expose the impossibility of dogmatic statements it is compelled to assume a variety of dogmas which can never be directly given in phenomenal experience, but can only be derived from them by those very processes of reasoning whose legitimacy is contested. The ten τρόποι or logical grounds of doubt, which Sextus begins by rehearsing, all come to this, that sensations by themselves cannot discover to us what is the nature of the object which excites them. The first τρόπος calls attention to the different organisations of different animals; when it goes on further to the proposition that by reason of this any object must appear different to the senses of one animal from what it does to those of another, it appeals to the Dogma that unlikes cannot be affected alike by likes. Nothing short of this argument would have justified his conclusion, for as we cannot place ourselves inside an animal's consciousness, this supposed difference between the sensation of one animal and that of another is a conclusion given by reasoning, which can never be established by immediate perception. More than this, the argument affirms too much; there is nothing to prove that visible differences in bodily organisation are an invariable indication of corresponding differences of feeling; no one will easily believe that a cat, by reason of its elliptically shaped pupil, must necessarily perceive the world of space differently to a man with his circular one.

The second τρόπος applies the same argument within the

circle of human beings. They too in their turn are variously organised; if then, the τρόπος argues, it were proposed—though we have no grounds for so doing—to give the human sensations a preference over the animal, and to regard these as true and adequate to the thing itself, we are again defeated by reason of the individual differences which exist between man and man. So that all we can say is, that to one man the thing appears in one way, to his neighbour in another way; how it is in itself remains unsettled.

The two next τρόποι lead to the same result; the third appeals to the differences among the senses themselves; to the eye honey is yellow, to the tongue sweet; it may be that there are other forms of sensation, lacking to us, to which it appears something different again : what it is in itself must therefore be relegated to uncertainty, as we have no reason for accounting the deliverance of one sense truer than that of another. Even supposing however that we keep to a single sense, the fourth τρόπος points out that here too there are variations of feeling, according to age and state of health, according as we are hungry or satisfied, asleep or awake, so that still we can only say how a thing appears to our sense under each of these varying conditions, but not how it would appear to a subject which was experiencing none of them.

These four τρόποι were concerned with the nature of the subject which frames judgments; the four which follow relate to the objects. The fifth reminds us that distance and position alter the appearance of one and the same thing : the sixth points out that no object produces in us the impression of itself unmixed with those of others; the seventh that the composition of various elements in single objects causes qualities to appear in them which are entirely wanting in the simple elements themselves, and effaces others which belonged to them; so that we can never do more than state how each one appears in its several combinations with other things, nor what it is like in itself and by itself apart from the various phases which by reason of those relations it passes through. It is impossible to read the examples to these last τρόποι without a feeling of astonishment that the scepticism of antiquity should have seen in them throughout only impediments to scientific knowledge. In modern science they have become one and all starting-points of enquiry. Modern science has not been content with raising a general lamentation over the changeableness of phenomena under changing conditions; it has questioned experience; it has enquired what are the special connexions which obtain between any one of these conditions and this or that particular change in the phenomenon, and it has in this way arrived at a knowledge of the general laws which govern this endlessly changing play of events. We have not indeed learnt what a thing is like in itself when it stands wholly apart from all the conditions of its manifestation to intelligence; but that the problem so presented is absurd the ancient scepticism was itself aware, as we find it expressed in the eighth τρόπος: Everything stands in relations of one kind or another, if not to other things, yet always at least if it is to become an object of apprehension, to the subject apprehending it; what it is like in itself, apart from all relations, remains therefore beyond our power to say.

The last two τρόποι are of less interest for us: the ninth reminds us that our estimate of the magnitude and the value of things is conditioned by their rarity or frequency, by custom and by contrast; the tenth appeals to the diversity of national manners and morals as an evidence that here too we can only say what appears good and bad to one person or another, not what is good and bad in itself.

311. The further development of the Pyrrhonian ὑποτυπώσεις of Sextus, from whose first book the doctrines I have cited are taken, I here pass over. It will here be evident that so far the Scepticism we have been considering does not deny the reality of truth, for it is the impossibility of

attaining to truth which it laments over, and one can only make that an object of quest in the reality of which one believes. Nor does it doubt that conformity to the laws of thought is the necessary condition of any thought being true. It is incessantly enumerating, in disjunctions alleged to be complete, sets of cases which are inferred on the basis of these laws to be possible and to exclude one another; and it is by this same logic of thought that it undertakes to bring us to acknowledge the necessity of withholding judgment altogether. It is true that this procedure has to be subsequently corrected. The sceptical argument is at pains to include itself in the uncertainty to which, by one of those very affirmations which it seeks to get rid of, it condemns the whole of our pretended knowledge. The forms of argument which are employed for this purpose are many and curious. If the Sceptic arrives at his negations by a process of demonstration, he is not, it is said, in so doing, here any more than elsewhere, laying down any positive doctrine; he is simply stating that to him, here and now, at this particular moment of his life, and in the particular state of mind in which he happens to be, the opinion which he has announced appears to be the true one. He does not guarantee its continuing so to appear even to himself at every future moment; if he is driven to acknowledge some one else's argument to be convincing, he can always answer, the truth Z which this man teaches, has up to this moment been unrecognised, yet all the same if it is truth it has been so always and been always valid; and where is our security that some third person may not hereafter discover and demonstrate a new truth to upset Z in its turn, which at the present moment, though it already holds good, is neither recognised nor capable of being either apprehended or proved?

These questions are independent of the relation of our knowledge to an object outside itself; they concern the ground of certainty generally, and our right to the confidence we repose in the truth of any thought in our minds; in this view we reserve them for consideration later. But apart from this the arguments of Sextus involve at once a prejudice and a fallacy; the prejudice of the existence of that World in itself with which knowledge was contrasted, a prejudice which may be just or the contrary—that cannot be decided here—the fallacy that the conception of a knowledge which apprehends things not as they are known but as they are, means anything intelligible at all, as to the possession or non-possession of which it is possible to raise a controversy; whereas the truth is that upon this at least thought is perfectly clear and at one with itself, that knowledge under whatever form can never *be* things in themselves but only represent them.

312. There will be a disposition to express this contention in the form that we only know phenomena, and not the essence of things in themselves, and so stated to recognise it as the primary truth of every theory of cognition. I avoid that particular form of statement because it still contains a prejudice which I should wish to see abandoned. The actual assumption indeed of the existence of this world of things which is given by the categorical form of the proposition might be avoided by transforming it into the hypothetical: *If* things exist knowledge apprehends only their appearance, not their essence. But even then the proposition plainly carries the idea of a thwarted purpose. That 'only' implies that our knowledge which was intended by rights for the apprehension of the higher, the essence of things, has to be content with the lower, the phenomenon. Such a valuation is once more a prejudice, it may be legitimate, it may be not legitimate, as the further progress of Science may decide which we are not here in a position to anticipate. But we can see at once that it is an arbitrary proceeding to place knowledge in the position of a means which is *not* adequate to its supposed end of apprehending things as they are. And we may at once pronounce an opposite point of view to be conceivable, which should regard things as mere means to produce in us in all its details the spectacle of the ideal world. If this were so we should not indeed know things as they are, but we should not therefore fail of any end or aim; in the appearances which things present to us would reside then that element of higher dignity and value which we sought to indicate by the name of essence; and in the discovery of the purport, the connexion and the laws which govern this inner world of phenomena, the knowledge of truth would lie not indeed exclusively but pre-eminently, and at least as truly as in that which we are now so painfully anxious to arrive at, the apprehension of that which must always remain outside our own and every other intelligence, the system of means through which the series of phenomena is called into existence within us. But to continue this discussion further would be to overstep the limits of my undertaking. I repeat once more what I desire the reader to understand this to be; let us leave entirely out of the question the opposition between our world of ideas and a world of things; let us look upon the former alone as the material we have to deal with; and let us endeavour to ascertain where within this world the primary fixed points of certainty are to be found, and how it may be possible to communicate a like certainty through the medium of these to other ideas which do not in themselves equally possess it. By following certain circuitous paths which will be found to be no deviation from our proper route, we may perhaps arrive at clearness on this subject.

CHAPTER II.

The World of Ideas.

313. THE problem which we have set before us is one which ancient philosophy long ago declared again and again to be insoluble. That all is in flux was the familiar doctrine of Heraclitus, a doctrine however of which it is difficult to determine the precise significance. That it was understood in the half pathetic sense of a lamentation over the rapidity of change appears in the heightened form subsequently given to his saying that it is impossible to cross the same river twice—'it is impossible,' it was added, 'even once.' But against the testimony of observation to the transitoriness of things the most ordinary experience might have set counter examples of duration through incalculable periods of time; philosophical reflexion could only have universalised the former set of experiences into the doctrine cited by establishing in opposition to superficial appearances, that the latter also do but veil a slow process of change to which in fact they are always subject. We do not know how far this actually took place and whether these speculations passed over without notice the circumstance that the differences in the speed of one set of changes and another at once introduce into the play of phenomena a contrast between the relatively fixed and the more transitory which might be turned to fruitful account. Once more, that nothing can wholly withstand agencies of change operating from without, that everything therefore must be *susceptible* of change, is a conviction too easily derived from the experience of every-day life to have needed a philosophy to discover it. But it remains doubtful how far Heraclitus passed beyond this, and taught that there are changes in all things springing from causes in their own nature and not merely occasioned by outside influences, and whether he taught this simply as a fact of experience, or whether he held continual movement to be the condition of the possibility of all natural existence, and that stable equilibrium and permanence were impossible.

There is much to lend probability to a view which should credit him with this more advanced conception, but the question can as little be certainly decided as the more important one what precisely is to be understood by the 'all' to which he ascribed this ceaseless mutability. The expression included beyond question the things of sense; in fact the very starting-point of the doctrine could have been found nowhere else but in the changing combinations of sensible qualities and relations. But did it include at the same time the content of the ideas by means of which we think this world of sense? Was it intended that not only all that is real but all that can be thought as well is subject to this eternal flux? I doubt if Heraclitus held this latter opinion; the universal instability of all determinations of thought would of course render all enquiry and all affirmation impossible. We may however assume from the lively picture which Plato draws in the Theaetetus of the later activity of the school, that they at all events had no hesitation in giving this extension to their master's doctrine.

At this point it is taken up by the Sophists. I do not mean that section which under the leadership of Protagoras acknowledged only the subjective validity of every perception for the person who experiences it, I mean those who, disciplined in the Eleatic dialectic, set themselves to demonstrate that every conception signifies at once what it does mean and what it does not mean. This contention was met, principally in the field of Ethics, where it produced its most pernicious effects, by the sound instinct and sense of truth of Socrates, who called attention to the fact that the conceptions of good and bad, just and unjust, are fixed and unchanging, and cannot be determined now one way and now another at the pleasure of individuals, but that they have to be accepted as permanent and self-identical conceptions to which everyone has simply to subordinate his own ideas on these subjects. Plato followed, at one with these aims of his master, but impelled by more many-sided motives, and expanded the convictions received from Socrates into his own doctrine of Ideas, a first and most characteristic attempt to turn to account the truth which belongs to the world of our ideas in itself, without regard to its agreement with an assumed reality of things outside its borders. The philosophical efforts of antiquity have the attraction of exhibiting in full detail the movements, the struggles, and the errors of thought, into which every individual still falls in the course of his development, and which notwithstanding the culture of our own day has no longer the patience to follow up and investigate. I shall permit myself to enter therefore into a review of this doctrine of Plato, approaching it at various points which seem pertinent to our present enquiry.

314. The Platonic expression Idea[1] is usually rendered Universal conception[2], and the rendering is so far correct that there are Ideas, according to Plato, of everything which can be thought in a universal form, apart from the particular perceptions in which it is presented. At the same time it is only for the purposes of a later set of conceptions which we shall meet with presently, that it becomes important to be able to think of the ideally apprehended content[3] as something common to many individual contents, that is

---

[1] ['Idee.' Where the term 'Idea' represents 'Idee' and not 'Vorstellung' it is printed with a capital 'I.']

[2] ['Allgemeinbegriff.']   [3] ['Inhalt.']

as a universal. What is essential here at the outset is not so much that it can be separated from different particular instances which contain it, as that it has been distinguished as a content with a meaning of its own which we *present to* ourselves, from a mere affection which we *experience*. In the latter sense it might have been involved by the Heraclitic or pseudo-Heraclitic doctrine in its ceaseless flux of events, of which each one only is in the moment in which it occurs, and no one has an abiding habitation or significance in the world, because there is no reason why having once occurred it need ever recur again in identically the same form. The former conception on the contrary turns the mere affection of our sensibility into an independent objective[1] content whose significance once is its significance once for all, and whose relations to other contents have an eternal and self-identical validity even if neither it nor they should ever be repeated in actual perception.

I have had occasion to explain my meaning here in an earlier part of this work (§ 3). Perception shows us the things of sense undergoing changes in their qualities. But while black becomes white and sweet sour, it is not blackness itself which passes into whiteness, nor does sweetness become sourness; what happens is that these several qualities, each remaining eternally identical with itself, succeed each other in the thing, and the conceptions through which we think the things have themselves no part in the mutability which we attribute on account of their changes to the things of which the qualities are the predicates—and even he who attempted to deny this would be affirming it against his will, for he could not represent sweetness as passing into sourness, without separating the one property from the other, and determining the first for his own thought in an idea which will always mean something different from the second into which it is supposed to have changed. It is a very simple and unpretending, but yet a very important

[1 v. § 3.]

thought to which Plato here gives expression for the first time. The continual change which goes on in the external world may affect us like a restless whirling eddy, bewildering our intelligence, yet it is not without a pervading truth. Whatever mutability the things may display, that which they are at each moment they are by a transient participation in conceptions which are not transient but for ever identical and constant, and which taken together constitute an unchangeable system of thought, and form the first adequate and solid beginnings of a permanent knowledge.

For it was one of the conclusions at which we arrived before[1], that to the making of this earliest immediate stock of knowledge there contribute not merely the separate unity of each conception in itself, nor again simply the fact of a mere uniform contrast between this and all other conceptions, but also those graduated relations of resemblance and affinity in which different conceptions stand to each other. If the white becomes black and the sweet sour they do not merely become different in the abstract, but pass over from the domain of the one conception in which they participated before into that of another which is separated from the first by a fixed and determinate degree of contrast, a contrast stronger for example than that which obtains between white and yellow, and altogether incommensurable with that absolute gulf of separation which exists between white and sour.

315. I refer to these simple examples once more in order to make it clear how a knowledge may be possible the truth of which is wholly independent of the question of Scepticism as to its agreement with a world of things outside it. If the current of the outer world had brought before us only once in a transient appearance the perception of two colours or two sounds, our thought would immediately separate them from the moment of time at which they appeared, and fix them and their affinities and their con-

[1] [Cp. §§ 13-16.]

trasts as an abiding object of inner contemplation, no matter whether they were ever presented to us again in actual experience or not. Again supposing we could never learn how these ideas are able to appear as predicates in things, and in what that which we have called the participation of things in them exactly consists, a question would indeed be left unanswered which might in the course of our reflexions prove important, but still the certain knowledge would remain to us undisturbed that the series of colours and the scale of musical tones themselves are each a connected whole with fixed laws, and that in regard to the relation of the members to each other, eternally valid true propositions are vitally opposed to eternally invalid false ones. And finally the question whether after all colours in themselves and tones in themselves are not different from what they appear to us, is one which no one will care to raise again. Or rather we do meet with it again in the confused notion that sounds are in fact merely vibrations of the air, colours merely quiverings of the ether, and it is only to us that they appear in the form of the subjective feelings which we know. It is unnecessary to enlarge over again on the consideration that these feelings do not cease to be real, and are not got rid of and banished out of existence as intruders, because we have discovered certain external causes not resembling them, which are the occasions of their making their appearance to us. Even if these vibrations of external media appeared to differently constituted beings in the form of modes of sensation entirely unknown to us, still the colouring and tones which we see and hear, would constitute for us, when once we have experienced them, a secure treasure of knowledge with a validity and an orderly connexion of its own. The feelings of such other beings would remain unknown to us and ours to them, but this would only mean that we have not *all* truths for our portion, but that what we do possess we possess *as* truths in virtue of the identity of every such content of perception with itself, and of the constancy of identical relations which obtain between different contents. Thus we readily understand the significance of Plato's endeavour to bind together the predicates which are found in the things of the eternal world in continual change, into a determinate and articulated whole, and how he saw in this world of Ideas the true beginnings of certain knowledge; for the external relations which subsist between different Ideas, and through which some are capable of association with each other and others exclude each other, form at all events the limits within which what is to be *possible* in experience falls; the further question what is real in it, and how things manage to have Ideas for *their* predicates, appeared to Plato not to be the primary question, and was for the time reserved.

316. There is one wide-reaching difficulty connected with the first-named aspect of this question. How precisely are we to conceive colours when they are not seen, or tones and their differences when the former are not heard and the latter not apprehended by comparison? Are we to say that they are nothing or that they do not exist, or are we still to attribute to them some predicate which we can hardly define, some kind of being or reality? We shall not be disposed at first to consider them to be nothing at all; for as long as we fix them in our thoughts, as at present in searching for an answer to this very question, every tone and every colour is a determinate content distinguishable from every other, and so a something and not a nothing. Still this decision becomes doubtful when we consider the answer which we feel ourselves compelled to give to the second part of the question. In regard to things we do imagine ourselves, dimly enough, to know wherein their being consists even when they are objects for no intelligence, but exist purely for themselves; but what is meant by a tone when it is heard by no ear and when even the silent idea of its sound is not called up by any mind, we can no more say than what a pain is when no one is hurt by it. But how can that which is not either in itself or in our consciousness, be any longer anything at all or be distinguished from anything else? Still this conclusion again we hesitate to affirm. There is clearly in our first conclusion, speaking quite generally, a certain element of affirmation, which is not entirely to be cancelled by the denial contained in the second. Perhaps it may appear to us a way out of the difficulty to turn the categorical form of our judgment into a hypothetical; two sounds which are neither heard nor imagined are not indeed actually anything, and stand in no actual relations, but they *will* always be something and the one will be different from the other, and stand in a definite relation of contrast to it, *if* they are heard or imagined. Yet even this does not at once satisfy us, for in order even to imagine how the notes a and b can be subject to this varied fortune of being presented to imagination at one time and not so presented at another, and then how it happens that when they are presented in experience the relation Z is necessarily thought along with them, whereas whenever certain other sounds are presented, they are no less necessarily accompanied by a different relation Z^1,—in order to imagine this we are constrained to ascribe to them existence and definite existence, at a time when according to this view they did not in fact exist at all; for so alone can we explain their subsequent existence and the definite form which their relations then assumed.

I will not pursue these refinements further, but will conclude with the following remarks. We have undoubtedly a conception of affirmation or 'position' in an extremely general sense, which meets us in various fields of enquiry, and for which languages, dealing as they do in their early stages with highly complex and concrete notions, and not with the simplest elements of thought, have commonly no abstract term which expresses it with the requisite purity. But it would not be wise to invent a technical term to represent it, the meaning of which would always be doubtful, because it could never come naturally to the lips or to the thoughts of any one; the very term 'position' which is frequently used for it suggests by its etymological form the entirely alien sense of an act, or operation of establishing[1], to the execution of which that state of affirmation which we wish to express then seems to owe its being. It is best however to keep to ordinary speech, and select a word which can be shown to express in common usage, approximately at all events and unmistakeably, the thought with which we are concerned. We may express it in our own language by the term Reality[2]. For[3] we call a thing Real[4] which is, in contradistinction to another which is not; an event Real which occurs or has occurred, in contradistinction to that which does not occur; a relation Real which obtains, as opposed to one which does not obtain; lastly we call a proposition Really true which holds or is valid as opposed to one of which the validity is still doubtful. This use of language is intelligible; it shows that when we call anything Real, we mean always to *affirm* it, though in different senses according to the different forms which it assumes, but one or other of which it must necessarily assume, and of which no one is reducible to or contained in the other. For we never can get an Event out of simple Being, the reality which belongs to Things, namely Being or Existence, never belongs to Events—they do not exist but *occur*; again a Proposition neither exists like things nor occurs like events; that its meaning even obtains like a relation, can only be said if the things *exist* of which it predicates a relation; in itself, apart from all applications which may be made of it, the reality of a proposition means that it holds or is valid and that its opposite does not hold.

---

[1] ['Setzung.']
[2] ['Wirklichkeit.']
[3] [Cp. 'Metaphysic.' p. 1, and for 'Objectivität' contrasted with different forms of 'Wirklichkeit' see above, § 3.]
[4] ['Wirklich.']

Now misunderstandings must always arise, when under the persuasion that the object which we are considering must have some sort of reality or affirmation proper to it, we endeavour to attribute to it, not that kind of reality which is appropriate to it, but a different kind which is alien to it. Then arises the conflict just noticed between the conviction on the one hand that we are right in asscribing to it some sort of reality, and on the other that the particular form of reality to which our misconception has brought us is inadmissible.

Now Ideas, in so far as they are present in our minds, possess reality in the sense of an Event,—they *occur* in us: for as utterances of an activity of presentation they are never a Being at rest but a continual Becoming; their content on the other hand, so far as we regard it in abstraction from the mental activity which we direct to it, can no longer be said to occur, though neither again does it exist as things exist; we can only say that it possesses Validity.

And finally we must not ask what in its turn is meant by Validity, with any idea that the meaning which the word conveys clearly to us can be deduced from some different conception; as if, for example, it were possible to find certain conditions by the operation of which either the Being which belongs to things could be so modified and attenuated, or the momentary act of Becoming or occurring, in which the transient reality of ideas regarded as excitations of our consciousness consists, could receive such fixity and independent existence, as that both the one and the other in different ways might pass into this conception of Validity, which at once excludes the substance of the valid assertion from the reality of actual being and implies its independence of human thought. As little as we can say how it happens that anything *is* or *occurs*, so little can we explain how it comes about that a truth has Validity; the latter conception has to be regarded as much as the former as ultimate and underivable, a conception of which everyone may know what he means by it, but which cannot be constructed out of any constituent elements which do not already contain it.

317. From this point of view some light I think is thrown on a surprising statement which is handed down to us in the history of Philosophy. Plato, we are told, ascribed to the Ideas of which he had achieved the conception an existence apart from things, and yet, as these same critics tell us, of like kind with the existence of things. It is strange how peacefully the traditional admiration of the profundity of Plato acquiesces in the ascription to him of so absurd an opinion; we should have to abandon our admiration of him if this really was the doctrine that he taught, and not rather a serious misunderstanding to which in a quite intelligible and pardonable way it has laid itself open. ⌈The expression of philosophical ideas is dependent upon the capabilities of each language, and it is hardly possible, in giving utterance to our meaning, to avoid using words which language has coined to express a merely cognate thought which is not our real meaning at all.⌉ And this is pre-eminently the case when a new field is being opened out, and the necessity of distinguishing the precise meaning intended from the ordinary meaning of the word is as yet little felt. This is I think the explanation of the misunderstanding in question. The truth which Plato intended to teach is no other than that which we have just been expounding, that is to say, the validity of truths as such, apart from the question whether they can be established in relation to any object in the external world, as its mode of being, or not; the eternally self-identical significance of Ideas, which always are what they are, no matter whether or no there are things which by participation in them make them manifest in this external world, or whether there are spirits which by thinking them, give them the reality of a mental event. But the Greek language then as afterwards, was wanting in an expression for this conception of Validity as a form of Reality not including Being or Existence; and this very expression Being came, often indeed quite harmlessly, but in this instance with momentous consequences, to fill the place.

Every possible content of thought, regarded as an individual unity, distinct and separate from others, all that class of things for which the language of the School philosophy in later times invented the not inappropriate name of *Res rationis*[1] was to the Greek a Being (ὄν or οὐσία); and if the distinction between a really valid truth and a pretended truth came in question the former was distinguished as ὄντως ὄν. ⌜The language of ancient Greece never found any term to express the reality of simple Validity as distinguished from the reality of Being, and this constant confusion has prejudiced the clearness of the Platonic phraseology.⌝

318. We may easily see that everything Plato says of the Ideas presents itself when understood in the manner so explained as natural and necessary, and that the various devices to which he resorts in setting forth their nature have this purpose and no other, to exhaust the conception for which no adequate term could be found, by the help of a variety of expressions limiting and supplementing each other. Eternal, without beginning, and imperishable (ἀίδια, ἀγέννητα, ἀνώλεθρα) the Ideas could not but be named in the presence of the flux of Heraclitus, which seemed in danger of sweeping them away along with the sense-world in its stream. The reality of Being indeed they have or have not, according as transient things of sense are clothed with them or not; but that reality which consists in Validity, which is a reality all their own, remains untouched by all this change. Their independence of time, when brought into comparison with that which comes and goes in time, would hardly be otherwise expressed than by this predicate of eternity which

[1] ['Gedankending.']

at once partakes of time and denies its power, just in the same way as we should most easily recognise that which has no validity and could have no validity in itself by the fact of its never occurring at any moment of time.

Again, we understand the ideas being called separable or separate from things (χωρὶς τῶν ὄντων), first because the image (εἶδος) of their content can be still called up to memory after the things which originally occasioned its appearance in us have vanished from real existence, and next, because the content is taken to include what can be apprehended in a universal form, and remains the same in different external manifestations, so as to be independent of the mode in which it is realised to sense in any particular instance.

But it was not Plato's intention to represent the ideas as independent merely of things while still depending for their special mode of reality upon the mind which thinks them. Reality of Existence it is true they enjoy only in the moment in which they become, in the character of objects or creations of an act of presentation now actually occurring, members of this changing world of Being and Becoming; but on the other hand we all feel certain in the moment in which we think any truth, that we have not created it for the first time but merely recognised it; it was valid before we thought about it and will continue so without regard to any existence of whatever kind, of things or of us, whether or not it ever finds manifestation in the reality of Existence, or a place as an object of knowledge in the reality of a Thought. This is what we all believe with regard to truth when we set out to search for it, and it may be lament over its inaccessibility at least to any form of human knowledge; the truth which is never apprehended by us is valid no whit less than that small fraction of it which finds its way into our intelligence.

The independent validity of the Ideas Plato emphasises again in a somewhat different form, in answer to the doctrine of Protagoras, rescuing them in their character of being in themselves that which they are (αὐτὰ καθ' αὐτὰ ὄντα) from the relativity in which the famous dictum of that Sophist was in danger of involving them. Even granting that his doctrine has its truth so long as it is confined to the impressions of sense, and that viewed in this relation Plato's opposition to it rests upon a misunderstanding, granting that is to say that my sensation is as true for me as yours which differs from it is for you, Plato would still be right in insisting that for neither of us could the sensation be possible at all, unless that which we felt in the sensation whatever it be, red or blue, sweet or bitter, had a definite and constant significance of its own, as a member of a world of Ideas. This world of Ideas is the permanent and inexhaustible treasure-house from which the things of the external world draw all the diverse and shifting attributes they wear, and the mind the varying series of its experiences; and a sensation or idea whose content has no fixed and determinate place, no fixed relations of affinity or difference in the universal world of thought, but stands in complete isolation, bare of all relations to anything in that world, the possession of a single individual mind alone, is in fact an impossibility.

While Plato by thus describing the Ideas, takes security for their independent validity, he has at the same time abundantly provided against the confusion of the validity thus implied with that wholly distinct reality of Existence which could only be ascribed to a durable thing. When he places the home of the Ideas in a super-celestial world, a world of pure intelligence (νοητὸς, ὑπερουράνιος τόπος), when again more than this he expressly describes them as having no local habitation, such language makes it abundantly clear to any one who understands the mind of Greek Antiquity, that they do *not* belong to what we call the real world. To the Greek that which is not in Space is not at all, and when Plato relegates the Ideas to a home which is not in space, he is not trying to hypostasize that which we call their mere validity into any kind of real existence, but on the contrary he is plainly seeking to guard altogether against any such attempt being made. Nor is it any objection that the Ideas are called unities (ἑνάδες, μονάδες), for there is no occasion to interpret these titles from an atomistic standpoint, whether in the sense of material indivisibility or of a self-identity resembling that of a self-conscious subject. For in fact what constitutes the *meaning* of an Idea, and of a complex no less than of a simple Idea, is that it manifests itself as a unity, unifying the elements which cohere in it and rejecting that which is alien to it. Nevertheless although these various expressions point one and all to the fact that Plato never asserted the existence of the Ideas but only their eternal validity, he had still no better answer to make to the question, what then are they, than to bring them again under the general denomination of οὐσία. Then the door was opened to the misunderstanding which has since widely spread, though no one has ever been able to say what the nature of that existence, into which he is accused of having hypostasized his ideas, precisely is.

319. There are two objections which may be taken to the view here maintained. First, the use which Plato makes of the Ideas to explain the course of the world, in which they assert their influence not merely as valid truths but as operating forces—this is a point to which I shall come later; and in the second place, the attitude of Aristotle. For it is really the very definite language of Aristotle which has established the doctrine of the reality of the ideas as a dogma of Plato, whereas Plato's own statements are in no way inconsistent with the other interpretation which we have preferred. It seems incredible that the most acute of Plato's disciples, informed by personal intercourse with the master, should have misunderstood him in a point of such serious moment as this. At the same time we are justified by the nature of his polemic not against particular statements of Plato but against the doctrine of Ideas altogether, as well as by many details in his criticisms, in assuming that his attack is in part directed against certain misunderstandings of the Platonic doctrine which had gained hold in the Academy at an early period. For he could not well have challenged Plato himself to show *where* the Ideas are, when Plato had said in plain terms that they were nowhere. He could not have directed against Plato the criticism that there must logically be Ideas of products of art, for one passage at least is to be found in the Republic which is entirely in agreement with that criticism, and how far Plato was from having overlooked the difficulty there involved, is evidenced by the opening of the Parmenides. Finally as to Aristotle's objections to the Ideas that they are superfluous, being mere copies of individual objects, and the assumption from which his elaborate analysis frequently starts, that there are as many examples of every Idea as there are instances of its application in reality, these are criticisms which do not really apply to the doctrines of Plato himself. That every Idea is what it is once for all, that what we are to understand by it is not an individual thing but a universal comprehending many things, and that all its manifestations are only copies of this one essential reality, is the doctrine which he never abandons, whatever obscurity may still attach to that operation on the part of the individual things, described as imitation or participation, by which they provide the one Idea with a countless number of realisations in the world of actual existence.

The discussion therefore which fills the XIIth (XIIIth) book of Aristotle's Metaphysics and of which the purport is to exhibit the absurdity of attributing to the Idea a reality identical with the reality of actually existing things, I cannot regard as a refutation of the pure Platonic doctrine, and the less so inasmuch as at the end Aristotle himself equally fails to find a decisive and unambiguous expression for that more appropriate form of reality which he desires, in contradistinction to this, to ascribe to them. To him the only genuine οὐσία is the individual thing, and there we must certainly agree with him; to the individual thing alone belongs the reality of Existence; still for Aristotle as much as for Plato the object of knowledge is always the universal; not only in the sense that we are incapable of exhausting the meaning of the individual thing, but that so far as we investigate it in its nature and its workings with any prospect of a result, we invariably proceed according to universal principles. But Aristotle is entirely at one with his predecessors, that that which is not, or has no reality in any sense, cannot be an object of knowledge either, and so in regard to the universal we cannot say that it simply is not, but that in a sense it is and in a sense it is not.

I do not propose to enter into Aristotle's further treatment of this question in detail. I must however remark that by placing the universal and the Idea within the Individual things and not outside them he does not explain the possibility of knowledge; for the mere fact of the presence of the Idea in one individual does not entitle us to transfer all the consequences which flow from it to a second individual in which it happens also to be found; it can only justify us in concluding from the doings of one real thing to those of another, if it includes within itself a number of characteristics so related that the appearance of any one necessarily implies the presence of the rest. Such considerations would at once conduct Aristotle back to the admission that the Idea is certainly in a sense χωρὶς τῶν ὄντων; but in what sense it is so was impossible for him to define, since he no more possessed than his master did a technical equivalent for our term validity; and thus eventually the universal conception or Idea came to be for him also an οὐσία, not indeed a true or πρώτη οὐσία but still a δευτέρα οὐσία.

320. It may appear to us a strange spectacle to see two of the greatest philosophers of antiquity struggling with imperfect success to arrive at clearness upon so simple a distinction as that which we have been considering. But such a view would do both of them injustice. The appre-

hension of the simplest relations of thought is not the simplest act of the faculty of thought, and the whole long history of philosophy teaches how ready we all are at any moment to be guilty of a degree of obscurity in the application of ideas which if reduced to its simplest terms would appear to us incredible. Whenever men have believed themselves to have discovered a principle which appears to represent the universal element in the constitution and development of the real world, they invariably go on to exalt it into the position of an independent reality and to represent it as a pure form of being, in comparison with which the individual things retire into a position of subordinate and even unreal existence. I need not even refer to the latest phase of German philosophy which aspired to set on the throne of the Platonic Ideas the one absolute Idea, for the same tendency is apparent enough in spheres of thought outside the circle of philosophy. How often do we hear in our own day of eternal and unchangeable laws of nature to which all phenomena and their changes are subjected; laws which would indeed cease to manifest themselves if there were no longer any things for them to control, but which would even then themselves continue in their eternal validity and would revive with their old effective power the moment a new object presented itself from any quarter for them to apply to; nay there is not even wanting on occasion, the enthronement of these laws above all existing realities in that very super-celestial habitation which with Plato is the home of the Ideas. Nevertheless those who hold this language would indignantly repel the imputation of ascribing to those laws an existence whether as things or as persons outside the things which are governed by them, and Plato may resist with equal justice a similar misinterpretation of his doctrines.

Finally it must be added that we ourselves, in drawing a distinction between the reality which belongs to the Ideas and laws and that which belongs to things, and calling the one Being or Existence[1] and the other Validity[2], have so far merely discovered, thanks to the resources of our language, a convenient expression which may keep us on our guard against interchanging the two notions. The fact which the term validity expresses has lost none of that strangeness which has led to its being confounded, as we have seen, with existence. It is merely that we have been so long accustomed to it; we use our thought as we do any other natural faculty without troubling ourselves about it, and take it as a matter of course that the content of manifold perceptions and phenomena does invariably adapt itself to general conceptions and can be read by us in the light of general laws, in such wise that the consequences which those laws lead us to predict are found to coincide with the actual phenomenal order which supervenes. But that this should be the case, that there should be universal laws, which have not themselves existence like things and which nevertheless rule the operation of things,—remains for a mind which realises its meaning, a profoundly mysterious fact which might well inspire rapture and wonder in its discoverer; and that he should have made the discovery will always remain a great philosophical achievement of Plato, whatever the problems it may have left still unsolved.

321. One of these problems is that of the exact nature of the relation of things to the ideas which Plato describes by the terms participation or imitation. I do not propose at present to discuss this question at large; but there is one defect in the doctrine of the Ideas which a criticism of Aristotle's—in itself not well-founded—may suggest to us. Among the reasons which led him to regard the Ideas as both superfluous and useless, he especially emphasises the fact that they supply no beginning of motion. However true this objection may be in itself, the fact that they do not perform this task proves little against the doctrine of the

---

[1] ['Sein.']   [2] ['Geltung.']

Ideas; the real objection is that they do not, as we shall see, adequately perform the task for which Plato intended them. As concerns Aristotle's criticism let us turn to the sciences of our own day. What shall we say of our Laws of Nature? Do they contain in themselves a beginning of motion? On the contrary, they all presuppose a series of data which they cannot themselves establish, but from which, *once given*, the necessary connexion one with another of the phenomena which ensue is deducible. No natural law ordains that the different bodies in our planetary system should move, or that their course should be directed towards one and not another quarter of the heavens, or that the acceleration which they impose on each other by the force of attraction should have the particular amount which it has and not a different one. But is the whole system of mechanical truths useless and mere empty babble (κενολογεῖν) because it leaves these first beginnings of motion to be explained from some other source, and starting from the fact of motion as it actually finds it, is satisfied with explaining its different phases in their necessary connexion with each other? There may be obscurity enough—though after all not more than in our own mode of representing the matter—in Plato's relegation of the primary motive impulses upon which the succession of phenomena depends, to that dim world of ὕλη which represents to him the material which is given for the Ideas to be applied to. But for all that to see in the world of Ideas the patterns to which all that is, *if* anything is, must conform, was a thought of which the importance is unfairly ignored by Aristotle. For he was himself on a later occasion to have recourse to that very same thought, for the explanation of individual phenomena: he too found himself unable to allow the cause of motion which communicates the actualising impulse also to control its issue; this had been decided from all eternity by those universal laws, which in their turn take no part in the communication of the impulse.

On the other hand it must undoubtedly be admitted to be a deficiency in the Platonic doctrine that this, which was its actual undertaking, it only half accomplishes. An account of the necessary connexion of two contents of thought must always assume the logical form of a judgment; it cannot be expressed in the form of a mere notion which does not in itself contain a proposition at all. Thus we have always employed laws, that is to say propositions, which express a relation between different elements, as examples to explain the meaning of Validity in contradistinction to Existence. The term cannot be transferred to single concepts without some degree of obscurity: we can only say of concepts that they *mean* something, and they mean something because certain propositions are valid *of* them, as for example the proposition that the content of any given concept is identical with itself and stands in unchangeable relations of affinity or contrast to others. Now Plato apprehended the elements of the world of thought which he discovered almost exclusively under the form of the isolated concept or the Idea. We need not look beyond the general impression which his Dialogues leave with us to be aware how rarely by comparison we meet with general propositions; they are by no means entirely absent, on the contrary they are made on occasions the subject of important disquisitions, but that it is propositions as such and nothing else which must necessarily form the most essential constituents of the ideal world, is a truth which never forced itself upon Plato's mind. His peculiar point of view is not without modern parallels. Kant himself in his search for the *a priori* forms which were to give the unity of an inner coherence to the empirical content of our perceptions, made the mistake at starting of developing them in the form of single concepts, the Categories, and that in spite of the fact that he derived them from the forms of the judgment itself. And now having got them, as he thought, in his Categories, it became the more evident that there was nothing to be made of them, and thereupon followed the attempt to derive judgments out of them again, and so he arrived at the 'Principles of the Understanding' which it was now possible to apply as major premises to the minor premises furnished by experience. It seems therefore that this disposition to bring into the inadequate form of a single concept truths which can only be adequately expressed through the proposition, is natural to the imagination at all times, and is not peculiar to the plastic mind of ancient Greece. It may however be remarked in passing how dangerous a tendency it is, leading the mind as it does away from the full concrete reality which is the true aim of its enquiries to a barren playing with empty ideas which have become separated from their natural foundations.

Thus we find our present requirements hardly at all satisfied in Plato, and even the need of satisfying them not clearly or adequately recognised. It is true the abstract thought that the Ideas are not only a multitude of individuals but that they make up all together an organic and articulated whole—this thought is the soul of all his teaching, and he describes with enthusiasm the delight which he finds in the dialectical exercise of resolving the complex structure of the Ideal world into its elements, following the natural joinings, and then putting them together again; even the different degrees of agreement or of contrast between individual ideas and the possible modes of combining them are mentioned as subjects worthy of investigation. But in the examples which he gives of the application of his method, the art of Dialectic ends almost invariably in a mere classification of Ideas, by which we are shown the place which belongs to any one Idea in a system of division in virtue of the elements which it combines, but which furnishes us with no single proposition, adds no jot to our knowledge concerning the nature of any one of the Ideas which could not have been arrived at equally without this circuitous route of classification. If we want to know what can be said or cannot be said of any Idea we have still to learn it, after the classification as much as before, from other sources. The joinings and articulations of truth which Plato's sole aim was not to mutilate he ought to have investigated with a firmer hand; instead of making a systematic collection of the flora of the Ideas, he ought to have turned his thoughts to the general physiological conditions which in each single plant bind limb to limb according to a law of growth. Or, dropping the figure, the existence of a world of Ideas possessing a definite meaning and an unchangeable validity being once clearly and emphatically established, the next task was to investigate the universal laws which govern its structure, through which alone, in an Ideal world as elsewhere, the individual elements can be bound together into a whole. Thus the question to be dealt with at this point was what are those *first principles* of our knowledge under which the manifold world of Ideas has itself to be arranged. This is the more precisely defined form which the systematic enquiry into Truth and the source of Truth now assumes for us.

CHAPTER III.

The a priori and the Empirical Methods.

322. WHEN we feel in doubt about any particular point of belief within the sphere of our knowledge we endeavour to clear it up by analysing the conditions which have led us to entertain the belief; we expect to learn from the history of its origin whether it is true, or if it is false how it must have grown up. And whenever in the history of philosophy the question has arisen as to the capacity of the human mind for the attainment of truth in general, mankind have thought that the same path would lead there also to the goal. It has been supposed that the claims of our ideas and our judgments to the name of truths could be decided by considering the process by which they have been formed. This belief, which is worth considering inasmuch as it lies to a great extent at the root of certain tendencies of philosophical enquiry even in our own day, leads me to quit for the moment the subject upon which I have entered. It is necessary to attempt to point out, that this method of criticising our Ideas by tracing their genesis does not present the advantages as applied to the subject of human knowledge generally which it does undoubtedly possess in the case of particular beliefs or ideas.

For the two cases are not alike. If we desire to test the accuracy of any particular opinion, we have a basis for our decision in other truths of which we are in acknowledged possession, on the one hand general principles with which all other propositions if they are to have validity for us must be in agreement, on the other hand established facts, which must not be contradicted by those other facts which are either affirmed or assumed by the view under question; finally we have certain laws of thought by which, given certain valid premises, logical conclusions derived from them are distinguished from illogical. Throughout we start from some truth which operates upon the mixture of our thoughts which is submitted to the test like a fermenting matter, assimilating that which is akin to it, and rejecting that which is alien. Such a standard given us to start with and itself independent of the subject-matter of enquiry, is wanting when we turn to the larger problem; to test the truth of human knowledge in general is impossible, without assuming as the basis for our decision the very principles which are on their trial.

This logical circle according to which our knowledge has itself to determine the limits of its own authority, we have already seen to be unavoidable; but we increase our difficulties, if, instead of regarding those principles themselves as the one element of certainty in our knowledge, from the vantage-ground of which we may go on to take possession of the rest of its domain, we explicitly attribute this certainty not to those principles themselves but to a particular unanalysed application of them, viz. to our supposed insight into the *origin* of our knowledge. The theory is that the mode in which knowledge originates is to decide its claims to truth, that truth moreover, as is supposed by this view, having regard to a reality which is foreign to and transcends knowledge. But if this is our aim we cannot move a single step without making certain more definite assumptions; first as to the position of the knowing subject as regards those objects of its knowledge, next as to the nature of that relation, *between* it and those objects, by which the process of knowledge is carried on. For it is only by understanding these circumstances that we can learn to estimate the dangers which stand in the way of the formation of true conceptions.

The pretence therefore of setting to work to ascertain the process by which knowledge comes to us, by a simple act of observation, discarding all prejudice and eschewing all admixture of principles whose validity can be called in question, is in fact a groundless illusion. Every attempt to carry out such an undertaking is necessarily full of metaphysical assumptions, but assumptions disconnected and uncriticised, because they are merely taken up at the moment as they happen to be wanted to clear up a difficulty. The circle is inevitable, so we had better perpetrate it with our eyes open; the first thing we have to do is to endeavour to establish what meaning it is possible for us to attach to knowledge in its widest sense, and what sort of relation we can conceive to subsist between the subject which knows and the object of its knowledge, consistently with those yet more general notions which determine the mode in which we have to conceive the operation of anything whatever upon anything else. What we have to do is to obtain the last-mentioned conception, which amounts to a metaphysical doctrine, and to treat the relation of subject and object as subordinate to it; we are not to begin by setting up some chance theory more or less probable as to that one relation, and then to use this as a test of the capacity of the human mind for apprehending truth at all. I say nothing of the question how far it is really in our power even to establish the facts regarding the gradual development of our world of thought; certainly the process of that development cannot be directly observed, for every observer has left it long ago behind him. And even though in many cases the developed consciousness may still retain the recollection of the road by which it has come to its present set of ideas, it will be admitted on the other hand that in many other cases these pretended observations of the development of our ideas are merely somewhat fanciful theories of the mode in which we think we may conceive it to have taken place.

323. If we follow the attempts which have been made to arrive in the first instance at some fact beyond the reach of doubt, from which we may proceed with security to test the origin and the truth of human knowledge, we are met at the outset of modern philosophy by the maxim of Descartes, '*cogito ergo sum*,' the one certain truth which the doubt of all received opinions seemed to him to leave standing. This proposition has been frequently taken as a point of departure, and it has always approved itself, from as far back as Augustine, in whose writings we first find it, for a truth as unquestionable as it is absolutely barren. Not the smallest step towards the establishment of any theory of knowledge whatever has it been possible to take from this proposition by itself, without calling in other and wholly independent principles to help. The very criterion which follows next in order, that all ideas are true which are equally clear and evident with this, Descartes himself did not venture to derive from that primary principle, without securing himself by the roundabout argument, alluded to in a previous chapter, against the objection that we may be all the while deluded by entirely false ideas possessing an equal degree of evidence with the true.

In point of fact it is easy to see that from this beginning we never can get to anything further. If we take the proposition in its negative sense, that is to say that nothing is certain for us except the fact of our own thought alone, and there is no such certainty in regard to the real existence of an external world, then I recall an observation already made: even if such external world be really existent, still it is only an ideal picture of it and not that world itself which can be present in us: the fact therefore that nothing possesses immediate certainty for us excepting our own world of thought, can never settle the question whether it alone exists, or whether there is a world of existence outside it to which it enters into relation. And even if the idea of this external world could be proved to be a necessary product of our thinking activity which we are compelled to form through the organisation of our mind and the laws of interconnexion to which our thoughts necessarily conform, if that is to say we could deduce from the fact of the *cogito* that our assumption of an external world of existence must necessarily have a *subjective* origin in the laws of our own minds: even then the truth of the assumption would be neither proved nor disproved; for even if that external world does really exist, it would be impossible for us to arrive at the idea of it unless the nature of our mind and the workings of our thoughts were such as to render it indispensable for the avoidance of contradiction within the world of thought itself.

On the other hand if we turn our attention to the affirmative aspect of the proposition, we find that it is not formulated in a way adapted to its purpose. It is no longer the expression of an immediate fact but of an abstraction. I do not complain of Descartes for keeping to the first person of the verbs '*cogito*' and '*sum*,' for obscure as the idea of the '*ego*' may be which they contain, and provocative as it is of further enquiry, it does unquestionably belong to the original form of this simplest of all experiences, and a theory which seeks to supplant the '*cogito*' by the '*cogitare*' and the '*sum*' by the '*esse*,' as the primary and most certain fact of experience, has no claim whatever to the credit of resting on a basis free from all presupposition and prejudice, which it is its ambition to share with the exact methods of the natural sciences. There never meets us as the simplest of facts an idea which merely exists and which no one has; we never meet with a consciousness which presents itself simply as consciousness and not as the consciousness of an '*ego*,' which in it is conscious *to itself* either of itself or of something else. Science may attempt afterwards to separate by one means or another the occurrences of thought and knowledge from this their constant condition of reference to a subject whose nature remains impenetrable: but they are originally given and their certainty along with them only in the form '*cogito*' 'I think,' not in that of the infinitive '*cogitare.*' But while Descartes is entirely correct in employing the personal form of the verb, it must be acknowledged that its significance was overlooked by him, and the interpretations which it received at the hands of Kant we cannot enter into here.

We may add that Descartes' principle was expressed in an unserviceably abstract form, emphasising as it does in the various mental states which carry with them this immediate certainty of personal experience, exclusively their universal quality—that is to say it emphasises exclusively the fact of cogitation or consciousness in the widest sense, which is an element entering equally into very various mental states, sensations and ideas, emotions and the will, distinguishing them all alike from that which we suppose ourselves to conceive as the condition of a being without a self and without a soul. No doubt this element of consciousness enters into every one of our mental states which we observe, but what can be the use of noticing this common quality alone to the exclusion of those concrete elements apart from which it cannot really exist or become an object of direct observation at all?

The really fruitful starting-point of enquiry would have been, not the fact that the '*cogito*' is found in every form which consciousness can assume, but the question, what are the forms in which it is found? Not the bare fact *that* we are conscious or think teaches us the truth we know; it is *what* we think, the matter or content of our cogitation, which supplies not only the original datum from which we start, but the sole source from which that which we ought to think or that which we cannot but think can be derived. Descartes himself points out that even the Sceptic in his doubt or in his denial of all knowledge, by that very act confirms the fact of cogitation, and just because it is associated indifferently with all true knowledge, and with every act of doubt, and with every kind of error, it cannot possibly serve to distinguish the true from the false.

324. Thus a fresh starting-point for the enquiry into human knowledge was unavoidable. It was given by the belief in the truth of innate Ideas. We must not allow the expression 'innate Ideas,' which has introduced a long controversy into the history of the theory of knowledge, to excite prejudices in our minds which a little care and consideration may certainly allay. Even the ancients in speaking of that *quod a natura nobis insitum est*, and all philosophers who have used the like expressions, were certainly very far from assuming that a truth, in itself foreign to the mind, was stamped in upon it at some particular moment when its life was beginning, and became thenceforth a permanent object of its conscious thought. What they meant was no more than this—the mind is of its own nature so constituted, that under certain operative conditions it necessarily develops certain habitual modes of combining its ideas. These constitute, to begin with, a method which the mind follows unawares, but finally as it comes to reflect upon innumerable acts of thought performed in accordance with them, the rules of its procedure hitherto unconsciously followed become themselves the objects of its conscious reflexion. These Ideas were called innate from the impression that it was not sufficient to represent the mind in which they were supposed to grow up as merely possessing a certain formal character, or general capacity for ideas, in such a way that given the same conditions the same set of Ideas would necessarily grow up in every being so endowed; it was held essential that every mind should have its determinate natural capacity, such as might conceivably distinguish it from other thinking beings, dictating the form which its thinking activity should take, and in which its particular acts of thought should be combined. It is true there was no occasion to take this assumption of a *possible* distinction between different beings endowed with a like capacity of thought for anything more than a fiction, which served to illustrate the truth that no adequate basis of human knowledge is to be found in the mere abstract fact of consciousness (*cogitatio*), but only in definite and concrete forms of it which at the same time are in fact shared by all minds in common. Nevertheless when once the conceivability of such a distinction had been admitted, it was no longer possible to resist the question what would be the result if it were accepted as real? And then the two sides of the Cartesian conception, the *a priori* character of the Ideas and their truth, parted asunder. To each individual that must necessarily appear to be truth which follows from the laws of its own nature; and so if each is furnished at birth with a stock of Ideas in the way supposed, then it is a mere act of faith, a faith quite irrational however firmly held, to imagine that the Ideas which are allotted to mankind contain a higher measure of truth than those which it may be force themselves with a no less convincing evidence and with a divergent message upon beings of a different constitution. It will be seen that such doubts are justifiable not only when we contrast the general sum of our knowledge with an objective world of existence of which it is supposed to be the copy, but even when—a thing which seems still more unavoidable—we insist on counting that only as truth which appears to all minds equally necessary, as distinguished from that which presents itself differently to different minds. This is the point from which the modern polemic against the Ideas takes its start, insisting that if our Ideas are innate they have no claim to truth, and that such a claim can only be allowed if they are regarded as independent of the possible differences between one mind and another and dependent only on the nature of a world of objects common to them all.

325. Before we enter upon the arguments on either side in regard to the questions which are here raised, it is incumbent on us to realise that we have now arrived at a point at which, instead of the unavowed assumptions to which we are in the habit of surrendering ourselves, it becomes necessary to make one express assumption which we admit in plain terms to be such. No enquiry of this nature can establish its conclusions, whatever they may be, without making some kind of assumption by the way as to the mode in which the object of knowledge may be conceived as operating upon the subject which apprehends it. Let us, instead of thus assuming our postulate by the way, place it at the head of our enquiry, in the shape in which the varied experience of the human mind has taught us to formulate it. Wherever between two elements A and B of whatever kind any event which we call the influence of A upon B occurs, such influence never consists in a constituent element, or predicate, or state a separating itself from A to which it belonged, and just as it is, and without undergoing any change, passing over to B, to attach itself thenceforth to this new object, or be adopted by it, or become one of its states (however we like to phrase it); what happens is, that a, the property residing, or change arising in A, becomes the cause by reason of which, given a relation C already established or coming for the first time into play between A and B, B also is necessitated in its turn to evolve out of its own nature and as a part of itself its new state b.

How this necessary connexion between the states of A and B is brought about, how it happens that B is necessitated to follow the changes of A, what again the relation C, which may be constant or may vary in different cases, but which is essential to the production of the effect in question, consists in;—all these questions, as well as the preliminary one whether they admit of an answer at all, may be left outside our present enquiry; for us the abstract principle enunciated is sufficient, no matter what the mode in which it is realised in fact. That principle however gives us this result, that the form of the effect b can never be independent of the nature of the object B which experiences it; it changes with that object; and the same relation C which obtained between A and B, will as between A and B^1, produce in B^1 a new effect b^1 quite distinct from b. As little is the effect b independent of the nature of the active agency A or of the relation C; it changes with both; if A^1 instead of A enters with B into the relation C, it will become β, and β^1 if B and A enter into the relation C^1. But all these different results b, b^1, β, β^1 will make up in themselves a complete series of events which are only possible in B, and A and C are only to be regarded as exciting causes, determining which of the many effects of which the nature of B is susceptible are to be realised at a given moment, and in what order they are to come about. If we like to apply here the favourite designations, receptivity and spontaneity, we may say that every object is receptive of various kinds of stimuli to its spontaneity, and never operates spontaneously without such stimulus.

326. The operation of objects of knowledge upon a subject apprehending them comes under this general principle. Every assumption, to begin with, is wholly inadmissible which places the origin of our knowledge exclusively in the object: a very little attention will discover to us that even in the '*tabula rasa*' to which the receptive soul has been compared, or in the wax, which it has been supposed to resemble in being a mere recipient of impressions, a spontaneous reaction of the recipient subject is indispensable. Only because the tablet by virtue of certain modes of operation peculiar to its nature and consistence retains the coloured points and prevents them running into each other, only because the wax with its cohesive elements presents the properties of an unelastic body readily receptive of the stamp and capable of retaining it—only by virtue of this peculiar nature of theirs are the tablet and the wax adapted to receive the colours or the stamp impressed upon them; an object which presented no such qualities of its own to meet the stimulus from without would not possess so much as the character of pure receptivity ascribed to it.

Further it is necessary clearly to understand, that in an act of knowledge the direct contribution from the side of the object may be absent, but never that which is furnished by the subject's own nature. For it is conceivable that two ideas a and β, having once arisen in the soul through a stimulus from without, should then combine in obedience to laws having their source in the constitution of the mind alone, and without any renewal of the external stimulus, in a new result γ; but it is quite inconceivable that we could receive an impression from the world outside with the shaping of which our own nature had nothing to do. And therefore we cannot assent to the distinction between the matter and form of knowledge as it is drawn by Kant. The idea is indeed perfectly just, but he formulates it inaccurately when he ascribes the entire content to experience and the form alone to the innate activity of the mind. Kant was well aware of the fact which we are here emphasising, that even the simplest sensations, which in the strictest sense furnish the original content of all our perceptions, do not come to us ready made from outside, but on the contrary (if we are to hold to the conception of an external world) can only be considered as reactions of our own nature of combined sense and intellect in response to the stimuli coming from that world. They are the *a priori* capacities of experiencing sensation having their seat in ourselves which the external forces do indeed summon into actual existence in a definite order, but never transmit simply to us ready made. And when we pass to the composite result of these simple elements, the image of a particular form presented in space, the succession in time of the notes in a melody, or of a series of events, these too, in every particular and detail of the picture, are no whit less the product of the thinking subject, no whit less therefore *a priori*. For even if we assumed that things exist in a real extended space or occur in a real order of time in the same positions or in the same order in which we thereupon apprehend them, even then our temporal and spatial idea of them would be something quite different from their temporal and spatial *existence*; we could not manage to bring our ideas a, β, γ, into the same order as obtains among their objective causes a, b, c, unless our own nature and the laws of our mind enabled and obliged us to do so.

327. Or do we wish to delude ourselves with words and to reply that this trifling business of *copying* may be taken as a matter of course and requires no such labour of re-creation as we have attributed to the mind? But what do we mean by this word copy, and how is an image or a picture produced? We will say nothing at present of the eye, *for* which alone after all a picture is a picture, and we will ask only what are the conditions which make it possible for a mirror to present to the eye the image of any object? It can only so present it by reflecting the rays of light which it receives from the object in a fresh direction, while maintaining their original arrangement relatively to one another, and for this office it is absolutely dependent on the smoothness and the shape of its surface. It depends on these qualities of its own whether it scatters the rays in such disorder that no eye can combine them into a picture, or whether it so reflects them that although they diverge they can still be collected by the eye, or so that by converging they compose a real image which becomes visible to the eye as a new object.

But even when all this is done the mirror only supplies the stimulus which acts upon the organ of sight similarly to the object itself, and can be taken therefore to represent it; but if we ask how it is brought to pass as a result of this stimulus that the picture reflected can be seen, we are at once sensible how inapt the comparison of knowledge with a copy is. The apprehending consciousness is no resisting surface, curved or plane, smooth or rough, nor would it gain anything by reflecting rays of light no matter in what direction; it is in itself and its own co-ordinating unity, which is not a space, and not a surface, but an activity, that it has to combine the separate ideas excited in it into the perception of a spatial arrangement, which perception again is not itself an order in space but only the idea of that order. For even if, as some persons may perhaps imagine, the idea of a point to the left were actually placed to the left in our consciousness side by side with that of another point to the right, and the idea of an upper point above that of a lower, still this fact would not by itself give us the perception of this fact; all that this by itself would do would be to place us this time *really* in no better condition than that of a mirror in which some other mind might discover the disposition of the points, but again only on the supposition that *it* succeeded in accomplishing that which our own mind had not done, that is to say that it not merely received and retained the impression of the rays with their order of arrangement as reflected from our mind, but also turned those impressions to account, by producing, on occasion of them, a co-ordinating perception of that order.

Nothing is left therefore of this inexact comparison except the conviction that even the mere perception of a given state of things as it really is, is only possible on the assumption that the perceiving subject is at once enabled and compelled by its own nature to combine the excitations which reach it from objects into those forms which it is to perceive in the objects and which it supposes itself simply to *receive* from them.

That the case is the same with all the ideas which we form as to the inward connexion between one perception and another, is a fact to which I need only briefly advert, for it is here that the criticism has been most generally admitted. It is allowed on all hands that we do not see the causal connexion between two events, but that on the contrary the idea of such a connexion has to be superadded by ourselves to that mere succession of events in time which is alone directly perceived; and the admission of the *a priori* origin of the causal nexus has been used by one school of philosophy to establish for it the superior dignity of a necessary idea of universal validity, and by another to deny it all validity whatever in relation to the world of things in our perception of which its origin is not to be found. `Both the one deduction and the other is unsound. In regard to the second I recall once more this simple consideration; even if a causal connexion does exist between the events of the world outside us, it still could not possibly be presented to us as the direct object of a purely receptive faculty of perception; the mode in which individual impressions are connected can never do more than afford a stimulus to thought to introduce the conception through its own activity, nor can such stimulus actually operate unless our intellectual nature is itself necessitated, in order to complete and account for the observed combination of impressions, to supplement it by that conception.

328. The *a priori* character however, which we thus claim in so broad a sense for our knowledge, is only one side of the matter. If we regard all forms of sensible perception, our intuition of space, our conceptions of thing and quality, of cause and effect, lastly the ethical ideas of good and evil, as modes of manifestation innate in the mind, then and for that reason the ground for this and that particular application of them, one necessarily excluding another, cannot possibly be found in the mind. In our perception of space there are innumerable figures possible, but at a given moment we only observe certain definite ones; we are capable of seeing many different colours and hearing very various successions of sounds, but we cannot alter the red which we have before us here and now, though blue or yellow in the same place would be equally perceptible to us, nor can we substitute for the melody to which we are now listening any other of the countless melodies which we have heard at other moments; events follow one another independently of us, now forcing us to recognise a causal connexion between them, now making such an assumption impossible; finally this grouping of the incentives which are offered us to the exercise of our *a priori* faculties varies as between one individual and another, and cannot therefore have its foundation in the common nature of the mind.

To what it is that we are to attribute them is here indifferent. It may be that the ordinary opinion in which we all acquiesce in practical life, and from which the present discussion started, is the true one; that there does exist a world of things outside us, in which we have ourselves our assigned places, and which affects us in varying ways according to the changes which take place in itself and to the different and varying positions which we occupy in it. In that case the complex web of ideas which forms itself within us, cannot indeed claim the name of truth in the sense of presenting to us a real likeness of that which exists or occurs in the world of things; still each several conjunction or separation or transformation of the phenomena which float before our consciousness, will in its character of a *consequence* bear witness to a definite process of change, though it may be of a different order, in the relations of that world of things which operates upon us. And we should be led to the same conclusion by the rival doctrine of Idealism which never becomes natural to us in ordinary life, and is recommended solely by arguments which lie purely within the field of philosophy. It may be, as this belief supposes, that there is no world of things or events outside us, but *only* the appearance of such a world brought about within individual minds, and nowhere else, by a single unknown power which penetrates them all, and that in such a manner that the pictures of the world which different minds seem to themselves to see around them, fit in one with another, and all are presented to themselves as members, each in its own place, of one and the same universe. This theory, like the other, has necessarily to admit that the stimulus which excites any individual mind to create *its* particular picture of the world, is a stimulus foreign to itself, and at the same time not explicable from the universal spiritual nature which it shares with all other minds. Wherever it may come from, it remains an empirical or *a posteriori* element in our knowledge. And again: every conjunction or separation or diversification of the phenomena which so arise in us, will point to a distinct occurrence elsewhere, to changes taking place, not indeed any longer in the relations of manifold external objects, but in the action of that one power which creates within us this dream of an external world. Here finally as on the former hypothesis it would be well worth while to establish by observation and comparison of the phenomena those unchanging laws which they follow through all the play of change; and the accomplishment of that task will still give a knowledge of truth, even though there were no means of deciding what is the nature of that distinct set of laws obtaining in an unknown outer world which are the source of the orderly government of our own world within. The view I am here representing is in essentials that of Kant, and is one which German philosophy ought never to have deserted. But in so doing I expressly decline to give any answer to the question last alluded to. Let a man believe himself ever so much to possess an immediate certainty of the existence or the nonexistence of an external world of things; the nature and the manner of that existence can still only be unriddled by conclusions drawn from phenomena. Here therefore our footing must be secured to begin with; we must first establish those certain principles which are to determine the judgments we form in regard to the system of this inner world, before we can talk of applying the conclusions so obtained to the further metaphysical question.

329. But now supposing that we assume certain truths as innate, in the previously accepted sense of the word, whence do we arrive at the knowledge of them, unless it be by discovering them within us, that is to say, by inward experience? So that after all experience will be the sole source of all our knowledge? This criticism has been made, and it will be felt *prima facie* to be as barren as it is unanswerable. For certainly to know a truth we must be conscious of it, and if we were not conscious of it before, then the passage to the knowledge of it is an event which we must necessarily live through or experience; in this sense of the word our whole existence is a fact which only experience discovers to us. This objection therefore to the *a priori* nature of innate ideas cannot hold; on the contrary, supposing there to be innate ideas, supposing them to exist even in the sense of being unceasingly present to consciousness, still the mind reflecting on them could, to begin with, only be aware of their presence as a fact given in its experience or its conscious life. Taken then in this broad acceptation the conception of experience no longer offers occasion for a difference of opinion; the only point of importance is *as what* do we experience the thoughts in question? Do we experience them as innate truths, or as matter of experience in that narrower sense, in which they indicate in contradistinction to such truths that their origin is foreign to the mind itself? With this distinction the question about experience seems at first sight to take a more urgent form; if, that is, we go on to ask for marks which may distinguish the one of these cases from the other. We then find that the impressions which come to us from outside are forced upon us and we cannot alter them; but the *a priori* truths also present themselves as unavoidable and unalterable; that the compulsion in the first case comes from without, and in the second is that of our own nature, we may indeed conjecture, but how are we to prove it? The truth however is that if we take the unsophisticated intelligence we find that *this* which to us in the course of our methodological investigation was the most important fact, is not *to it* the primary one at all; the truths in question are not matter of experience in respect of their alleged quality of being innate in us; what first strikes us is that as a matter of fact what they assert is self-evident, so that when once we have had occasion to think of them in any particular instance, we see them to be independent of any further confirmation through fresh instances, and thus independent of experience which might supply such instances. And hence *universality* and *necessity* have always been the two characteristics which have been ascribed to *a priori* knowledge. We understand by the term *universality* that invariably as soon as the subject is thought of the predicate which belongs to it appears in self-evident conjunction with it; and again it is in this self-evidence and in nothing else that necessity or necessary validity in this sense consists, for clearly necessity attaches to universal truths in quite a different sense from that in which it belongs to those conjunctions of various objects which our changing experience brings before us. These objects, it is true, are also presented to us in such a way that at the moment in which they occur we cannot dissolve the conjunction at our pleasure; but though the content of experience possesses necessity in the sense in which every fact which cannot be denied does so, still it lacks that perfect self-evidence which consists in an inherent connexion of elements which are unthinkable apart from each other.

But after all, what gives us the right to affirm that that which may appear to us self-evident at this particular moment will appear so equally at every other, that is to say, to ascribe to it a *universality* which can make it a fixed principle of judgment in face of a perpetually changing experience? This question was raised by the early Sceptics and led them to declare *all* general propositions inadmissible. And in point of fact, whatever principle we may choose to devise to justify us in concluding from the certainty of a proposition at the present moment to its certainty for all future time, must itself be subject, *as* a universal principle, to the precise suspicion which it was intended to remove. Thus we should have no means of assuring ourselves of the universal validity of any proposition if we cannot be satisfied with the self-evidence with which its content, once thought, claims for itself eternal validity in anticipation of experience. And it would have to be a matter of consideration that this incapacity for attaining to universal truth could not be deplored as an infirmity peculiar to the human intelligence; it would be shared by all minds whose experience as being developed in time at all resembles ours; the very truest truth which might be innate in such a mind could only come into its consciousness at a definite moment, and all the self-evidence it might possess for it at that moment would not remove the uncertainty whether it would remain a necessity of thought in the next.

330. This result will perhaps be eagerly admitted, and it will be urged that it proves the futility of our defence of *a priori* truths; even when the mind has got them it has no means of distinguishing them from the results of experience. Or in other words it is only experience which teaches us that they have universal validity; that is to say, when we find their self-evidence confirmed by each successive attempt to think them, we have not indeed strict proof but we have the strongest probability that they are valid without exception, and it is to this gradually increasing empirical probability that the whole of our knowledge is in fact restricted.

In this there is an element of truth which I shall consider presently; but taken as a whole it is a false position. If we assume, as this view admits, that the certainty of a given proposition as experienced at one moment does not guarantee the experience of its certainty in the next, then just because this is so a thousand repetitions will not make it a whit more probable in the thousand and first case than it was in the second or third. If after a series of cases of the connexion of two events a and b unbroken by any instance to the contrary, we look for fresh instances with constantly increasing confidence, we do so on the strength of very definite assumptions. If the connexion of a and b is not of such a kind as to make it self-evident the moment it is presented to the mind, if its eternal validity is not at once apparent, then we explain its constant occurrence by the fact that the conditions which might have produced a different result have not so far come into operation; that they are not likely to do so at any future time we conclude after numerous instances of similar experiences on the strength of one special assumption and not otherwise, the assumption that the course of the universe in general and of this part of it to which the events in question belong in particular, proceeds in a fixed order, which by examination of a sufficient number of instances, becomes discoverable. Then, starting from this assumption that a particular set of conditions whenever they recur in the future will be equivalent to what they were when observed in the past, we draw our conclusion: given like conditions a like result must present itself. If we are wrong in that assumption this will mean that we have set up as universal a false generalisation concerning a matter of fact, which will be refuted by future experience. On the other hand, if our universal principle, that under like conditions like consequences follow, is no longer to be regarded as really universal, then the entire method of logical procedure by which we expect to pass from particular experiences to propositions of even probable universality, is absolutely baseless and vain. For every time we argue from m to $m+1$, whether we are undertaking to establish a strictly universal or a merely probable conclusion, in either case we assume the strict universality of that logical principle.

It is clear therefore that the attempt to derive the entire body of general knowledge from experience, that is to say from a mere summing up of particular perceptions, breaks down. We have invariably to help ourselves out by assuming at one point or another some one of those self-evident principles, some principle to which when once its content has been thought we at once concede with intuitive confidence that universal validity to which it makes claim.

331. Now in practice as a matter of fact there has never been any dispute on this point. Mathematical demonstrations have often been subjected to fresh examination, but never with any other object than to establish whether each one of the several propositions which made up the chain of reasoning was either itself self-evident or was logically derived from others which were so. We never set to work merely to prove over again the self-evident propositions themselves, to see whether some moment may not arrive in which their direct contraries, the equality of unequals for instance, or that the part is greater than the whole, would be equally self-evident; and even supposing so unexpected an event had on some occasion occurred, no one would have doubted that there was an error somewhere, which could only be attributed to an oversight in the calculation. On the other hand much difference of opinion does exist as to the extent of these universal and self-evident truths, and here we are brought in view of that element of truth which I could not help allowing above, in the theory just combated. I by no means intend however to imply that experience as such could help us to establish what holds universally not merely as a universal fact, but as a self-evident and necessary truth; on the contrary it is precisely experience with its repeatedly recurring uniformities which at last deludes us into taking for necessary and self-evident truth, that which is merely matter of fact, or not even that.

I have spoken before of the delusive certainty which many principles assume, merely because our limited experience has constantly presented them to us without any instance to the contrary. The psychological association which establishes itself under such conditions between the ideas a and b, representing two events which have constantly followed each other, very soon assumes the appearance of a self-evident connexion in fact between the contents of the ideas so presented. I observed then that the attempt to think the direct contradictory of a proposition which has come to be thus self-evident may serve sometimes to dispel the illusion, and we then find to our astonishment that a hypothesis which contradicts our apparently self-evident proposition presents no difficulty to thought, that it is just as much thinkable as the other, and that accordingly the certainty which we ascribed to our belief cannot depend upon any universal self-evident connexion in its content. I was obliged however even then to add that this attempt to think the contradictory will not always be a decisive test; the influences of previous experience which nullify its value are in fact very various. If we could be certain, in applying it to any proposition, that we have not only determined with perfect exactness, with nothing lacking and nothing over, the meaning of the subject a, and the predicate b, and also of the copula c or whatever the connexion may be which we wish to establish between them, but also that in the final decision as to whether that relation c which we have established is self-evident or not, we have been guided by no sort of consideration save the fixed meaning of the three conceptions; then undoubtedly we should all agree in our conclusions, positive and negative alike. And wherever these conditions are susceptible of fulfilment, as is the case in mathematics, such agreement is in fact found. The complex notions on the contrary of real objects are very far from admitting the same exactness of analysis, and every reasonable man looks for results in this sphere only from experience or rather from the accurate manipulation of our experiences. Finally those simplest and most universal conceptions and principles to which we should desire to subordinate that manipulation, would unquestionably admit of the highest degree of such accuracy, did not the influence of past experiences come in the way. We certainly intend something very simple and definite when we use the words, being, thing, cause, force, effect, matter; but in our use of any one of them we are commonly determined by our limited circle of experience or our favourite study or pursuit. Thus we are led on the one hand to apply them only to a fraction of the subject-matter which we in fact hold that they ought entirely to dominate, and yet on the other hand to bring them into a variety of connexions which are not indeed impossible to them but still do not essentially belong to them. Thus we might perhaps if we were required to define one of these conceptions agree in our definitions, yet the ways in which we actually look at its meaning might be different enough, as different at all events as in the case of the same objects seen in different lights. Now all these unanalysed sidethoughts, the emotional suggestions and the wishes which thus attach themselves unawares to the object of thought, and give it its characteristic colouring, dispose us to find the certainty of self-evidence in predicates which we should not be warranted from the nature of the object alone in applying to it at all. This is at once the value and the danger of experience; except as suggested by experience the universal principles of our judgment cannot be presented to consciousness at all; but as thus occasioned they are at the same time subject to one-sidedness, deficiencies in one direction, superfluities in another, from which later reflexion has much ado to purify them. Here begins a work of criticism which has to be unremittingly pursued; the useful labour of investigating the psychological origin of the particular form which these conceptions have come to assume in our consciousness; the object being not so much to show how all certainty and truth arises little by little out of the deliverances of experience, as, on the contrary, to make it clear how much foreign matter due merely to the peculiarities of the instances observed, has incrusted itself upon the substance of those original truths, truths which, if once they were seen in their simplicity and purity, would be not only recognised as necessary and self-evident, but would prove so in all their applications.

332. Such a criticism of prejudices, as I may shortly call it, cannot I conceive be conducted otherwise than piece by piece in connexion with definite problems which offer themselves for solution; for it is only difficulties which rise upon us in working out individual problems, which lead us to suspect the soundness of our principles and to cast about for the sources of the errors we have fallen into. I refrain therefore from entering into the subject here in detail; on the other hand it is necessary that I should vindicate the method I have thus far pursued as against the opposite theory, which not content with freeing the primary truths by this process of psychological analysis from the erroneous side-thoughts which have grown up about them, aims further at giving a systematic explanation of the nature of thought and demonstrating the validity of its first principles. I have maintained the opinion throughout my work that Logic cannot derive any serious advantage from a discussion of the conditions under which thought as a psychical process comes about. The significance of logical forms is to be found in the meaning and purport of the connexions into which the content of our world of ideas ought to be brought; that is to say in the utterances of thought or the laws which it imposes, after or during the act of thinking, not in those productive conditions of thought itself which lie behind. Conditions of this kind there must certainly be, not only those conditions of a psychical mechanism which determine at every single moment every single one of its motions, just as every feature in an event of external nature is determined by the physical conditions which are given at the moment of its occurrence,—but more than this, the necessity with which, speaking generally, thought follows unawares those logical rules of its procedure which later reflexion formulates into consciously apprehended principles, must be an unavoidable consequence of the nature of the mind itself, which it belongs to Psychology to investigate. But if we knew all that we could desire to know on the subject, it would still be a delusion to suppose that we should be thereby any the better able to judge of the truth of our logical principles; on the contrary the validity of those principles themselves would still be the necessary postulate without which the successful enquiry into their psychological history could not have been undertaken at all.

To touch here for the last time upon this logical circle which has wearied us so often already; it must be clear enough that no sensational or empirical theory of the origin of thought and knowledge can possibly either prove or disprove the principle of identity or excluded middle; in every step of the argument it needs them both. As little can it be left to such a theory either to establish or to destroy the validity of the law of causation. For every attempt to reduce our application of it in the field of experience to the association and reproduction of ideas presupposes its validity in another form in relation to the interaction of psychical states; so that it can neither be accepted nor rejected unless its validity be established to begin with—a premiss from which certainly the rejection of it could only be arrived at by a very curious sort of logical suicide. Nothing then remains but to restrict this psychological analysis to the task of showing how truths which have their own validity in themselves find realisation in thought and for thought, regarded as a psychical process, as rules of its procedure which it follows unawares.

333. And now I should like to make clear that of all that we might wish to know in this direction we in fact know nothing at all, and that Logic would have to renounce for a long time yet any profounder understanding of the operations of thought if she had to look for it in the psychological analysis of their origin. In the works of the sensational school, which have been produced in such numbers and such variety on the model of Locke's Essay—which is here unrivalled—and of Condillac's bold venture, I can find nothing that answers in a general sense to this requirement. Regarded as a criticism of the prejudices of human thought, Locke's work has enjoyed the full measure of influence in the development of modern philosophy to which the wide horizon which it opened and the keenness of its analysis entitled it. But in dealing with all the variety of those inner processes of the mind, which he undertakes to criticise, Locke has no other instrument to apply but 'common sense,' a faculty which, versed in the criticism of the course of events in the outward world, imagines that the very respectable and probable but quite unsystematic maxims there acquired are sufficient to meet all emergencies. It is more to my purpose at present to consider the attempts which have been made in this direction in German philosophy. When we speak of explaining any set of processes, and regret its non-accomplishment, we think, as the type of the wished-for ideal, of the body of the natural sciences. By the strict observance of the laws of thought and the careful application of them to the results of exact observation, natural science has succeeded in arriving at a small number of original facts from the interaction of which exceedingly various phenomena can be shown to follow with logical necessity. A series of happy inspirations[1] have within quite recent times added to this domain a portion of the inner life of the soul, at least in regard to the dependence of sensations upon external stimuli. And this result

[1] [For an account of these investigations, see 'Metaphysic,' § 258.]

was due not to attempts to construct the entirely peculiar set of events which we call psychical out of physical processes, which can never be brought into any comparison with them; but to investigations of which the aim has been simply to apply exact quantitative determinations to the members of the two series which the order of nature does actually unite together, though in a manner unknown to us, and from the pairs of correlated values thus ascertained to develop the laws of their correspondence. And previously to these enquiries a valuable attempt had been already made[1], not indeed resting on the exact observation of special facts, but upon hypotheses suggested by experience generally, to bring the purely inward phenomena of mental life under a mechanical theory of their origin. At the same time all these achievements which have given the psychology of the present day a very great superiority over the views of earlier times, do not reach those obscure regions of enquiry, the illumination of which might open new paths to Logic. They merely instruct us concerning the interaction of different psychical states to which measurement has been applied, in regard to the changes they severally undergo when brought into connexion with each other, and thus in regard also to the total state of the soul at any moment, considered simply as the mechanical result of all these reciprocal influences. But they do not equally explain the fresh reactions to which the soul is stimulated by each one of these states of itself as they thus arise, and which are not calculable consequences of certain quantitative relations in the co-operating conditions, but depend, in obedience to a necessity of a wholly different order, shall we say a dialectical or teleological necessity, upon the meaning or the idea which the soul is destined to realise.

The investigation of external nature leaves questions of this sort behind, but for its purposes it does not need to answer them. In what way it happens, by what means it

[1] [An allusion to Herbart, see 'Metaphysic,' §§ 269, 270.]

is brought about, or to what purpose it tends, that particles of matter attract each other with a force determined by their distance, are questions which may be left undecided. When once the law of this reciprocal influence is ascertained, it can be reckoned as a constant element in the course of nature, that is to say in the present case as an element into the determination of whose variations in each several instance the given circumstances enter. The more we succeed in reducing all natural processes to homogeneous motive forces of this kind, the more possible will it become to construct even the form of every single natural event out of the conditions which occasion it. This would all be altered if the natural sciences had cause to suppose that the material elements which had hitherto been regarded as unchangeable, experienced under the operation of forces of this kind certain inner changes which had the effect of stimulating them to wholly new modes of reaction, giving them a new influence in the play of events. No doubt those new influences so far as they operated to bring about changes in the physical surroundings could still be directly connected with the ascertainable outward conditions under which they arise, or, to express it in general terms, they could be regarded as functions of the conditions; and thus there would be apparently no interruption in the continuity of the scientific construction, only an increased difficulty in carrying it out. But in point of fact a breach of continuity would certainly have taken place. For the simple fact that given a certain set of physical conditions m a new mode of operation μ will make its appearance and given another set n a second new result v, would remain after all a new *datum*, a fact known indeed from experience, but not to be derived analytically as a necessary and self-evident consequence from the physical conditions given.

Now the case in which we find ourselves in regard to the present question is analogous to this. All the mental processes which psychology teaches us are necessary presuppositions for the realisation of any act of thought, are merely the conditions m or n which give occasion to the logical reactions μ and ν to present themselves. They cannot explain the fact that μ and ν do thus appear upon the scene, nor again do we find in this fact in itself the least explanation of the further relations of constantly increasing complexity which thought establishes between its μ and ν or other of the elementary products of its activity.

I should dwell upon this point further were it not that the subject of the following section will oblige me in any case to call attention later on in detail to the deep gulf which remains unfilled between the psychical mechanism and thought; I content myself here with the expression of my conviction that all logical reactions of the mind have to be conceived as a connected whole, as expressions of a single tendency whose separate utterances can in so far as their *meaning* is concerned be apprehended and arranged in an intelligible series, but in their origin as psychical processes remain wholly incomprehensible. It is an illusion in psychology and a corruption of logic to take the conditions which occasion the logical operations of thought for the operations themselves. There is only one delusion more desperate still,—to imagine that a complete physical theory of the nervous system will explain that which is itself the condition of any theory being possible at all.

CHAPTER IV.

Real and Formal Significance of Logical Acts.

334. FACTS of perception we acknowledge without question; our misgivings begin with the interpretations of those facts by discursive thought, more especially when we consider the protracted and intricate web of ideas which thought spins in abstraction from the facts of sense, yet always with the expectation of reaching a final result which perception will confirm. Thought as an activity or movement of the soul follows laws of the soul's own nature; will these laws which it necessarily follows in the connexion of its ideas, lead to the same result as that which the real chain of events brings round? Will the outcome of the process of thought, when at the close of it we turn once more to the facts, be found in agreement with the actual results which the course of nature has produced? And if on the whole we consider it improbable that thought and being, which it is natural for us to regard as made for one another, should be entirely divorced, are we also to suppose that every single step taken by thought answers to some aspect of that which actually takes place in the development of the things thought about? Such are the doubts which give rise to the theory of the purely formal or subjective validity of thought. That theory is perfectly clear in what it affirms; the logical forms and the laws of their application are the conditions through the fulfilment of which thought satisfies its own requirements, and brings the connexion of its ideas with one another into that form, which for it, for thought itself, is truth ; but it is not at all clear what is the relation—though some such relation cannot be dispensed with—in which these forms and laws stand to the content which they do not create but find, and from the manipulation of which alone after all that which is truth for thought draws its material.

Can an object, we ask, be brought into forms to which it is not adapted? Or even supposing that we are able to force our material into a form which it does not naturally assume, still must there not be some quality in the material which at all events makes such an operation possible? Must not every given subject-matter therefore, which thought casts into its own forms, possess some relation and affinity to those forms, of which the most we can say is that it may be misused? Finally, must not this assumption hold as regards every single logical operation? Not one of these could be carried out even as a mere subjective process of thought, unless the object upon which it is exercised contained in itself some characteristic which invited or at least allowed it. Now we know that the distrust of thought spoken of above, does not find confirmation in experience in the universal sense we dreaded. However wrong we may go in protracted chains of reasoning, daily life shows how well our conclusions taken in the average agree with the actual course of events. Why should we not hold fast to that confidence in the veracity of thought which is the natural attitude of our minds before scepticism disturbs them? Why not mount a step higher still, and regard the objective[1] content of our world of ideas as bound by no other laws than those which thought imposes on it? Then we should need nothing more than careful attention to the subtle and intricate logical processes of the mind, to find reflected there as in a mirror the real

[1] ['Der sachliche Inhalt des Vorstellens.']

or objective forms in which all existence appropriately developes.

In this way the belief grows up in a Real significance of thought, a belief which in its more general features appears in the history of the human mind earlier than its opponent, but which stated in these explicit terms and in this thorough-going form, is a product of recent times. Between this and the opposite theory the history of philosophy has a long controversy to recount. We cannot decide it by placing the logical forms and laws side by side with those of real existences and events and comparing the one with the other, for we have no knowledge of the latter in which thought is not already present and operative. But we can ask what is the judgment of thought itself on its own operations, and how far it pronounces the forms which as a psychical movement of the thinking subject it is constrained to assume, to be a determination belonging to the object-matter upon which it operates.

335. To whatever act of thought we direct our attention we never find that it consists in the mere presence of two ideas a and b in the same consciousness, but always in what we call a Relation of one idea to the other. After this relation has been established, it can in its turn be conceived as a third idea C, but in such case C is neither on the one hand homogeneous with a and b, nor is it a mere mechanical effect of interactions which in accordance with some definite law have taken place between the two as psychical processes with definite magnitudes and definitely various natures. We may take as the simplest examples of what I mean the identification and the distinction of two ideal contents. If we assume a and a identical[1] with each other, then unquestionably the idea a is present twice over in our mind, but the only result to which this circumstance can

---

[1] ['Gleich,' i.e. the same both in quantity and quality. Neither 'equal' nor 'like' fully render this meaning. Cp. 'Metaphysic,' § 19, note.]

lead us on mechanical analogies will be either that the two ideas must count as one because they exactly cover each other, or that as similar affections of the soul they will become fused into a third idea of greater strength, or that they simply remain apart without any result at all. But that which we call the comparison[1] of them, which leads to the idea of their identity C, consists neither in the mere fact of their co-existence, nor in their fusion; it is a new and essentially single act of the soul, in which the soul holds the two ideas side by side, passes from one to the other, and is conscious of experiencing no change in its condition or in the mode of its action during or by reason of that passage from the one idea to the other.

Again: let us compare two different ideas a and b, red and yellow. Two external *stimuli*, which acting by themselves would have awakened severally one of the two sensations, might acting simultaneously coalesce in the nerve, through which they propagate themselves still as physical states, into a third excitation intermediate between the two so as to occasion in the soul only a third simple sensation. But two ideas which have once arisen as ideas in the soul, never experience this sort of fusion. If it were to occur, if the distinctive existence of the two ideas were to vanish, all opportunity and possibility of comparison, and therewith as a remoter consequence, all possibility of thought and knowledge, would vanish also. For clearly all relation depends upon the preservation in consciousness of the different contents unfalsified by any interactions of one upon the other; the single undivided energy of thought which is to comprehend them must find them as they are in themselves, so that passing to and fro between them it may be conscious of the change which arises in its own condition in the transition.

In using this language I am fully aware that it may be

[1] ['Vergleichung.' The emphasis on the connexion of 'Vergleichung' with 'gleich' cannot be rendered.]

fairly objected that my designation of the energy in question contains mere descriptions which cannot be embodied in a construction. But this is exactly the point upon which a clear understanding is essential,—that the intellectual processes upon which all thought depends do bear no sort of resemblance to those physical events on the analogy of which such an objection would like to see them modelled. An activity which cannot be said simply to *be* a movement but which executes a movement, which relates itself to two objects without introducing any change into them, which finally becomes conscious of the direction and the length of the path it has travelled by the differences which it experiences in its own states,—such an activity cannot be brought under the ordinary category of unchanging elements with changing relations, or of the equality of action and reaction; and yet at the same time it is something whose reality we all feel; it in fact and nothing else is the instrument by means of which we accomplish those much admired constructions which we would fain apply to it. These characteristic peculiarities we have simply to acknowledge, and to look for a new set of conceptions which may enable us to formulate them without falsifying their nature, an order of conceptions which are still a desideratum in philosophy, and which I by no means consider my own very incomplete formulae to have supplied.

336. In the instances taken above, a and b, red and red, or red and yellow, were objects directly given in perception. The ideas of identity or difference C which we obtained as the result of the act of relation introduced by the mind, are no longer of this character. As a relation of one *to* the other, the identity of *a with a*, or the difference *between a* and *b*, they cannot be really thought without at the same time recalling on the one hand the ideas of a and b, which form the terms in the relation, and on the other that movement of thought which carried us over from the one to the other. Thus every time we use the term identity or difference we are called on to renew once more all those operations of thought through which alone it is possible to use them with a meaning; but when we express the final result which we wish to produce by the process of thought, by saying that a is the same as a, or a is different from b, we are implying that the objective knowledge which it was our object to arrive at lies entirely and exclusively in this final step of the completed comparison. It is not to a and b that we ascribe the movement backwards and forwards between them through which we discovered their relation to each other; this movement is merely a psychical process, without which indeed our result could neither be obtained in the first instance nor repeated afterwards in memory, but which has nevertheless to be abstracted from the real significance of the act of thought to which it ministered, as a scaffolding is withdrawn when the building is completed. Thus we see at once in an example of the simplest possible kind the antithesis between the merely formal significance of an act of thought and the real significance of its product. Before I follow up this line of thought further I wish to advert to two sets of processes which add a confirmation on a large scale to the conclusions which we have seen suggested by a particular instance.

In the first place we receive the sensible perceptions from which thought starts almost without exception under the form of space,—in spatial shape, arrangement or relations; hence we come to apply terms of space symbolically to every sort of complex relation in order to give it that vividness to the imagination in which it would otherwise be deficient. We represent ideas of difference by terms of distance, distance long and short, in this direction and that; the multiplicity of what is the same by distribution at different points of space; the self-identity of unity[1] by the notion of an unchanging place which we assign to the idea in question whenever we think it; lastly we find it difficult to

[1] ['Identität des Einen mit sich selbst.'

make our conceptions clear, wherever the manifold orders of relation which present themselves to thought are such as the formulae derived from space are inadequate to express. And yet for all this we are conscious that these formulae do not reach the heart of the matter; all these symbols are, we are aware, mere subjective aids to the understanding, convenient paths for thought which has to travel up and down to reach its goal C, which is in itself wholly distinct from them; what we *mean* is independent of the mode in which we *figure* it.

Secondly we are accustomed to clothe our thoughts in speech, and even in the silent processes of thought it has long become habitual to us to call up the appropriate words before the mind; perception, recollection, expectation, hardly reach perfect clearness until we have found adequate expressions for them in spoken propositions. The advantage thus gained is not in its own nature dependent on speech and its sounds, but rather on an inward act of analysis and combination which would remain the same if it employed other forms of communication; still in point of fact, now that speech is there for the purpose, it is undoubtedly the case that the forms which the processes of thought assume and the facility with which they are conducted are dependent upon the means which speech provides, and thus present even national differences, when many and various causes have combined to render the formation and syntax of different languages dissimilar. Thus the logical meaning of a given proposition is indeed in itself independent of the form in which language expresses it; but in practice all human thought is compelled to represent its meaning by separations, combinations, and readjustments of those ideas which the growth of language has attached to single words. It is only in this its discursive character, in contradistinction to Perception, that thought is a psychical fact. It is in this character also that it has been the subject of our logical treatise. . Logic has never concerned itself with a thought which did not make its various ideas, one after another, the object of its attention, which did not move amongst them comparing and relating them to each other, which did not symbolise abstract ideas by spatial images, which finally did not express its thoughts in the forms and constructions of a language. We must expect therefore to find in what we call logical operations, logical forms and laws, a considerable amount of purely formal apparatus which although indispensable to the exercise of thought, yet lacks that Real significance which for the ultimate results of its activity thought does undoubtedly claim.

337. Let us now return to consider this result. When in comparing a and b we are conscious of a change C which we experience in passing from one to the other, there is no doubt that C must depend upon the nature of the two terms of the relation, for it would alter and become C^1 if they were replaced by c and d. At the same time the connexion of C with that objective relation seems to be one of dependence merely, and not to consist in being an identical copy of it; as a subjective excitation in us it falls short of the objective reality towards which knowledge is directed. I should not advert to so subtle a refinement of criticism were it not that it gives me an opportunity to return once more to the difficult subject of the nature of the act which presents ideas. The act of presentation is not that which it presents, the idea is not that which it means. And this not merely in the obvious sense that neither the one nor the other is the fact presented: but I mean that even the very simplest ideas, the content of which can only exist in thought and is not a thing, have not their content as their own predicate; the idea of yellow is not yellow, the idea of triangularity is not itself triangular, or the idea of timidity timid, or the idea of a half half as large as that of the whole. At the same time the act of presentation is not so completely separable from its content, that it could be, or occur, or experience change by itself; it *is* only in as far as it presents that which, itself, it is not; it changes only in exchanging one of these contents for another. Thus even the change of which it becomes conscious in its own condition can only consist in a change in the contents presented, which with its single activity it comprehends and compares; it cannot be sought in an affection of a wholly different character which the mind experiences merely as an after *result* of the stimulus given it by those contents, and which becomes observable to consciousness apart from those contents as an idea C having no resemblance to their own relation. He who finds red and yellow to a certain extent different yet akin, becomes conscious no doubt of those two relations only by help of the changes which he himself as a subject of ideas experiences in the transition from the idea of the one to that of the other, but at the same time he never entertains the apprehension that the relation of red and yellow may be something quite different in itself from that of the affections which they occasion in him, that red for instance may be in itself exactly like yellow and only appear to us different from it, or again that in reality there is a greater difference between them than we know and that their apparent affinity is an appearance only. Such scepticism might not be groundless if the question was one concerning the relation of our world of thought to a world of things assumed to be external to it, but so long as we are considering not this external world, but our own ideas, we never doubt that the relations of likeness and difference which we experience in the comparison of them, on the part of our presentative susceptibility, signify at the same time an objective relation on the part of those contents which our ideas present to us.

338. But now after all how is this in strictness possible? How can the propositions 'a is the same as a,' and 'a is different from b,' express an objective relation, which, as objective, would subsist independently of our thought, and which thought could only discover or recognise? We may suppose ourselves to know what we mean by a self-existent identity of *a* with *a*, but what are we to make of a self-existent distinction *between a* and *b*? And what objective relation can correspond to this 'between,' to which we only attach a meaning so long as it suggests to us the distance in space which *we*, in comparing *a* with *b*, interpolated by way of metaphor for the purpose of holding the two apart, and at the same time as a connecting path on which our mind might be able to travel from one to the other? Or otherwise expressed: difference being neither the predicate of *a* taken by itself nor of *b* taken by itself, of what is it the predicate? And if it has a meaning only so far as *a* and *b* have been brought into relation to each other, what objective connexion, we must then ask, obtains between them, if we consider the relating activity through which we have conjoined them in our consciousness as not being exercised? Many errors in ancient Dialectic were occasioned by the fact that these questions were ignored. Attributes which can only belong to things in the reciprocal relation which our combining thought establishes between them, were predicated of them, not without violence to the logical imagination, singly and by themselves. In order that *a* and *b* might be represented as different, without thought being required to establish the difference, the attribute was ascribed to each separately of being in itself a ἕτερον, and the act of comparison with a second thing, which alone gives any meaning to the term, was to be left wholly out of account. The negation which thought, comparing and distinguishing, expresses in the proposition '*a* is not *b*' was then treated as a positive predicate of *a* as such, the negatived term *b* being dropped out. That is to say it was treated as a not-being which yet is, and became thus credited with a reality of its own; and this confusion was reckoned an important and profound discovery. If *b* is less than *a* and greater than *c*, it was a riddle which much vexed philosophers, how the two predicates, less and greater, which, once separated from the terms of the relation to which they belonged, stood in direct opposition to each other, could be associated in the same *b*.

It would be a task not without interest from many points of view to follow up these erroneous conceptions in detail, but it would lead us too far afield for the purposes of the present discussion, which I may be content to close with the following remarks. If *a* and *b* are as we have thus far been regarding them, not things belonging to a reality outside and independent of our thought, but simply contents of possible ideas, like red and yellow, straight and curved, it will follow that a relation between them can exist only so far as we think it, and by the act of our thinking it. Only such is the constitution of our soul and such do we assume that of every other soul to be which inwardly resembles ours, that whenever and by whomsoever they may be thought, they must always produce for thought the same relation, a relation which has its being only in thought and by means of thought. This relation therefore is independent of the individual thinking subject, and independent of the several phases of his thought; this is all that we mean when we regard it as subsisting in itself as between *a* and *b*, as an object having a permanent existence of its own, which our thought discovers. It has in fact this permanent and assured character, but only in the sense of being an occurrence which will always repeat itself in our thinking in the same way under the same conditions. And this holds not only of difference but of every relation whatever which we may discover between *a* and *b*. Every time that any mind forms the idea of a perfect circle it will be found, in this case, it is true, only through a chain of intermediate ideas, that the ratio $1:\pi$ obtains between the diameter and the circumference; this proportion therefore is valid in itself; but although thus possessing objective Validity, it possesses Being only in the form of the thought which apprehends it.

The case is different if *a* and *b* are taken expressly to

signify realities, things, beings, which we do not create by thought but recognise as objects outside thought. In that case the name Relation expresses *less* than we have to suppose as really obtaining between the related things. Only so long as we are merely placing the thinkable contents of this *a* and *b* by a voluntary act side by side for comparison, would a proposition affirming a relation between *a* and *b*, or more properly in this case between the ideas or thought-pictures of them, adequately express our meaning. If on the other hand we are led in order to explain some connexion between these ideas which perception has thrust upon us, to have recourse to a relation C such as to subsist not between the ideas but between the things *a* and *b* themselves, of which the ideas are the thought-pictures, then we must recognise that this C which we have invoked cannot be a relation *between* *a* and *b*, cannot any longer therefore be a relation in the ordinary sense of the word at all. For it is thought and thought only which, passing from the idea *a* to the idea *b*, and becoming conscious of the transition, creates that which we call here a 'between,' and presents it as a mental picture which thought finds intelligible; accordingly it must always be a vain endeavour to attempt to ascribe to this relation, which at once separates *a* and *b* and brings them together, and which is nothing more than the recollection of an act of thought performable only by the unity of our consciousness,—to ascribe, I say, to this relation a real validity in the sense of being something in itself apart from the consciousness which thinks it. This supposed 'relation' can only subsist independently of our consciousness, or objectively, if it is something *more* than relation, and then it subsists not *between* *a* and *b* (for this 'between' has no existence except in us), but rather *in* them, as an influence which they reciprocally exert upon and receive from each other. It is merely for us when we think it that such influence takes logical shape in the weakened form of a relation, which no longer expresses its full significance.

I must leave it to the Metaphysic[1] to show what are the conclusions to which this observation leads; to certain questions nearly connected with it I shall return directly.

339. The comparison of *a* and *b* does not lead merely to the affirmation of identity or difference; we also try to present identity *in* difference under the form of a universal as the content of a separate idea *C*. It is a criticism frequently made in Logic that our general conceptions do not possess the fixity with which ordinary thought credits them; their content is formed and their structure developed little by little, and the same conception means different things at different stages in the evolution of our growing knowledge, as fresh experiences continually enrich it. This is very evidently true of those conceptions whose content is drawn purely from experience, and therefore can only become gradually known to us; on the other hand the conceptions of an integer or a fraction, a line or a figure, will not be found necessarily imperfect in the same way. The conception of a triangle as such contains in it no more to the geometrician than it does to the scholar who follows him; the difference is that to the geometrician it *suggests* numerous relations which the scholar is as yet unacquainted with, and in this way the conception of the triangle as such appears to be richer in content to the one than it is to the other, whereas the truth is that it is only his knowledge about it which is more extensive. But leaving this, the point I wish to emphasise is that a general conception, even if we consider merely its content at any one moment, indicates a task which no actual idea, that can be presented to the mind, can fulfil. A specific red or blue colour we can see, colour in general can neither be seen nor yet presented in the same sort of imaginative embodiment as the images of red and green recalled in memory. He who speaks of colour in general reckons on his hearer first of all summoning up the mental picture of some definite colour, red

[1] [Cp. 'Metaphysic,' § 80, and Book III. ch. 3.]

perhaps, which however is accompanied at the same time by a negation by which it is made to stand not for itself, but as an example of colour in general. To this negation however, if it is not to deprive the idea of all content whatsoever, he can only give effect by calling up at the same time the ideas of other definite colours to his imagination, and becoming aware in passing from one to the other of the common element which remains constant throughout the changes of his conscious states.

It is a series of psychical operations of this nature which is the task prescribed to us, when we hear the name of any universal; but that towards which those operations are directed can never be presented as an actual idea; we can never separate that which makes red and green colours from that which makes red red and green green. It is commonly admitted as a self-evident truth, that the class to which a real object belongs is not itself real; this individual horse we see, horse in general is nowhere to be found; but it has to be understood that in thought too the universal is never more than an idea strained after but always unrealised, floating over the forms of the individual instances of it which are imaged in the mind. To these purely inward operations of thought no objective significance can attach; they remain subjective efforts of our mind, and the very form in which we express the result to which they lead us, ' in intension the universal is included in the particular, in extension the particular in the universal,' merely indicates in the symbolism of space those operations of thought through which the mind endeavours to represent as an idea the objective relation between them. And now inasmuch as, more than this, we never find the object of our search, our universal, in actual presentation at all, we are led to ask whether it really has any objective significance? Or are we to approve an opinion widely current, that it is merely the mechanism of the mind which misleads us into grouping similar impressions under general names by blurring the real distinctions between them to the prejudice of accurate thought? This theory however in fact acknowledges that which it sets itself to deny. In order to make the fact intelligible that not all but only similar ideas are thus drawn together under a common name it presupposes the fact of that similarity, and clearly, with it, only in another form, the objective validity of our assumption of a universal, which, however inseparably, is contained in them. On the other hand, if we could merely point to an innate tendency of thought to *search* for a universal, such tendency might very well be without any objective significance, but the fact that the object of the search is *found* gives it such a significance at once.

This is only an apparent contradiction to what I was saying just now, for although the universal cannot be held before the imagination, the effort to think it is still not without result. We could not so much as bring red and blue under the general name of colour, did not that common element exist in them, to our consciousness of which we testify in framing the name; we could form no class notions of animals and plants if the marks of individual plants or animals, and the modes in which those marks are conjoined, did not really possess such points of comparison as allow us to arrange them under general marks and forms, and thus by setting these in the place of the merely individual, to construct the thought-form of the class, however impossible it may be to picture it to the mind. Thus in the fact that we are *able* to think a universal, there is undoubtedly contained a truth of real and objective validity; the contents of the world of ideas which thought does not create but finds do not fall into mere individual and atomic elements, each one admitting of no comparison with the other, but on the contrary resemblances, affinities, and relations exist between them, in such wise that thought as it constructs its universals and subordinates and co-ordinates the particulars under them, comes through these purely formal and subjective operations, to coincide with the nature of that objective world.

340. If we pass from these more simple instances to the main forms of logical thought, and enquire into the significance of universal notions, we are met by the controversy between Nominalism and Realism, which excited such passionate agitation in the middle ages. To both parties the question at issue had other than a purely logical importance; the metaphysical interest predominated, leading them to think of the world of ideas mainly in its relation to the world of things. Thus Realism first misunderstanding and then exaggerating the independence of the Platonic Ideas, came to look upon the general notion as the only real existence in things, all distinctively individual characteristics being relegated to the position of merely transient and subordinate though mysterious appendages to the eternal substance of the universal. Nominalism starting from the sound Aristotelian doctrine, that reality of *Existence* belongs only to the individual thing, found no way of reconciling this with the *Validity* of the universal. Thus the Nominalist came to regard general notions as at the best mere aids to the mind in the arrangement of its ideas, possessing no significance whatever in relation to the things which the ideas represent. They even erred so far as to deny them so much value as this, and to declare them to be mere sounds which may be uttered and heard, but are wholly devoid of content or meaning.

I am desirous in the first place to avoid dealing with the subject thus exclusively in relation to the question of existence, which involves an undue limitation of the issue. In Mathematics where we find ourselves dealing not with existing things and their essence at all, in Moral Philosophy and Jurisprudence where we speak of virtues and crimes, which *ought* or ought not to exist, more than this, when in actual life we endeavour to arrive at a decision in a matter of importance by bringing the given case under a general notion:—in all these instances we meet with the universal and its laws, in dealing with objects which are given us as matter of knowledge although they are not things[1].

341. If we can get out of the habit of always thinking exclusively of class notions in natural history as examples of the universal, if we recollect that we also frame general notions of figures and numbers, events and relations, truths and errors, the wild ambition to ascribe to general notions as such a reality like that of things, or at any rate of some actual existences, vanishes at once. To the original forms of substantial existences, of the plant, the animal, the human being, our imagination may if it pleases attribute an independent and eternal existence in a hypostasized world of ideas, as objects of intuition to souls which are yet unfettered by the limitations of an earthly existence. But the general notions of rest and motion, resemblance and contrariety, activity and passivity, could not possibly *exist* side by side with the former even in a world of ideas, they could only possess *validity* as predicates of the ideas. This fact, from which it is easy to see that there is no escape, we do indeed sometimes forget. We are tempted to treat qualities, relations, or occurrences, to which some prominent interest attaches, objects of our reverence or of our dread, as universals with a reality like that of an actual existence, misapprehending their purely predicative nature. We speak for instance of 'the beautiful' as of a being which is merely to us unapproachable, but in itself an object of possible intuition; we speak of 'sin' not merely as of an act which becomes real when we commit it, but as if it were a substantial force which operated upon us with an independent reality of its own. We confound the importance which belongs to the content of such conceptions in the entire system of the world with a form of reality which it cannot possess, and in attributing which to them we are merely expressing in the most emphatic terms at our command

[1] ['Sachlich, aber doch nicht dinghaft.']

their independence of our recognition of them. This mistaken habit of thought, which is not altogether harmless, is however here easily renounced; it is only from that class of general conceptions the nature of whose content necessitates its being apprehended from the first in a substantive form, that this hypostasizing tendency continues to draw support. Here too however it has to give way before a very simple consideration. We are not content to frame, starting from the particular of perception, a single universal Q, but we go on to combine this with others like it in a higher universal P, and as we proceed with this operation, it rests within wide limits with our own logical good pleasure to determine through how many such links in the chain of universals we may choose to connect our Q with the highest universal A, at which the process of abstraction will be arrested. Each one of these universals would have an equal right to such substantial existence; side by side with animal in general would appear vertebrate in general, mammal in itself, one-toed animal in general, horse in itself, black horse in general, all equally real. I say deliberately side by side with each other, for in fact our imagination is totally unable to transfer that relation of subordination through which in our thought one such general notion includes another, to beings such as these, which are conceived as possessing all alike actual existence. Placed thus however side by side with one another they could no longer have the meaning which they purport to have. Thus we find ourselves confirmed in our conviction that this Reality which we desire to recognise in the general notions which are created by our thought is a reality which is wholly dissimilar to Existence, and which can only consist in what we have called Validity or in being *predicable of* the Existent. But how much of the full meaning of a general notion possesses this validity, and what is the meaning of possessing 'validity' at all, are questions which need some further discussion.

342. I remind my readers to begin with that we are not concerned with the question of the objective value which may attach to one or another of the general notions evolved by thought in virtue of its content being correctly constructed; the question relates to the general significance of the logical *form* as such. That this like every other of the forms which logic prescribes as ideals may be given a content which is not adapted to it, needs no special mention, but a critical review of the countless modes in which the form of the notion may be applied is not our business here. To proceed then: we saw that any content of thought S is conceived under the form of the notion, when we do not merely grasp its manifold constituents as some sort of whole, but present to ourselves at the same time a universal M whose general characteristics $P, Q \ldots$ standing in determinate relations to one another, become severally modified and defined in S in the specific forms p', q'. This constitution of the logical notion does not correspond to anything which takes place in things or external objects[1] themselves; and neither does it answer to the actual nature of a content which is presented to us as matter of knowledge but not as a substantial thing. There is no moment in the life of a plant in which it is merely plant in general or conifer in itself, awaiting some subsequent influences answering to the subsequent logical determinations in our thought, to settle the question what particular tree it is to grow up into. It is true that the plant is not while still in the germ its future self in perfect miniature; still its manner of development is not that certain conditions superadded from without produce a special determination of characteristics which were present in a general and indeterminate shape; on the contrary its characteristics are already fully determined when the conditions enter in. From the two in conjunction new results are produced of which it is mis-

[1] ['Eines Dinges oder Gegenstandes,' contrasted with 'Inhalt' (content) and 'sachlich' (matter of knowledge) in the following clause.]

leading to say that they were contained in the earlier and more general properties as mere potential species and are now for the first time actualised to the exclusion of all other alternatives. An ellipse has no natural existence and development like a plant; still here too it is not the only way of arriving at a true apprehension of its nature to think of it first as a curve possessing the general properties of all curved lines, and then to define those properties further till we reach the particular form of them which belongs to this particular curve. We *may* indeed arrive at the conception of it in that way—supposing for instance an unpractised memory only allows us at first to recall the general outlines of the figure required, and we need subsequent reflexion to draw it exactly; but in the mathematical equations, whether they refer the shape of the line to arbitrary points of origin, or take account of some graphical method by which it may be generated, the curvature itself is not directly expressed at all; it only appears as a consequence which may be deduced from the definite ratios of the co-ordinates. These considerations hold equally as concerns the subordination of notions to one another in classification; it has no real significance in relation to the actual structure and development of things themselves. This horse was not to begin with animal in general, then vertebrate in general, later on mammal, and only at the last stage of all horse; nor can we by any means at any moment of its life separate off as an independent set of qualities the more fully defined group of properties which make it a horse, from the more general and less determinate which would make it a vertebrate, or from those most indeterminate of all which would merely constitute it an animal as such. Add to this that not only do different classifications of the same objects conflict owing to imperfect knowledge and observation, and thus introduce various and diverse ladders of universals between the highest universal and the objects, but the logical right of thought is incontestable to start from any point of view it pleases, and so to subsume the same object S under different general notions, or to construct its conception of the object by means of several widely divergent series of successive determinations. In such a case we are at liberty to ask with a view to the particular purpose of any enquiry, which of these various constructions is to be preferred, as presenting the object in the form in which it can be brought most conveniently under the principles which happen on the particular occasion to be our guiding principles; and if we knew ourselves to possess a knowledge of the supreme principles of the universe, such as would contain within them the key to all problems which could arise, then we might go on to select out of the various possible conceptions of an object that highest or best conception, which would indicate its place in this supreme classification, and in which all the other conceptions of it would be contained as logical consequences. Still greatly as the *value* of this conception for knowledge would be enhanced if this ideal were attained, from the importance which would then attach to its content and to the mode in which this content would be internally connected, for all this the Logical structure which belongs to it as a conception would still represent no Real structure corresponding to it in the object itself.

This value for knowledge however, which we do not dispute, gives us the other side of the question, that which we mean when we all insist in spite of everything, that the general notion and that classification do at all events contain something which has to do with the thing itself. We shall perhaps be disposed to express it by saying that the whole series of intersubordinated universals are contained not *actu* but *potentiâ* in the essence of the thing itself; and this proposition will be extended to other and different ways in which a given content is constructed or conceived: not really but potentially is every mark of division contained in the continuous magnitude which we break up by means of it; potentially all simple motion in a straight line contains in it the two component motions into which we may choose to resolve it; 7 *is* not 4 + 3, but certainly it admits of those figures being substituted for it for purposes of calculation. We may interpret these phrases into more definite language; all the processes which we go through in the framing of conceptions, in classification, in our logical constructions, are subjective movements of our thought and not processes which take place in things; but at the same time the nature of those things, of the given thinkable contents, is so constituted, that thought by surrendering itself to the logical laws of these movements of its own, finds itself at the end of its journey if pursued in obedience to those laws, coinciding with the actual course of the things themselves. The paths however which it can pursue with equal prospect of success in passing from one element of its content to another, are many and not one; in countless directions the world of possible ideas extends and is knit together, a diversely articulated system of coherent connected series, and thought when it moves from one member in the system to another, choosing its path at pleasure but always observing its own laws, resembles in some sense a melody whose course we cannot predict yet which strikes always definite intervals in the scale each with its determinate harmonic relations.

343. When we come to the *judgment* we find that not only its logical form but its content for knowledge which is expressed through that form has in itself no direct Real significance. We give utterance to the categorical propositions 'This tree blossoms,' 'Atmospheric air is a permanent gas,' 'Every triangle has its angles equal to two right angles.' In the first case it is merely thanks to the subject-matter of the proposition that we are able to ascribe to the tree an existence which really is independent of the temporary condition of blossoming, that is to say that the subject and the predicate are actually related and separated as we divide and connect them in the form of the judgment.

In the two other cases this separation is not to be found in the thing itself, it is a purely subjective movement of thought arbitrarily selecting one particular constituent in a whole which is really a unity, to be made the object of separate attention. The differences in the copula again in the three propositions are due merely to the imagination, which adapts itself to the peculiarities of each separate subject-matter, and finds an expression for them in language; logic itself testifies by representing all judgments under the symbolic form S is P, that in the uniform copula 'is' all objective distinctions in the connexion between S and P are obliterated. They may be related as whole and part, as a thing to its transient states, or as cause to effect; in the form of the judgment they appear solely as subject and predicate, two terms which denote merely the relative positions which the ideas of them assume in the subjective movement of our thought, and tell us nothing as to the objective relation in itself which *if* it becomes an object of thought compels the ideas to assume those positions in our thoughts. Once more, in Hypothetical judgments we do indeed appeal to an objective relation of this sort, but in the form of the judgment we neither express it nor make it intelligible. The conjunction of antecedent and consequent in the form, 'If B is true F is true,' in itself affirms no more than the proposition that B and F belong both together and in some way not defined to a single notion M. The fact that we notwithstanding divide this coherent unity and place one part of the notion in front of the other, so that by reason of the inseparable connexion between the two, the one becomes antecedent, the other consequent,—all this is once more simply one of those subjective movements of thought which do *not* take place in the content of the notion. And this subjective character of the movement is shown by the fact that we have it in our power to reverse its direction. We say, 'Every equilateral triangle is equiangular,' or 'If a triangle is equilateral it is equiangular,' but we might say equally well 'If it is equiangular it is equilateral.' That which constitutes the objective content here is the undivided thought or the intuition of the equilateral and equiangular triangle; the two constitutive elements, equality of sides and equality of angles, are simultaneously present in it, but thought taking an arbitrary starting-point at one or the other moves up and down between them dividing and uniting in its own fashion. This holds of all judgments which like those of mathematics are occupied with the ideal and not with the actual. They would all admit of simple conversion, if their expressions in language through the medium of propositions allowed of all the conceptions which occur in them being as precisely defined as is the case in the form of the equation.

If on the other hand our hypothetical judgments relate to data of reality, in such cases our intention is certainly that the antecedent and the consequent are to be taken as not interchangeable, but the hypothetical form of the judgment does not in itself express the condition which makes that assumption true. For given the antecedent B there is logically no interval left which separates its validity from that of the consequent F; the two together constitute, in perfect accord with that which the hypothetical form of judgment itself affirms as its result, a single process M which can be expressed in a judgment. And further inasmuch as if we take our conception accurately, leaving nothing out and adding nothing to it, no F^1 can be connected with our B but F only, and no B^1 with F but B only, it follows that we pass in thought with equal right and necessity from either of the two starting-points taken at pleasure, to the other, from B to F just as much as from F to B; we know the consequent from the antecedent and the antecedent from the consequent. That in actual fact there is here some circumstance which makes B and B alone the *Antecedens*, and F and F alone the *Consequens*, we are very well aware, because we are acquainted with the subject-matter under consideration, but it receives no expression through the form of our logical act. For that form depends upon nothing more than the abstract notion that F is in a general sense *conditioned* by B; but this, a mere abstract relation, is as shown already, something less than anything that we obtain in reality between B and F as things or events. A relation through which B and B only is to be the antecedent, and to be a real antecedent, can only actually obtain if B is cause and F effect; but in the hypothetical judgment instead of this real and specific relation of causality we have nothing but the vague and general relation of conditioning in the abstract, which thus has no significance for reality whatever.

Finally Disjunctive judgments do not even purport to express any reality at all; the process of wavering undecided between several mutually exclusive predicates can answer to no process in the real world; it remains a state of our thinking, to which the adequate data for the knowledge of reality are lacking.

344. A brief consideration of the various forms of Syllogism leads us to similar results. We shall be most readily disposed to ascribe a Real significance to those Figures of Subsumption which arrive at their conclusions by bringing the particular under the universal, for this subordination we do certainly regard in the sense already sufficiently explained as a notion which possesses an objective validity in relation to everything that can be presented to the mind as an idea.

Still here also the logical form of the argument does not correspond to anything that takes place. In mathematical syllogisms the universal major premiss, from which we derive our more particular conclusion, has no priority of truth as compared with the conclusion or with the minor premiss; all three are parts of one eternal truth, all possess a simultaneous validity. The priority of greater simplicity or more immediate evidence the major premiss may indeed possess, but both the one predicate and the other would belong to it in relation to our thought only, without giving it any superiority in itself over other propositions of equal certainty. Lastly there is nothing in the form of inference by Subsumption which obliges it to start from a major premiss of this simple character at all; on the contrary the simultaneity of the connexion which obtains between the entire body of mathematical truths allows the simpler among them to be derived as limiting cases from a logical connexion of less simple, no less than the other way, and always in this figure of Subsumption.

This purely subjective significance of the form of the syllogism we sometimes forget in applying it to matters of fact. So long indeed as the universal major expresses a highly concrete and specific truth, when for instance we say 'All animals breathe,' we never question that such a major premiss cannot designate any reality which is prior to the validity of the conclusion 'Fishes breathe,' anywhere but in our thought. Yet when we turn to the most universal principles of the system of things, the impulse comes back upon us to give to the expression of those principles, the most universal laws of nature, which present themselves as major premises in our enquiries into the order of the world, a real priority, which is in fact wholly inconceivable, to the processes in which they are to hold good. This impulse is not without danger to the soundness and consistency of our metaphysical theories; it leads to a superstition which has far reaching consequences, that the reality of the world may be derived from something which is unreal and which is ye essential and possessed of a regulative power, whereas on the contrary we have thoroughly to convince ourselves that all necessary truths, to which we imagine that we can subordinate the existent as if it were something merely secondary and additional, are simply the nature and self-consistency of the existent itself, and are only disengaged from it by a reflective act of thought and credited accordingly with a prior and regulative character to which they have no claim.

Inferences by Induction do not give occasion to this sort of misunderstanding; no one fails to see that the synthesis of particular facts in a general, not merely a universal[1], proposition is not the real ground of the validity of the general proposition but only of our apprehension of that validity. Still more convincingly does the variety of forms, which a Proof may assume, witness to the merely subjective significance of the several inferences of which it is made up. How many different proofs, direct and indirect, progressive and retrogressive, all equally adequate, may be given for one and the same proposition! How many even in the form of direct progressive argument alone! And supposing that in fact one out of the many could possess the prerogative of alone exhibiting the essence and actual structure of the thing, still the mere fact that other forms of proof are possible would always show that it is not the logical Form by itself which occasions or expresses the Real validity of this particular form of proof, but that its superiority over other forms of proof lies in the content which we have taken and conjoined in this form. Lastly in regard to the final operations of thought with the account of which the doctrine of pure Logic concluded, we saw there that Logic does in those operations strive to discover some Forms in which the proper essence of the thing, as distinguished from our mere subjective and haphazard notions about it, may be exhibited. But there too we come to the conclusion that those Forms turn out to be far wider than that which they purport to contain. If the proper essence of the thing does make its way into our thought, it can only be apprehended under these Forms, but the Forms do not create it and do not fully express it; they admit always of fresh applications which issue as we are ourselves conscious in merely subjective notions, and from among which the

---

[1] [See § 68, sup.]

selection of the more trustworthy in relation to reality cannot be made by the help of Logic but only through knowledge of the subject-matter, if such knowledge is forthcoming.

345. It is now time to determine more exactly the meaning of certain expressions in the use of which I have hitherto been somewhat less precise. We have spoken of Subjective and Objective, of Formal and Material[1], of Formal and Real significance, as applied to the Forms of Thought. The three pairs of antitheses do not coincide. If we distinguish, as we have done, between the logical act of thinking, and the thought which it creates as its product, the former can claim only a *Subjective* significance; it is purely and simply an inner movement of our own minds, which is made necessary to us by reason of the constitution of our nature and of our place in the world, and through which we make that Thought, for instance the distinction which exists between a and b, or the universal C which is contained in them both, an object for our own consciousness. In the same way every one who desires to enjoy the prospect from a hilltop has to traverse some particular straight or winding path from the point at which he starts up to the summit which discloses the view; this path itself is not part of the view which he wishes to obtain. The Thought itself on the other hand in which the process of thinking issues, the prospect obtained, has *Objective* validity; the various paths followed by various travellers once traversed and left behind, the scene which opens before them is the same to all alike, an object independent of the subjectivity of the individual; it is not merely one more affection of his consciousness which he experiences, but an object presented to his thought which also presents itself as the same self-identical object to the consciousness of others.

The second antithesis[2] throws light on the same state of facts from another side. It would not be sufficient to call

[1] ['Sachlich,' opp. to 'formal.']   [2] ['Formal' and 'sachlich.']

the operations of our thought Subjective and nothing more. The term would simply separate them from that which actually goes on in the object-matter[1] with which they deal, leaving it quite obscure what the relation is in which they stand to it; yet after all some such relation there must be, if the Logical Thought in which they issue, is to possess an Objective validity which does not belong to the thinking act which issues in it. Accordingly we call the logical operations not Subjective *merely* but *Formal* because their characteristics though not the actual determinations of the matter they deal with[2], yet on the other hand are Forms of procedure the very purpose of which is to apprehend the nature of that subject-matter, and which therefore cannot stand altogether out of connexion with that which there has place.

Upon this point the illustrations adduced above will remove all uncertainty. The limitation to a *merely* Formal validity showed itself in the fact that there may be several processes of thought equally successful in view of the result arrived at, all, that is, leading to the same final thought-product, or the same material result. No one of them therefore can have an exclusive significance as regards that determinate matter and content with which all are equally concerned; all alike are merely forms of procedure, employed to reach a certain result which once obtained is valid independently of the path which led to it. But clearly it would be impossible to arrive by all these different paths at the summit from which this prospect opens, if they were not all included with their determinate positions and relations the one to the other within that same geographical territory, the remaining part of which is what constitutes the landscape which is commanded from the summit. Herein consists the positive element which this second antithesis affirms of the processes of thought[3]; each is one

[1] ['Von dem Verhalten der Sachen.']   [2] ('Der Sachen.']
[3] [They are not merely 'subjective' but also 'formal.']

among the various ways in which the variously ramifying systems of the world of fact make it possible for us, by reason of its universal interconnexion, to arrive by a process of movement from point to point within that world, at a determinate objective relation, although the particular movement chosen neither is nor yet copies the way in which *this* relation itself arose or now obtains.

The third antithesis[1] is not merely another way of expressing the second; it relates to a specific question. We regard every content of thought as having a material value[2] if it has a fixed Objective significance in the sense above explained—ideas of the non-existent no less than of the existent; by the term *Real*[3] we should have to understand only things and events in so far as they exist and occur in an actual world of their own beyond thought. Now it is out of the question that this kind of Reality should move and have its being in the forms of the Concept, of the Judgment or of the Syllogism, which our thought assumes in its own subjective efforts towards the knowledge of that reality. But even the logical thoughts which are the issue of those operations have not in relation to Reality in this sense the immediate and material validity which belonged to them in relation to every content of thought as such. It will be better to reserve for the Metaphysic[4] the fuller discussion of this important point; a reference to the illustrations already adduced will suffice in the way of a preliminary elucidation.

We saw that the notion of a condition is inadequate to denote that which we mean by a relation which subsists in actual fact between two real elements; so to subsist, it would have to be more than a relation, it would have to be nothing less than interaction. This being so, it was in that Real connexion between the Real elements that the cause resided which brought their phenomenal appearances for us

---

[1] [In German 'Formal' and 'Real.'] [2] ['Sachlich gegeben.']
[3] [German 'Real.'] [4] [See 'Metaphysic,' § 81.]

into that particular formal relation which we now, employing a merely logical term, *call* a conditioning of one by the other.

The same is true of all logical Forms. No real S can be subject and nothing more to a real P, which is its predicate and nothing more; in actual fact P can only attach to S either as a state which it passes through, or as an influence which it exerts, or finally as a permanent quality which belongs to it in the sense (a sense it is true at present somewhat obscure) in which we contrast the metaphysical notion of a Quality with the merely logical notion of a Mark. It is not till one of *these* three relations has been affirmed that we understand what the meaning is *realiter* of the logical conception of S as subject and P as predicate. It is not till then that we have an actual state of things answering to the logical copula, which in itself leaves it quite undetermined what precisely we are affirming to have occurred to the real things in question, when we feel ourselves necessitated thus to connect the ideas of them. When then we employ such expressions as unity, multiplicity, equality, contrariety, relation, condition, so long as we use those terms by themselves, we have said absolutely nothing about the existent. We have still to show how it is brought about that the unity of the One is proved to be an actual reality, not merely a barren logical title; how it is that what are many but identical, although in thought they simply are identical, nevertheless in real existence break up and become many; what is the one kind of reciprocal influence in which the opposition, what is the other kind of reciprocal influence in which the relation, of different existing things, shows itself to be real.

CHAPTER V.

The a priori truths.

346. LET us put together once more the conclusions to which we have been brought. Neither in the content of our ideas nor yet in the reality which we regard as its source outside, was there anything to correspond to the logical processes of thought, which choosing their path at will, connected or separated the several constituent elements of which that content was composed. On the other hand, at least in relation to this content, without regard to that reality which may be its cause in the world outside, the Thought-product, in which it was the aim of the Thought-processes to issue, had, we saw, an objective significance. The differences, the resemblances, the contrasts, the subordinations, of which we could only possess ourselves in consciousness by help of the discursive activity of Thought, passing backwards and forwards from point to point, had we saw an actual *validity* as applied to the apprehended content, although the content itself in no way participated in such movements. They subsist, as we saw, independently and objectively in the sense in which any other relation may subsist between the terms related. Real existence, that is to say, they can never claim except at the moments in which they are thought; but on the other hand, such is the common constitution of all minds, that whenever the given terms of the relation a and b are thought, one and the same judgment C affirming this relation between them is immediately and invariably pronounced.

We are here brought back to the Platonic world of Ideas. All contents of possible ideas stand in fixed and unalterable relations, and by whatever processes or movements of thought, as our own pleasure or as chance determines, we may carry our attention from one to another, or in whatever order they may be one after another brought to our perception by occasioning causes even unknown to ourselves,—we shall invariably find the same relations obtaining amongst them which are given us once for all in the objective and endlessly complex structure of the world of Ideas.—So often as this proposition is insisted on it will be regarded as an entirely superfluous affirmation of that which is perfectly self-evident, and just as often I must repeat that the very existence of this self-evidence is the most astonishing thing in the world. Although an indispensable foundation of all thought, and just on that account passed over by us in our presumption as a mere matter of course, it is not even, as I observed before, a necessity of thought in the sense in which that character may be claimed for the particular relations which it includes within it. We cannot indeed fully realise in thought what the state of things would be if this fact were wanting, but still we can imagine a world in which it did *not* obtain; in which countless contents presented themselves for our minds to form ideas of, but each one standing in no relation to the rest, all so entirely disparate in nature that no two of them could be combined as allied species under any common universal, nor any two of them be pronounced to differ from each other more or less or otherwise than any other two. One postulate alone, in such case, Thought would be in a position to make, in obedience to its own law of Identity, namely, that each one of the contents must be identical with itself. This postulate would be the condition of their being presented to thought at all, and it might be fulfilled by such a world as I am supposing. But beyond this we cannot go. Thought may wish, in order to the possibility of its further operations, but it cannot demand as a necessity of thought, that between the different objects there should be found that graduated scale of affinities which alone enables it to accomplish the ends after which it strives,—it is not a necessity of thought that thought itself should be possible. And even supposing that by its own intrinsic power it could postulate those affinities, still it could not make them; it would always have to trust to their being given it by the grace of facts, ordered and arranged on principles which it could never have itself contrived, as series of tones or colours, or as differences in degree among things qualitatively the same, or in any other way.

But strange and important as is the fact that such affinities in the world of experience are actually found, it is not in this fact or in the consequences which follow from it, that the final goal of our enquiries lies. All that it guarantees us is the security with which thought is able to move within the world of ideas as such, to investigate the systematic and invariable connexions obtaining among the elements of that world, and by conjoining them one with another to construct new forms which will be found without fail in another and a predictable place in the world of ideas, so connected, finally, one and all together in various directions and at fixed distances, that the most diverse and the most roundabout tracks of thought may lead to the certain discovery of any one of them. This however by itself is not all that we are concerned to know. What we want to arrive at is the significance which is to be attached to this systematic arrangement of the world of knowledge in relation to that empirical and unsystematic order of events, in which a causal reality independent of thought presents contents of possible ideas to our perception. What we wish to understand is not only the classification of things which is eternal, but also the course of things which is in change.

347. The two are completely distinct. Perception does not present those objects to us in connexion which stand side by side as akin in the system of knowledge, nor is its entire history a periodically recurring procession of orders, genera, and species, following one upon the other in a descending scale as they do in the order of classification. Contemporaneous in different points in space, succeeding one another at different points of time, we find the most heterogeneous elements of that realm of contents phenomenally connected; if laws in this scene of change there are, they are of a different kind altogether from the logical laws which have hitherto been engaging our attention. If we agree henceforth to designate the empirical course of phenomena as it is thus presented to us, Actual Reality[1], then the question is as to the significance which our thought can claim in relation to it, since its affirmations even though retaining their validity, seem nevertheless to be incapable of controlling the order of connexion which the reality presents. For even supposing it to be true that a and b will exhibit, when given in actual perception, the same distinction and the same affinity which belong to them in our thought, still this tells us nothing as to whether they will actually be found in conjunction in perception, or whether that conjunction may not be an impossibility. Admitting the law of identity to hold without exception, still it does not profess to do more than affirm that now and always every $a=a$, and every $b=b$, *whenever* and *wherever* they may be found. But here at once the last clause is no longer part of the law of identity itself; we append it because we know on other grounds that possible objects of thought are susceptible, over and above their eternal validity in the world of ideas, of an alternation of temporal reality and unreality in the world of phenomena. Of this the law

[1] ['Reale Wirklichkeit.']

in question contains no indication, and cannot therefore in the least determine the order in which in that world whether in the way of simultaneity or succession, the two phenomena necessarily introduce or necessarily exclude one another. Again, the classifications by which we range our conceptions one under the other will be valid equally of our perceptions and of the timeless content of our ideas; but when we bring a perceived object S under the general conception M, although all the higher universal conceptions NLK which are contained in M are now valid of S too, still this deduction gives us no new objective knowledge, but only a logical analysis of what was already implied in bringing S under M,—correct if this was correct, incorrect if the contrary, but in neither case enabling us to combine the S given in the perception with a P which has not been so given.

Hypothetical judgments seem better adapted to an extension of knowledge. In so far as they apply to a subject S a condition x, and derive from the two together a predicate P, which was not already contained either in S or in x by themselves, they make at least a formal approach to that which we conceive to take place in reality. In the problematic antecedent they express the connexion of S and x as a possibility, and accordingly distinguish the thought content of it from the realisation which may be in store for that content in the actual course of events, and as to which they abstain from affirming anything. On the other hand, that condition once given, they do seem to anticipate the after perception and to define the new result which will necessarily follow in this perception. But now what is it that justifies us in subjoining to, or equating with a determinate $S+x$ a determinate P? In thought it can rest only on this, that by means of a logical determination x we transform the notion S, which previously did not contain P, in such wise that now it does contain it; and now it is of this new subject, not of the one we began with, that we affirm the predicate P, which in fact we have already taken into it. But that which is directly presented to us in perception is something different from this. When in actual perception a new phenomenon x enters into relation to a previous phenomenon S, what happens as a rule is not that from the conjunction of the two in thought there results the subject $S+x$, from which thereupon the resultant phenomenon P would follow as a matter of course as if they were equivalent expressions. On the contrary the question has still to be solved, how it is possible for x so to transform S, that there may spring from it the conditions for the realisation of P which were before wanting. Thus, wherever we apply hypothetical judgments to questions of the real world, they are always found to rest in the last resort upon certain presuppositions. They always assume the validity of certain propositions affirming the connexion of a particular condition with a particular consequence—a connexion which cannot be deduced from conceptions—to be a universal fact. If it is really universal, then thought can draw it out into its particular instances by a purely analytic procedure, but its real content appears, to begin with, as a synthetical judgment, which binds together as subject and predicate two conceptions, the contents of which mere logical analysis can never prove to be identical.

348. Our hope then of mastering by thought the course of events in the real world, rests on three points. First, to no single constituent b of the ideal world can thought ascribe, over and above the eternal validity which within that world belongs to it, a necessity of realisation in the order of events in time; it is only if this reality belongs as a matter of fact to a second such element a, with which b stands in necessary connexion, that it can then pass over to b also. All our knowledge therefore is in this respect hypothetical; it strikes in at a particular point in a reality which it finds as a matter of fact given to it, in order to deduce from this real premiss as themselves *real* the consequences which attached to the thought premiss as *necessary*; but it is never possible, starting from mere conceptions of thought, to prove the actual reality of that which is contained in them. And in fact the attempt has never been ventured upon except in the single instance of the ontological argument for the being of God. The temptation in this case was very intelligible. The conception of God as a necessary consequence *b* following from a reality *a* other than Himself, and given in perception, contradicted our necessary idea of Him, for this very idea demanded that He should be conceived as the ground of all consequences. Hence, it seemed, nothing remained but to seek the reality of God in the idea itself of Him. True all that could really be found was the *claim* to reality which the idea carried with it. Beyond question the idea of God includes the idea of Being, and more than this, the idea of living Being; for all other predicates by which we think of God as God, can only be unified, or even thought, when they are conceived as belonging to a real Being who fills time, and is capable of undergoing a change of states. But in this sense the idea of any being whatever includes the thought of that particular kind of reality which the nature and the mode of combination of its content require. The very notion of an organism is unthinkable without this assumption; the properties of nutrition, growth, propagation of its kind, have no meaning when applied to a subject which does not exist, and just as little when applied to one which exists merely and has no faculty of development. If therefore the objects of our conception are to have reality at all, they must have that kind of reality which answers to their nature, Beings that of existence not of occurrence, Events that of occurrence not of existence, Relations neither the one nor the other, but a reality which consists in being valid of reality. It was a mere illusion to suppose that the case was different with the idea of God, and that it was allowable to look upon that notion of the highest reality which is necessarily included in that idea as equivalent to the reality of the whole content which included it.

A class of arguments nearly allied to this, which pass from the incontestable *value* of an object of thought to the belief in its reality, have an appearance of committing a fallacy of the same kind, but in this case it is an appearance only. It is not altogether just to maintain that we believe in a supreme Good, in a life beyond the earth, in eternal blessedness, merely because we desire them. In reality such beliefs rest upon an extremely broad, though an un-analysed foundation of perception. They start from the fact of this actual world as it is given us in experience, in which we find certain intolerable contradictions threatening us if we refuse to acknowledge that these ways in which the structure of the world extends beyond our perception are real complements of that which we perceive. In form, therefore, this class of inferences is quite legitimate; starting from the reality of *a* as given in experience, they connect with it the reality of *b* which is not so given, but which appears to follow from *a* as a necessity of thought.

349. The second point alluded to is tacitly assumed in every argument, but seldom explicitly acknowledged as a necessary logical assumption. Clearly we could never hope to work upon reality through the medium of thought, if we were not in a position to assume in the empirical order of things the presence of universal law, which alone makes it possible for us to turn the formal laws of our thought to positive use. We saw that the real causes which determine the succession of our perceptions of possible contents of thought are wholly independent of the systematic relations which we find between those contents when regarded as objects of thought simply. Whence then do we derive our assurance that there are reasons of universal validity at all determining this order of succession, and that the unknown cause of the experienced series of our perceptions is not simply playing with the elements of our Ideal world and its systematic classifications, itself void of all principle, bringing before us like a self-acting kaleidoscope now one arrangement of the picture and now another, but observing no law or order in its combinations?

We have no ground whatever for representing the wild disorder which this supposition implies as unimaginable; there is a very great deal in the empirical world which we do not yet understand, that actually does still so appear to us; if throughout the world of reality all regular law and regular relations were altogether absent, all we can say is that the same spectacle would then be presented to us everywhere which meets us now in cases where the laws are concealed from us. The laws of our thought would still hold good, but in the sense of an empty postulate, to which reality would offer no counterpart, just as there are many events even now to which we seek in vain to apply them, events which seem with their like conditions and unlike results to mock at our principle of identity. Nevertheless this assumption of an independence of law in the real world is maintained by no one; in every case where observed phenomena might seem to force it upon us, we regard the state of facts so presented as simply a problem which awaits solution, and we never doubt that a wider experience will furnish links of connexion hitherto unobserved to restore order and regularity to the observed parts in which at present they are not to be found.

Now on what does this confidence rest? The universality of laws in the real world is neither in itself a necessity of thought, nor can it be deduced as a necessary consequence from given facts. We might have the right to say that the laws of space, even supposing space to exist only as an innate intuition in us, still must of necessity hold good of all objects of our experience, for nothing will ever make its way into experience without having been already moulded in that form of space through which alone it becomes an object for us at all. But we cannot attempt to prove in the same way that unless there was a connexion according to law in the real world the experience which we possess would be impossible. That which we actually possess is merely a succession of ideas; that this succession constitutes an unbroken connexion in accordance with universal laws, that is to say that experience in this heightened sense, as distinguished from mere perception, is also actually given us,—to affirm this is to confuse that which we know as a fact with preconceptions of our own which we bring to the facts. For our actual knowledge amounts to no more than this, that a large number of occurrences admit of being regarded *as if* they were conditioned by universal laws; there remains always a far larger number which we have not yet succeeded in thus reducing to order. A reign of law embracing all reality, and admitting of no exception to its rules, is therefore neither an actual nor a possible outcome of experience, but only an assumption with which every enlargement of our experience is accompanied.

We have therefore only two alternatives. Either we may acknowledge this assumption as an assumption and trust it, and thus credit ourselves with this one piece of certain knowledge, by the help of which our thought, crossing the boundary of its own domain, reaches one certain result as to the nature of reality; or we may look upon it equally as a mere assumption, and on that account *distrust* it, accepting thankfully such instances as confirm it, but always bearing in mind the possibility of finding ourselves stumbling at any moment upon ground where it no longer holds good. Whenever human reflexion has reached the point of a scientific view of the external world, it has without exception preferred the first of these two alternatives. Even those who are most careful to resist any undue encroachments of reason, and pride themselves on interrogating nature and nature only as to her own laws, never question the fact that such laws do universally obtain, they only insist that we know nothing about them. Only they do not observe, that in thus affirming the universality of law they are passing beyond the data of reality, and are making in one clause an *a priori* assertion about it which the next declares to be illegitimate.

The alternative theory may be thought to be discoverable in one particular instance, the belief in the freedom of the human will. As to the material rights and wrongs of this hypothesis, I am not here called upon to decide. But with regard to its form, it is only in appearance that it comes under the point of view in question. It does not assert that the same thing is free at one time and conditioned at another without any reason. On the contrary, subjecting as it does one sphere of reality permanently and without exception to determination by fixed laws, and connecting the fact of freedom exclusively with the presence of a particular spiritual nature in the subject which wills, it does in fact assume that the system of the world is throughout a system of law, and merely ascribes to it the peculiar property of admitting at particular points in its course of the entrance of unconditioned elements, which once admitted into the world of reality thenceforth produce results which are conditioned by law. This theory also then, and more clearly still any theory which, denying freedom, brings the inner world as well as the outer under a system of determinate laws, permits itself in so doing to make an *a priori* affirmation concerning the real world, the universal validity of which experience as such can never prove. Whether it is justified in so doing, can never be decided by strict logical argument, for every attempt to prove this affirmation a necessity of *thought*, would leave the question of its validity as applied to the real world undecided. On the other hand, to attempt to exhibit it as agreeing with the nature of reality, would only be to repeat in a new form the old claim which it is desired to establish, the claim to be able to make *a priori*, that is to say *universal* statements on the authority of thought alone, about that real world, of which experience can never give us universal knowledge. We have therefore the right to say that all our conclusions concerning the real world rest upon the immediate confidence or the *faith* which we repose in the universal validity of a certain postulate of thought, which oversteps the limits of the special world of thought. In point of fact this confidence which logic can never justify lies at the foundation of all logic, as it does also of that formula in which we described it as the universal tendency of thought to turn the observed fact of co-existence into coherent connexion. The methods of applied logic one and all have a meaning only on the assumption that that inward coherence and connectedness which this tendency ascribes to the real world does actually belong to it. To suppose it otherwise would be to cut away the logical standing-ground on which induction relies whenever it pronounces one inference drawn from experience to be even more *probable* than another; it would have to be content with rehearsing the premises, the conclusion would be wanting.

350. There remains the third question. The assumption of a connected system of uniform laws embracing all reality does not by itself teach us what the particular laws are, in accordance with which a definite event b is conjoined with another event a. Further we have already satisfied ourselves that the mere analysis of the contents of the notions of a and b as such could never enable us to affirm that the realisation of the one must necessarily be followed by that of the other. Two courses remain open to us: either to lay claim to an immediate certainty of the universal and necessary validity of synthetic judgments which nevertheless demand such a connexion, or else to content ourselves with extracting all the particular laws of reality one by one from the evidence of experience by the help of the methods expounded in the last book. At this parting of the ways I wish by one general formula of ready worship to purchase a dispensation from any further glorification of the second of these two alternatives. It becomes in time wearisome to be told over and over again in endless iteration, how reason is to come to nature in a spirit of self-renunciation, how indeed from her own resources alone she cannot possibly decide a single question, and how she at once wanders off into a world of brain-spun phantasies if she does not at every step apply to experience for her *data*. Unhappily we cannot affirm that such warnings are superfluous, or that they are nowhere applicable, for errors enough have been due to the neglect of them. Still any moral sermon becomes intolerable if it goes on for ever, and at last its only effect is that it moves us, as we are moved here, to ask the question whether the claims which the doctrine advocated holds up for our acceptance are not just as one-sided as confessedly those are which it undertakes to disprove. Can then, we ask, the purely empirical investigation of the laws of the actual world really solve its problem entirely from its own resources, calling in perhaps the aid of the law of identity, but otherwise without making assumption of any synthetic judgments *a priori*? That it cannot do this, was the doctrine of Kant; if we arrive at a similar conclusion, we shall be championing a characteristic tenet of German philosophy, which has brought on us assaults from all nations.

351. English scepticism in the person of Hume endeavoured to restrict us on the one hand to the expression of mathematical truths, which appeared to Hume to rest simply upon the principle of identity, and on the other to the narration of the facts of history, which having once occurred are thenceforth matter of actual experience, and

can be expressed in synthetic judgments *a posteriori*. No scientific inference was possible, he thought, which should predict the occurrence of a *b* in the future on the strength of a given *a* which was not identical with it.

Before I go on to discuss the last-named contention, it may be useful to point out, that if it is valid, then the previous contentions made with regard to mathematical and to historical truths cannot be. The possibility of synthetic judgments *a posteriori* is a point which does not sufficiently arouse our suspicions, because they are taken for simple expressions of experience, into which no admixture of too forward thought has made its way. But so long as they are judgments at all, no matter whether expressed in language or not, they are still not the facts given simply, but a preparation of the facts, made by reading into them an inner connexion which in immediate observation is not to be found. No narration of an event is possible except by combining together as subject and predicate one portion of the sensuous images which arose in us when we witnessed it, with another, and then going on to think in between the contents of these two conceptions a relation of action exerted on one side and received on the other, or again of mutual alteration of states, none of which relations are in the least degree given in the perceptions as such.

It may be contended that the proposition Cæsar crossed the Rubicon, means no more than that a certain partially changeable, but still coherent group of sensible impressions, which for shortness we call Cæsar, changed its position in space in relation to a second group of sensible impressions, which we call the Rubicon, in such wise as to be perceived by one and the same spectator first to the right of the latter group and then to its left. I answer with no less obstinacy: that this group was the same group on the left as on the right, that is to say that it has changed *its* position,—this does not lie in the simple data of observation, but is a hypothesis which covertly introduces under a connected and continuous alteration of the appearance a permanent substratum with merely changing relations. Whenever in recounting an event we speak of any sort of movement in space, we are giving not our perception, but a hypothesis about it. That one and the same real a^1 passed through one after the other the places m, n, p, is not a fact we have seen; the fact perceived is only that in successive points of time similar appearances a were observable in successive points of space. One who was under no necessity to explain this fact to himself by the hypothesis of a permanent subject, could not venture to affirm the proposition 'a has moved,' as a description of the facts, but merely as a convenient mode of expression, having in relation to fact no significance whatever. If he denies himself this introduction of certain points of view into the interpretation of the content of perception, then he must acknowledge all synthetic judgments *a posteriori*, all judgments indeed of whatever kind, to be inadmissible, and instead of a recounting of past facts there remains in truth merely the possibility of recalling in memory a series of perceptions, a reproduction of the raw material, out of which judgments might be formed, if only such a proceeding were allowable.

352. Turning to the question of the discovery of mathematical truth, we shall not dispute the validity nor yet the importance of the principle of Identity, but we must dispute its fruitfulness; we must insist that if it were the only principle we had to start from, mathematical truth could never be discovered at all. It is no doubt true that in any proposition affirming equality or inequality, $a = b$ or $a \gtrless b$, we have always to assume the validity of the principle of identity, according to which $a = a$, and $b = b$, in other words that every quantity which we desire to bring into any relation with other quantities, is identical with itself, for obviously every such comparison of different quantities

[1] ['Dasselbe reale a.']

loses its meaning if the quantities compared may have an unlimited variety of meanings. Here the principle of identity has a validity which is manifest enough and is the necessary security for truths of whatever kind. But it is precisely from this point of view that least attention has in fact been paid to it; that which has been more especially emphasised is that very different application of the principle, by which the two quantities compared are pronounced equal to *each other*. It is in this application of the maxim of identity that philosophers have found not only the guarantee of truth, but when repeated in frequent succession through a long chain of such equations, a fruitful method for its discovery.

I cannot think that either the one of these contentions or the other precisely expresses that which is intended. Equations either as in $\sqrt{4} = 2$ express simply the definite quantitative value which is arrived at by an act of calculation as applied to a given quantity, or else they express the fact as in $\sqrt{ab} = \sqrt{a} \cdot \sqrt{b}$, that certain operations, different in form, applied in a prescribed order of succession or of connexion to any given quantities within defined limits will give identical results. Now in both these cases the value of the entire mathematical process depends not solely upon the discovered equality of the result but rather upon the fact that different paths have led to the same goal, that is to say that it has been found possible to affirm the equality of different things. If I am answered that the quantitative values of the two different terms in the comparison have not been made identical as an after result of that operation but were so always, and that the identity was merely concealed under the different forms in which the two were originally presented, or that the one form of expression merely sets the problem of which the other gives the solution,—such a reply expresses precisely my own view, only that it takes as self-evident that which I cannot regard as being such.

For whence do we derive our confidence in the possibility of one and the same self-identical value being presented under different forms? Certainly not from the law of identity alone; for it contains not the slightest hint of an antithesis between Form and Content or Form and Value; nor supposing that we derived our idea of such an antithesis from some other source, could the law of identity even then tell us anything whatever about it. It could only tell us over again, every Form is identical with itself and every Value with itself. That one and the same Value can be present under different forms, it could never affirm, because it could never fix any limit to the validity of such a proposition except one which would reduce it to a barren tautology. For to the question *what* different forms of expression designate identical values, it could only answer, those in which one and the same identical value is contained.

I need not here enlarge on the fact, that it is in this possibility of affirming the equality of the different, and not in the bare application of the logical law of identity as such, that the motive force of all fruitful reasoning in mathematical science is to be found. We should never get any further, if we could never subsume under the subject of a given major premiss anything but a term absolutely identical with it; we do make progress just because by means of innumerable substitutions, by a process of analysis on the one side and recombination on the other we are able to bring a quantity given us in the form *a* into the form *b*, and thus to subsume it on any occasion under such a major term, as then enables us further by known methods of calculation to give it a predicate which was not deducible from it in its original form. Everything turns therefore on our right to affirm identity of the different, and this right does not follow, at all events as an immediate consequence, from the purport of the law of identity.

353. The remainder of my argument here must be taken in connexion with the considerations which I urged when

dealing with the subject of pure Logic as to the nature of judgments synthetic in form but identical in content. I there made allusions to Kant, who in endeavouring to prove the presence of synthetic judgments *a priori* in all branches of reasoning included under that category the arithmetical judgment $7 + 5 = 12$. My object at that point was to insist on the identity of content which must necessarily obtain in any true proposition between the subject and the predicate taken in their entirety. I was dissatisfied that this point should not have been more expressly insisted on by Kant, but I then reserved the right to revert again to the truth which his doctrine contains (§ 58). Kant held that we could not possibly recognise in the predicate 12 the solution of the problem expressed in the subject $7+5$, without an act of Perception[1]. Perception alone, that is, he insisted, can establish for us that the identity required between the two sides in order to the correctness of the equation is actually the fact. Considered for purposes of illustration, indeed, I think that Kant's example was not happily chosen, because it does not bring the formal difference which exists between the subject and the predicate, and upon which stress ought to be laid, into sufficiently clear prominence. It is true, indeed, that 12 is not merely another name for $7 + 5$, but expresses something quite distinct, viz. that the same quantity which is produced by the addition of 7 and 5 also occupies a place as a definite term in the numerical series between 11 and 13. But then the simplest idea which we can form of that series itself is to conceive it as arising out of repeated additions of the unit, that is to say out of the very same operation through which 7 and 5 themselves were put together. So that we conceive the left side and the right side of the equation equally as a sum of units and we merely analyse, on the left side, into two steps, as the idea of a sum allows us to do, that which on the right we take as a whole.

[1] ['Anschauung.']

On the other hand such a formula as $7+5=4^2-2^2$, though not in fact expressing any more completely than the other that which is essential in Kant's thought, yet would have better illustrated the point that there are various ways by which we may arrive at one and the same quantitative value. For that which all turns upon is in fact nothing more than the assertion which is contained in the sign of addition,—viz. that quantities *can* be summed so as to compose another and a homogeneous quantity; a proposition the importance of which we may once more be tempted to ignore, because it seems to us self-evident and a mere identical proposition defining the nature of numerical quantity as such. And so it undoubtedly is, but how do we arrive at this piece of self-evident knowledge? Not every ideal content will submit to the same operations; we cannot add red and green together and produce blue; the notes c and d do not admit of being summed so as to produce a third note x, such as to stand higher than d in the musical scale by the interval c, just as 12 stands higher than 5 in the series of numbers by 7.

But here the question may be asked in surprise, what does this last remark lead to? Of course, it may be said, mathematical operations can only be applied to quantities, whose nature it is to admit of them, and not, or at all events not immediately, to impressions which are qualitatively different. But this is really to be blind to what lies under our very eyes. This very fact, that there *is* such a thing as quantity to be found in the world of ideas, while yet our thought itself is not bound, on pain of not taking place at all, to be the thought of just these comparable quantities—this very fact is a fact of *immediate perception*, which if it were lacking to us, could be as little supplied through logical operations working on a different set of ideas, as could the conception of qualitative resemblance if the world of ideas presented no comparable impressions of sense such as colours or sounds. The proposition therefore that quantities can be summed is undoubtedly an identical proposition; but that the subject and predicate of that proposition appear as valid in the world of ideas, and that it has quite a different value from the equally identical proposition, all wooden iron is wooden iron,—this does not follow from the principle of Identity. It is not then the bare logical principle of Identity, but the perception of quantity, the peculiar nature of which makes it possible to frame a countless number of propositions in content identical yet in form synthetic, which at once guarantees the truth of arithmetical reasoning and is the source of its fruitfulness.

That which might here be added in the interest of mathematics, I must pass over; with regard to the logical question I confess myself in entire agreement with Kant in a further point, namely in maintaining the pure or *a priori* perception of numerical quantity in the sense of the word *a priori* explained above. It is true that neither the idea of quantity as such, nor the more defined conception of its capability of being summed, nor finally any one arithmetical proposition, ever enters into our consciousness without being occasioned, and the occasion can always be traced in the last resort to an external stimulus. We think them only when we are led in one way or another to frame the idea of numerable objects. But, when the occasion arises, we do not learn that $7 + 5 = 12$ from the content of this perception, in such a way that our knowledge of the truth in question would gain in certainty with every fresh confirmation by subsequent experience; but as a matter of fact the single presentation of the idea $7 + 5$, no matter whether mediated through external perception or not, is sufficient to teach us its identity with the term 12 once for all and as a fact of universal validity. And supposing that we found when we came actually to count external objects in a variety of further instances that our arithmetical proposition was in some cases confirmed and in others not, we should certainly all of us, even the most decided adherents of empirical theories, agree to correct not our arithmetical proposition by our countings but them by it.

354. The case is perhaps still clearer if we turn to geometry. As to Kant's particular instance of a synthetic geometrical proposition, a straight line is the shortest line between two points, I have alleged similar scruples as in the case of his arithmetical example just discussed. Here again the example is not happily chosen, because we have no other direct standard of measurement for the conception of distance which is contained in the predicate 'shortness' but the straight line itself, and thus the proposition suggests before everything else the complete identity of its subject with its predicate. And such identity does undoubtedly, in respect of their content, exist; the proposition would not otherwise be true at all; but once more, how do we establish that identity? By connecting the two points through a something which we say is 'between' them. Now it is clear that this expression does not mean merely that the two points are logically designated as not identical or as merely in some way or other different, for that is equally the case with green and acid, out of which a proposition of this kind could never be formed. Nor again is it merely that they can be compared, for so—again with no such consequence following—can green and red. What it means is that they are connected in a manner completely *sui generis*, which is thinkable and has a meaning to us through an original faculty of spatial perception and so only, and which in the absence of such perception could never be made intelligible to us through any logical operations working on a content of a different kind, and of which, finally, even now when it is familiar to us all, no form of words, unless tacitly implying such spatial perception, can by any possibility give us a clear idea.

Other instances of Kant's are more expressive. Take, he says, the proposition that two straight lines cannot enclose a space, or, therefore, make up a figure, and try to derive it from the conception of straight lines and the number two; or again the proposition that out of three straight lines a figure *can* be formed, and try to deduce this in the same way from the conceptions it contains. Your labour is all in vain, you find yourself driven to have recourse to Perception, as Geometry in fact always does. These words remain true, even though a slight inexactness in the form of expression may offer a handle to controversy. The complete subject, in the second example, to which the predicate of 'forming a triangle' belongs, is not simply 'three straight lines'; the lines must be in the same plane, they must not be parallel, they must admit of being produced at pleasure. Again in the first of the two examples, we have no right to require the impossibility of the closed figure to be deduced from the isolated conceptions of the number two on the one hand and of the straight line on the other; we must begin by representing 'two' as the number of the lines, and the lines themselves as included in the same world of space. If we add these fresh points, the predicate will be seen in both cases, though not in both with equal obviousness, to follow identically from the subject when taken in its full meaning, and so the identity of their contents, which is essential to the truth of the proposition, will be established.

But this mere matter of statement does not alter the question at issue. All these conditions, that the lines must belong to the same plane, must not be parallel, must be capable of being produced, have absolutely no meaning whatever, unless we assume the spatial perception to begin with. It is this and nothing else which is our evidence that anything answering to those expressions is to be met with in the world of ideas, and which alone assigning a thinkable meaning to the complete subjects of the propositions in question, gives a reason in so doing for the predicates identical with their subject, which in each case they contain. These propositions then are undoubtedly identical propositions, although under a synthetic form; but that their full content and the manifold relations contained in it exist, is not due to the principle of Identity. That is to say, it is not by means of the principle of Identity that we can pass from one form of expressing a geometrical fact to another equivalent to it; rather it is the peculiar nature of space which makes it possible for identical facts to be variously expressed. It is upon this fact, and more especially upon the unlimited power we possess of bringing any given figure in space by the help of artificial combinations under fresh mathematical points of view or fresh general ideas, and thus constructing predicates for it, which were not contained in our original conceptions of the figure,—it is upon this fact, and not upon the mere application of the bare principle of Identity as such, that the fruitfulness of geometrical procedure depends.

355. At this point I may expect the criticism that my argument has brought me to a different conclusion from that which it was aiming at. I began I shall be told by maintaining the necessity, in order to any extension of knowledge, or to the discovery of the laws of nature, of synthetic principles *a priori*. And now I am invoking the aid of Perceptions to supply both subject, predicate, and copula of the judgments in which we express those principles, a proceeding which seems after all to amount to no more than the not very helpful proposition, that we cannot think without having some idea of that which is to be the content of our thought; the fact still remains that the object in question is given not *by* thought but *to* thought, in a manner not essentially different from that in which every other object of consciousness is given, namely through experience.

In regard to this last point I repeat once more in one word what I have said already, that all knowledge whatever, whether innate or not, which as a matter of fact whether constantly or upon occasion makes its appearance in the consciousness of any one, is for him in the broader sense of the word, an object of experience. And further we have admitted from the first that no one of the principles which we regard as innate, can be operative in us even in the sense of a major premiss unconsciously followed in our judgments, until an incitation so to follow it comes to us in experience, while it can only become in the full sense an object for our consciousness through a definite act of reflexion upon those applications of it which have already been made unconsciously. In this sense then I have no objection to offer if any one insists on calling the apprehension of *a priori* principles itself an inner experience; I only regard it as a perfectly barren contention. Nor can the controversy between the *a priori* and the empirical view turn on the further point that the latter ascribes to outward that which we would rather attribute to inner experience. For this antithesis simply does not exist; whatever notions we may form about a supposed external world, our experiences can only be of the representations of it in our own minds, of the order and connexion of our own ideas. Upon this point I may be allowed to be brief. In Germany at all events the fallacy which has been imported from abroad does not yet find favour, that by measuring the solid and superficial angles of material forms we can confirm the propositions of geometry, or discover any others than those which we can develope with our eyes shut from relations assumed to exist between mere points of space. We are still aware that such measurements, supposing that we make them, relate directly not to the nature of the bodies which fill the space in question but to properties of the space which they fill; finally that they can only be made at all by the aid of contrivances and methods which are all founded to begin with upon the essential order and regularity of our spatial perception, and that we can never therefore employ the process of measurement to test this our geometrical knowledge by the standard of a knowledge which has a different and independent source, but that so far as we do employ it we are merely bringing a particular case of spatial Perception under the laws of geometrical Perception in general.

Thus the difference between us and our opponents comes back merely to this, that to us the simple principles of geometry, that every straight line may be produced to infinity, that the opposite angles of two straight lines intersecting one another are equal, that the sums of any two adjacent angles are equal,—such principles are to us truths which once presented to thought are valid always; whereas in the view of empirical philosophy each particular apprehension of them must in consistency be regarded as a psychical fact and nothing more, as to which there is no certainty whether it will recur in a similar case or not, and of which therefore universal validity can never be established as true, and can only be established as probable on the strength of the agreement of a very large number of instances in which as a matter of fact it has so recurred.

356. I must once more summarise my position in relation to this point of view. In the first place the contention that every truth of whatever kind requires this test of experience in order to be received as universally valid, would contradict itself. For on the one hand it must itself come under its own rule and by consequence cease to be universal; on the other hand, as we have already seen, without the assumption of the unconditional validity of some absolutely certain principles not drawn from experience the very deliverances of experience itself could be no one more probable than another[1].

On the possibility of an immediate knowledge therefore of *some* universal truth all certain belief depends, that of our opponents no less than our own; the difference between us can only be as to what the truths are which we hold to be accessible to this form of knowledge. But it is self-evident

[1] [§ 330.]

that in the case of truths which are to be recognised immediately as universally valid, their sole credentials must be the clearness and strength with which they force themselves upon consciousness and at once claim recognition without constraining it by any process of proof. Now any one has perfect liberty to allow this claim or to resist it; it is open to every one whether in all honesty to distrust the self-evidence with which this or that object of knowledge presents itself to his consciousness, or to insist (at all events for sophistical purposes) that no self-evidence in the world affords a proof of the truth of the thing evidenced; only in the latter case he must allow that a like vein of sophistry may contest the validity of any process of proof whatever and of his own contention along with the rest.

This sort of idle disputation for disputation's sake we may leave to itself; the former more honest variety of scepticism on the other hand is not without its justification, for undoubtedly that state of repose and peaceful equilibrium of the mind, in which the self-evidence of knowledge, regarded as a psychical fact, consists in the last resort, may also be produced by conjunctions of ideas of by no means universal validity. These false forms of self-evidence we have admitted to exist, and the logical processes have been given through which we seek to free ourselves from such illusions. These processes all resolve themselves into this—by shaping our investigations in various ways, adopting various starting-points and various methods, we arrive at separating from a subject S to which it is our object to ascribe a predicate P, all associated ideas x, not really contained in S but secretly affecting our conception of it, which might create in us the impression that our P which in fact belongs only to $S + x$ is an invariable attribute of S as such. Our method does not always assume the form of a direct proof; the proposition that a straight line may be produced to infinity is too simple to admit of any argument except one which brings us back by a complete tautology to immediate Perception; in other cases again proof will take the apagogic form of a *reductio ad absurdum*, a form of argument which does not deduce the truth of the given proposition from some other acknowledged principle but merely establishes the impossibility of denying it. When this has once been accomplished we regard the proposition in question as a truth of universal validity, needing no empirical confirmation from particular instances in which it is found to hold, but on the contrary standing over against all particular instances as certain *a priori*. We do not deny the possibility that this trust in reason may now and again deceive us; but we should not surrender the presumption in favour of a principle thus arrived at being true merely because it is *possible* to distrust it; we shall hold fast to it until either the results to which it leads involve us in contradictions, or until some other truth becomes plain to us, from which we are able to understand how a proposition now seen to be false came to present the appearance of a self-evident truth.

357. There are various points here which still need elucidation. The terms in which in the Kantian school pure Intuition[1] has been spoken of in contradiction to Thought, have led to its becoming associated with the idea of a peculiar and somewhat mysterious form of *procedure* through which the apprehending mind accomplishes something which is impossible to its discursive thought. The obscurity which attaches in consequence to this idea is due to this, that in fact it is just in the case of Intuition that no sort of procedure consisting of the connecting of various single acts is describable, whereas there is one in the case of Thought. The attitude of Intuition towards its content is that of passive receptivity, and its work is done so com-

---

[1] ['Anschauung.' 'Perception' is usually a better rendering of this word than 'Intuition'; but the latter is preferred in this passage for obvious reasons.]

pletely at a single stroke, that no steps or stages in it can be distinguished or could be described. This must not be misunderstood.

When geometrical intuition teaches us that two straight lines intersecting each other can only have one point common to both, there does undoubtedly take place, regarding the act as a psychical event, a certain succession of ideas, which we might describe if in any particular case it were exactly known to us. We might explain how we first think each of the two straight lines in itself, then place them in the same plane, make them from a parallel position converge, follow each to the point of section and then beyond it,—all this we can describe, but this is not the geometrical intuition itself: so far we have only brought into consciousness all the different points which go to make up the relation in question, and now intuition pronounces on these points of relation, as by a single instantaneous revelation,—the two straight lines can only have one point in common. How this final step is accomplished, the immediate apprehension of the necessary truth which is implied when once all the members of the relation are completely given, is a point upon which certainly at present, and in my judgment no less certainly for ever, any further psychological analysis is impossible. It is only in this sense of absolutely immediate apprehension that I have here employed the term intuition, and it leads me to a further observation as to the meaning of the expression *a priori* as applied by us to intuition.

I have explained before why it is that knowledge must necessarily consist not in the mere passive reception of impressions but in a reaction, the form of which reaction will depend on the nature of the mind which is stirred to it. I did not conceal my agreement with Kant in accounting Spatial Intuition as a form of such reaction, and therefore as *a priori* or innate in the sense in which that term may legitimately be used. For the question before us however this point is of no importance. It is not because the idea of space is innate in us, that we are in a position to frame universal propositions in geometry, which once thought are valid always; if it were at all intelligible without any such hypothesis how the idea of a particular combination of spatial points of relation could arise in us purely through external impressions, still, in presence of such an idea, the immediate apprehension of the universal truth contained in those relations, which is the service of intuition, would be not more inexplicable (though it would be equally inexplicable) and not less possible than if those same points of relation could only be brought into our consciousness by the help of an innate mode of reaction and spontaneity in the mind itself. I therefore reserve the question of the *a priori*, in the sense of the innate character of spatial Intuition, with any further question which may arise out of it, for the Metaphysic, and apply the term *a priori* to spatial intuitions in a restricted sense only, viz. to indicate that they are not derived by a process of induction or summation from particular instances which exhibit them, but are thought to begin with as truths of universal validity, and are thus prior to the particular instances in the sense of being rules by which they are determined.

358. This brings us to the last point which we have here to consider. Philosophers have spoken of pure Intuitions as an innate *possession* of the mind, in terms which could not but lead as a natural deduction to the idea that all truth which rests upon any such intuition is also an intellectual treasure always at hand, which we take with us to experience, and through which we judge it. And in fact Locke made use of this deduction as an argument against the doctrine of innate Ideas. It needs however only a brief consideration to see that such a deduction is illegitimate. Every one who speaks of innate knowledge includes in it most certainly mathematical truth, but mathematical truths had all to be discovered before they were known, and the universally innate possession of a spatial intuition was not the same thing as the possession of a knowledge of geometry. But the most elementary of these truths were discovered as soon as ever the mind was drawn to turn its attention away from the infinite variety of figures presented by bodies in space which surround us in the world of perception, to the simplest relations which are contained in all of them alike. Then at once the truth of each several principle one by one sprang to light self-evident and self-proved, just as Plato so admirably represents it in the Meno, only that it was superfluous to refer us to a previous state of existence from the memory of which this sudden emergence of knowledge was supposed to come, inasmuch as there also the *conviction* of the certainty and necessity of the truths which there were given to intuition in a universal form could only have arisen in the mind through the same immediate act of apprehension by which in our life here we recognise it in particular instances.

It is still easier to understand how it is that the more complicated mathematical relations should have had to wait for their discovery, and that an immense tract of ground should always remain before us, in which new discoveries are to be made. The consequences which follow from simple mathematical principles become science only by being deduced from them by reflexion, and this operation involves a labour of a most extended and constantly progressive character, the application of processes of exact definition, of analysis into varied elements, of synthesis into well-defined forms, to abstractions made by the mind itself, and this in order to establish even the subjects of the propositions required, the predicates being obtained, it may be, by processes no less elaborate.

Paradoxical therefore as it may seem we must disabuse ourselves of the false idea that the world of the self-evident lies of itself plain in its self-evidence before us, and that all we have to do is by the help of this comfortable possession of a self-evident truth to go on to subdue the intractable world of our perceptions. The fact is that even universal truths, for the apprehension of which the mind requires nothing outside itself, have yet to be found by searching, have to be abstracted and separated off from among the measureless host of ideas which form the world of consciousness. Nor can we even expect that the very simplest of innate truths, the highest principles of all, will be revealed to consciousness first of all by this process of self-reflexion. On the contrary, their first appearance is invariably occasioned by some particular instance which exemplifies them, or some particular case presented by perception or by imagination that the mind may pass judgment on it. But it may happen that our perceptions may be of such kind as never to present to us the case required in its purity, and in the same way to debar the imagination from conceiving the idea of it, and this though if once it were presented to consciousness, the mind would at once feel the conviction awakened of a truth of the most universal and fundamental kind, and would judge accordingly. Thus then it may be an extremely difficult task for knowledge, to remove all the obstacles which the actual connexion of our ideas, imposed upon us by experience, plants in our path, and to fight its way through to the knowledge of the self-evident.

359. In mathematics, where the matter of investigation can most easily be separated from the real objects to which it is attached in experience, it has speaking generally been possible to advance from the simplest truths to their derivative consequences, although, in spite of this, the fresh knowledge has afforded new and more comprehensive expression even for the principles which were known before. It has been otherwise in the science of mechanics, which applying itself directly to actual occurrences, seeks to prescribe laws to the interactions which obtain between real things. I use this much criticised expression[1] of Kant, in

[1] ['Vorzeichnen' (to prescribe).]

order to reduce the objections which have been made to it within their proper limits. No one could have intended it to mean that human reason can invent laws at its own good pleasure which nature is bound to follow. But supposing the idea of a relation between different elements to be presented to us in so simple a way as to exhibit an instance of the perfect purity required, in which true laws of nature are seen producing their simplest result, with no multiplicity of extraneous conditions to obscure it, why should it not be possible in such a case for reason, itself a member in the system of the world in which these operations take place, to have an immediate apprehension of the result in which the relation supposed must necessarily issue? This is not to thrust its own subjective laws upon nature, but to detect the real laws of nature herself, which become to it binding rules which it brings with it to the confused tangle of separate events wherewith to estimate and interpret them.

In this sense pure mechanics is an *a priori* science; it is quite true that many of its principles may have been first suggested and the enquiry after them occasioned by experience, but it was not by the testimony of repeated perceptions that they were discovered and reduced to the exact form of a law, it was by an operation of thought, apprehending with the clearness of immediate vision the self-evident law in an instance where it is presented in its purity, and in complicated cases finding means to reduce them to a similar simplicity. This is commonly expressed by saying that within its own province mechanics is an absolutely demonstrative science, which from pre-suppositions of its own creation evolves necessary conclusions with irresistible logic; but that, to compensate for this it has in relation to experience only a hypothetical validity, that is to say it is valid only on the assumption that real things exist which admit of being subsumed with perfect exactness under the conceptions from which its conclusions are drawn.

But such language allows too much to an unjustifiable

scepticism as to the tenableness of the hypothesis, and does not really answer to the facts. For the science of mechanics did not spring up in some meditative consciousness, playing with possibilities before experience existed, it arose under the persistent pressure of experience which called for explanation. The abstract universal conditions, from which in mechanics we derive definite consequences, are not Problematic schemes of something which might perhaps be found in reality, but reductions of that which is Assertorically given in experience to a form in which its validity is universal.

But that reduction to a universal form was necessary by reason of the one actual postulate with which the science of mechanics stands and falls, that a uniformity of law does hold good in the world of events. If this assumption is justified, and if there are many elements $A\ B\ C \ldots$ operating together in the order of nature, each under various forms $a\ a^1\ a^2 \ldots \beta\ \beta^1\ \beta^2 \ldots$, finally all of them in varying relations $M\ N \ldots$ each of which again may assume different values $\mu\ \mu^1 \ldots \nu\ \nu^1 \ldots$,—then any single event must be the joint effect of many single laws, each law concerning two elements $A\ B$ only and their relation M, and determining the particular operation E which results from these data, and which in turn will change to $e\ e^1 \ldots$, as $A\ B$ and M pass through their several changes in form or in value.

It may be that experience never affords a perfectly pure instance of one such single law; still it would be folly to find fault with mechanics for speaking of motion in the first instance without taking account of resistance which nevertheless invariably attends it; or of a homogeneous mass which is nowhere to be found, or finally of a perfectly rigid body, whereas perception presents us only with bodies which are elastic, yielding, of various degrees of hardness. It will be time enough to take account of the influence of these secondary conditions when we have learnt the universal laws upon whose consequences they exert their modifying operation; but even supposing that the theory of the resisting mediums, of the specific qualities of matter and its molecular properties, were never to reach the simple clearness of the other departments of mechanical science, it is certain that a philosophy of nature which was not even acquainted with the laws of the simple and pure cases from which every individual mixed case varies by a determinate amount, would be attended by still less success. For it is by no means for the mere convenience of shortening our procedure at the cost of its exactness, that we ignore the special peculiarities of the concrete instance, and begin by looking for the law of a universal and abstract instance; our assumption of the presence of law in actual events involves as a necessary and objective consequence that the joint operation of many elements is made up of the several operations, which each pair of elements, combining in a specific relation, generate on their own account, and which they alter in accordance with a fixed law as this relation alters.

360. The empirical content and course of our perceptions has rendered it by no means an easy task for mechanical enquiry even to form the ideas of the simple and pure cases upon which an immediate intuition of the truth could at once pronounce a judgment self-evident and universal; on the contrary, it is here more than anywhere else that experience has exerted the injurious influence already alluded to, drawing the mind away from the apprehension of the universal and the unconditioned, by constantly introducing to it the particular and that whose validity is conditional.

The entire period of antiquity passed away without the conception of motion, the central point in mechanics, having been reduced to a form simple enough to be immediately apprehended by the mind in its abstract character. Three great examples of motion were presented by experience to the imagination, the perpetual motion of the heavenly bodies, the rapidly ceasing motion of terrestrial bodies caused by external impulse, finally the energy of living beings, originating within but after a while wearying. The mind of antiquity never succeeded in separating the simple process in which all motion consists, continuous change of place, from the conflicting peculiarities of these different classes of instances in which it occurs. The phenomenon was never disentangled from certain assumed causes of it; the course of the stars was represented as a divine motion exalted above the general laws of nature, or else the motions of terrestrial bodies were attributed to an extraneous necessity and thus degraded to a position below the due and natural order of things. Add to this that the analogy of the wearying of human activity led men to regard cessation of all motion as such as the natural and self-evident law, its eternal continuance as a divine exception.

It was reserved for a much later epoch to conceive the essential features of all motion of whatever kind, as consisting simply in a relation between the three elements of velocity, duration of time, and space traversed, and by the modest formula $s = vt$ to lay the foundation of a scientific theory of motion. That formula once given, the law of the persistence of motion followed of itself: for although the discovery of the law was due to a generalisation from particular results obtained by experiment, showing that motion always lasted for a longer time in proportion as all external hindrances were removed, still no one doubts that directly it was discovered it expressed a tardily apprehended necessity of thought. That there is such a thing as motion had to be learnt from experience, but if it exists or is to exist at all, the idea of its persistence becomes a necessary postulate in order to make it even a possible object of intuition[1].

Similar difficulties had to be encountered in forming the conception of mass. The bodies with which we most ordinarily deal, whether solid or fluid, were observed to follow the downward tendency of weight, whereas vapours

[1] [See § 247.]

and fire tended upwards; thus the idea arose of two opposite impulses, both belonging essentially to the nature of bodies, but leading away from one another in two opposite directions, directions which might indeed have been correctly distinguished by a qualitative distinction of the ultimate points towards which they tend, but which were in fact confounded with the unintelligible antithesis of an above and below in an absolute space. It took a long time before the combination of more extended observations was able to compensate for the one-sided character of the facts as experience at first presents them, and to show that neither the direction nor the intensity of weight-pressure was everywhere uniform. Not till then did the natural idea make its way that the beginning of any new motion whatever must necessarily require something to determine its direction *a fronte* or *a tergo*, in the way of attraction or repulsion along a straight line, that is to say, that it takes its origin always from an interaction of different elements in space, and that the amount of such interaction depends on the quantities of a homogeneous real existence which are united in each one of the elements in question. The idea of mass, again, which was thus arrived at, in which regard is had only to the amount of the resistance of inertia on the one hand which real existence in space offers to any motion which is demanded from it, and to the magnitude of the power with which it enforces every motion of other elements which originates from itself,—this mechanical conception may very well stir new questions to which philosophy would have to find an answer; still when once a regular order of natural events is given or is assumed, in which each single event is taken as the condition determining the definite degree of another event following upon it, it is easy to see that such a conception involves as a self-evident postulate the commensurability of all real elements in regard to the magnitude of the effects they may be expected to produce, a principle which is expressed in the conception of Mass. But how great the power is which one-sided and partial observation exerts over our conceptions, is attested by the difficulty which the common imagination finds even in the present day in believing in the possibility of the Antipodes, and again by the errors of certain schools of natural philosophy, to which not indeed the eternal downward motion of the philosophy of antiquity, but still the concentric pressure of gravity, formed so essential a part of the general notion of material substance that the idea of mass without weight always seemed to them a contradiction.

Here I must break off; but any one undertaking to write the history of the development of mechanical conceptions would find it a suggestive task, instead of being content perpetually to repeat how we have come simply through the connexion of particular experiences to our knowledge of natural law, to go on to trace and explain how at first the partial and one-sided character of those experiences forced upon men's minds a number of false ideas, and hindered them from arriving at an earlier apprehension of self-evident truths.

361. There are conflicting opinions as to the logical character of the simplest mechanical principles. Just because they concern in the first instance not actual bodies but a certain postulated subject-matter whose nature is wholly determined by our definitions of it, we either consider ourselves bound to look upon them as analytical judgments the truth of which is guaranteed by the law of Identity, or else we regard them, even as taken in their purest and most abstract form, as still synthetic and therefore mere probable hypotheses, whose truth can only be established by their agreement with experience and the complete internal harmony of the conclusions to which they lead.

My own judgment in this controversy can be no other

than that already given in reference to the kindred problems in Arithmetic and Geometry, but I must content myself with briefly indicating my point of view without developing it in all the detail which might be desirable. In general I might express my position thus: the two given data A and B, as to whose connexion a mechanical judgment is to be affirmed, are not given to us merely one by one; our ideas of them are only intelligible and are only understood in and through a single Intuition, which embraces both together and which determines also in one and the same act the relation between them.

Let us, to begin with, turn once more to an example from arithmetic. The proposition $3a - 3a = 0$, we shall be disposed to refer immediately to the principle of Identity; nevertheless all that that principle tells us, taken simply by itself, is that $3a = 3a, -3a = -3a$, and finally $3a - 3a = 3a - 3a$; that this last expression $= 0$, we can only maintain on the strength of a direct intuition of the fact that there are two operations lying within our power, the addition of a to a and then the subtraction of a from $2a$, which exactly cancel each other, and in the repetition of which an equal number of times the subtraction will annihilate whatever quantity the addition may generate. For in fact in the expression $+ a - a$ the sign $-$ represents not merely an opposite to $+$, it indicates at the same time the mode in which this opposition is able to operate and is to operate, namely by subtraction. If we knew nothing of the possibility of such an operation, or if it could not be carried out, then we could as little evolve the result 0 from $a - a$, as we could arrive at a result from the mere combination in thought of the contradictory notions of possibility and impossibility; in their character of opposites these two notions can equally well be represented by a and $-a$, but this cannot be interpreted by a subtraction.

We see therefore that the proposition $a - a = 0$ may

be regarded with equal truth as at once identical and synthetic. It is an identical proposition, because it would be actually false if the two sides of the equation did not represent precisely the same content; but that the identity is there, no mere logical analysis of our a, $-a$, and $-$ signs, can possibly inform us; we learn this solely through the immediate intuition of the meaning which the sign $-$ is in this particular case capable of bearing, because it is related to the increasing or the diminution of quantities. Hence the proposition is a synthetic judgment of identity between two contents different in form, between a problem and its solution.

A similar instance is presented in the field of mechanics by the determination of the resultant of two motions the lines of which include an angle. I confine myself here to the postulate from which the ordinary attempts at demonstration start, namely that where two such forces are equal the resultant bisects the angle between them. This proposition is commonly regarded as self-evident, and we suppose ourselves to possess in this simplest possible instance an immediate certainty of a conclusion to which any more complicated problems would have to be reduced. And undoubtedly the most cautious mind will agree to recognise in it not merely a probable hypothesis but a truth which only cannot be proved, because it is too simple to admit of being proved from anything simpler. But the observation which is commonly added by way of elucidation, that there is no reason why the resultant should approach more nearly to the line of the one force than of the other, may serve to illustrate the logical character of the proposition in question. For it cannot in itself be a positive ground for the necessity of the assumed direction of the resultant, that grounds are absent for two other classes of directions, unless we start with the position that some direction must necessarily be taken, and that it cannot coincide with either of the two forces.

But now it is precisely this that we know from Intuition; a merely logical analysis would only teach us that under the condition a the element M moves in the direction α, under the condition b in the direction β. Supposing both conditions operating together, then M can neither move in the direction α nor in the direction β, because either one or the other would suppose one of the two conditions entirely inoperative. What then would happen? The two conditions being supposed of equal strength, it follows that either both the one and the other must be inoperative and M remain at rest, or else both must act and be counteracted in equal measure,—supposing always that there are ways and means by which that result can be brought about. But this last is the important question; that there are such ways and means, and what they consist in, this is what no method which thought can provide is able to inform us. But when we turn on the one hand to the Intuition or Perception of space which gives us the connexion between the different directions which are possible in it, and on the other to the Intuition of motion, there it lies all clear before us; there we find that M can satisfy completely both the two conditions at once, by so moving as at the expiration of the unit of time t to arrive at the same point (being the end of the diagonal of the parallelogram) at which it would have arrived in two such units of time taken in succession, had it pursued first the direction α or β simply during the one, and then the direction β or α simply during the other; that the path finally by which it reaches that point is the diagonal itself, follows from the fact that for any small fraction dt of the time precisely the same principle holds; the diagonal is the geometric locus of all the points at which M must necessarily arrive at the ends of the times dt, $2dt$, $3dt$ and the rest. Here again, then, and this time in a proposition of Mechanics, we have a synthetic judgment, which establishes the identity between a given problem and its solution through the instrumentality of immediate Intuition.

362. This for the present must suffice; I glance at the more advanced part of mechanics for a different purpose. Whereas its first beginnings by their very simplicity render formal methods of demonstration impossible, the problems later on become so complicated, that the solutions, although strictly following from those fundamental principles, do nevertheless, owing to the large variety of the points of relation which have to be kept in sight, necessitate very lengthy and circuitous processes of abstraction and calculation. Now indisputable as are the conclusions which are thus arrived at, yet nowhere has the desire been more keenly felt than in this exact science, to dispense with the scaffolding of the Calculus and reduce the results obtained to simple conceptions which only need the help of computation so far as is involved in their application to the conditions, determinate in respect of quantity, which particular cases present. I would only remind my readers of Gauss' principle of least constraint, which expresses in the most universal form the law of all motion as follows: a system of material points, however connected with each other and whatever may be the external limitations by which they are controlled, moves at every instant in the greatest possible accordance with the free movement of the points, or under the least possible constraint; taking as measure of the constraint which the whole system endures in every minute portion of time the sum of the products obtained by multiplying the square of the deviation of each point from its free movement into the mass of that point.

The second clause in this law supplies the general conception which is expressed in the first with the mathematical form by help of which, for every individual case, the purport of what the conception requires is precisely defined and made applicable to the given quantitative relations of that case; but in the first clause we are convinced that we possess not merely a general rule which is found as a matter of fact to hold good, but the veritable *ratio legis*, from which all the special laws of the various kinds of motion are derived. Applying it to the simplest case of all, the case of the resultant of two lines of motion, we have seen (§ 232 seq.) that various chains of reasoning will lead us with equal certainty to our conclusion. These forms of proof however serve only with greater or less cogency to *constrain* belief; on the other hand the reflexion that the motion in the line of the diagonal is that by which both motive impulses are completely satisfied, and in which no part of either is lost, presents itself to us, when once we comprehend it and find experience to confirm it, as a ground of judgment of an entirely different order, and of quite peculiar significance, which arouses in us at once the conviction that in it we possess not merely one of the rules by the light of which it is *admissible* to regard the order of events observed, but the supreme principle by which they are actually governed.

I added advisedly that we are obliged to presuppose the preliminary corroboration of our principle in experience; and in fact however convincing the proposition might be in itself, that the conflict of all motions is always so ordered that in the final result no element in the effects aimed at by the constituent is lost, still without such corroboration it would be of very doubtful validity. It would represent a principle after which we ourselves perhaps should order the world, if the task could be set us, and provided always that it was possible and that we had found the means really to carry out in every individual case the universal postulate which the principle contains. But that the actual world of reality or even that the world of thought does possess the particular content, form and constitution, and the particular combination of elements which renders it possible to unite under this single supreme principle all the particular events which take place in it, or even the several laws which abstract reasoning has presented to us as necessities of thought—this we learn only at the end of our journey.

We know how often in the history of mechanics attempts have been made to connect the entire course of the physical universe with some such supreme philosophical law; we have heard of the constant sum of motion in the universe, of the indestructibility of force, of a principle of least action, and of a law of Parsimony. All these attempts did not merely express the aspiration after a fundamental and self-evident idea from which the individual laws, mathematically determinable, which govern events, might be derived; they tell us something also of the direction in which the desired end is to be looked for. But it has never been found possible to determine distinctly and precisely, without superfluity or omission, of what subjects of relations so universal a conception could be enunciated as no less universally valid.

How far up to the present time any advances have been made in this direction, I have not now to enquire; all that I desired to emphasise was the fact of the eager ambition displayed by the mind to perfect the circle of its knowledge by the aid of principles of the most comprehensive order— principles once again which affirm in the form of *synthetic* judgments, which are nevertheless self-evident and universally valid, a connexion between two terms of a relation whose connexion no process of logical demonstration can show to be of an analytical or identical nature.

363. The final goal of knowledge is usually represented in different terms from this. What is aimed at is the reduction of all connexions which appear synthetic in character to an analytic form—more properly expressed to the form of identity—and we are even believed to be actually on the way to the consummation of that end.

At the commencement of our knowledge, we are told, a conception S is made up at first of the small number of marks $P\,Q\,R$, which we have already found to be connected together; then supposing that fresh experience presents in a particular instance a further characteristic Z conjoined with S, the proposition S is Z which gives expression to the observation made, is considered to be a synthetic judgment. If however this new fact of experience becomes established as obtaining in all cases of S without exception, Z is adopted forthwith into S, and the proposition S is Z has now with the enlarged signification of S become analytical. This in fact, it is said finally, is the goal towards which all knowledge is striving—to reduce those connexions of subject and predicate which at first appear so completely synthetic to this analytic form, that is to say, to resolve coexistence into coherence. And this is a perfectly correct description of the origin and growth of knowledge—for it must, alas! be confessed that beyond this point it seldom advances—yet it has to be remarked that this ideal described in the last words of the sentence is one which is attained only to a very modest extent, and that in the sense of the initial appearance of mere coexistence giving place to an intelligent apprehension of a self-evident law of connexion it is never attained at all.

If we had formed the conception of body to begin with out of the qualities of extension, impenetrability, and inertia alone, characteristics from which the necessity of mutual attraction does not follow, the proposition 'Body is heavy' would undoubtedly have been a synthetic proposition; but the same proposition does not become analytic, even if we take into the conception of body the universally observed fact of gravitation; this last property is just as little to be derived from the others as it was before, and therefore just as much synthetically connected with them as it was in the first judgment which expressed that association as a constant fact. Undoubtedly we are able, taking this synthetic conjunction of all the different marks of S as our datum, to submit them to the analytic method, and bring them one after another before the mind as separate objects of thought; but this recognition of the mere fact of constant coexistence where the coherence is not understood is in fact the renunciation of knowledge; the mind could only rest satisfied if the conjunction of any two such properties of S were a sure guarantee of the necessary presence of any third. And such demonstrations we are able to some extent to establish, and whenever we succeed in doing so it means that an advance in knowledge has been accomplished; but it is clear that no such result is possible, unless in the last resort we assume at some point or other a premiss of the form $A + B = C$, that is to say, a premiss which does not merely affirm identity of what is the same[1] by the bare principle of Identity[2], but affirms identity of the different where no reduction to the principle of Identity is possible. Thus the supposed transformation of all synthetic knowledge into analytical resolves itself after all into the enquiry, what are the simplest forms of synthetic truth?

364. This contention, though it may perhaps be said to amount to nothing more than a needless change of phraseology, will nevertheless be in the end admitted. But it will be urged in addition that this very necessity of allowing certain synthetic combinations to start with, proves the inability of human knowledge really to come to a final resting-place, and to obtain insight into the inner connexion of the coexistent; everywhere there remains a residue of mere facts, of which the connexion of one with another is unintelligible, and vouched for only by experience. I cannot agree with this opinion, according to which we attain to knowledge only where we can affirm exact identity of what is exactly identical. For after all whence comes the confidence with which we hold the proposition $A = A$ to be an *intelligible* truth, except from the immediate self-evidence with which it forces itself upon us, and which leaves us no room to wish for any mediate demonstration of its certainty

---

[1] ['Gleiches einander gleich setzt.'] [2] ['Princip der Identität.']

besides? But how it happens, by what means it is brought about, or from what inner coherence in the nature of things it follows that A is identically like itself, we do not know, nor will anyone believe that there is any meaning in asking such a question at all.

If then a perfectly simple synthetic proposition of the form $A + B = C$ presents itself to us with a like degree of self-evidence to recommend it, why should a question be raised in this instance which was meaningless in the previous one? Why should the latter act of equation only be allowed to be valid by the help of some intermediary process, to show us *how* C can $= A + B$, when in the former our intelligence was satisfied to know the fact *that $A = A$*? I will not again insist on the point that in the processes of our thought no such mediation could come from the mere law of Identity, that it would always have to begin with a proposition $A^1 + B^1 = C^1$, analogous in character to the one to be proved—for this reflexion would certainly not meet the complaints of the incompleteness of a knowledge which is said to be incapable of attaining to any supreme self-evident principle. But how are we to understand the requirement that we should accept some such synthetic connexion as given, as valid in itself, and only not accessible to our intelligence? Are we prepared to assume that as a matter of fact M and N are always conjoined in reality without affecting one another in any way? But if this is impossible, and if it is at the same time impossible that out of one and the same self-identical A two different results M and N should arise, what else is left to us but to suppose that there do exist in the real world certain natural and original connexions between things different, original syntheses the members of which are not joined together by any intermediate links, so that the tie between them could appear as even the most distant consequence of the law of Identity, yet are none the less immediately and really connected? If then in the world of Being this must necessarily be the case, how can it be demanded of knowledge that it should exhibit the certainty and the intelligibility of a given relation through a process of mediation which does not exist in that relation itself?

Thus then there may certainly be synthetic truths of an ultimate and absolutely simple nature, which as conceived in their purest and most simple form possess a validity guaranteed not merely by fact but by their own self-evidence, a self-evidence however which if we insist on grounding all logical truth on the principle of Identity, must no longer be called logical but aesthetic, and which accordingly will find the touchstone of its validity no longer in the unthinkableness but in the plain absurdity of its contradictory. To this class of truths belong the simplest principles of mechanics; that we regard them together with all truths of like kind with them not as the earliest constituents of our knowledge which have been there from the beginning, but as its final results, to be won only with difficulty and labour, has been explained above in terms sufficiently clear to make the repetition of it here superfluous.

365. Special lines of enquiry lead in the first instance to single truths of this nature, each one its own evidence and standing in no need of support from others. At the same time nothing prevents us from bringing them as members of one and the same world into connexion with each other and searching for a single supreme principle in which they may find their unity, just as each one of them had already supplied a centre of unity for a body of connected facts. It is possible that many such truths may lose in consequence their independent value, and that even logical analysis may reduce them to particular cases of a more general law, which we have found conceptions of a sufficiently comprehensive and exalted order of abstraction to express. It is just as possible and more likely that the self-evidence with which the coherence of the many single elements of truth enables them to be ranged under a single fundamental idea, may

rest upon that very same kind of aesthetic propriety on the strength of which the single laws themselves were formulated, affirming connexions which logic could not prove.

Such a development of synthetic truths out of a single supreme principle—a development itself synthetic and yet at each step necessary—was perhaps the problem of the Platonic Dialectic, though as yet but dimly presaged; it may be truly regarded as the end towards which the Hegelian revival of the Platonic scheme was directed. From these ambitions by which Germany was once inspired, our own age has passed with much sobriety to the order of the day, to that unremitting labour of empirical enquiry, the incompleteness of which paralysed the audacious flight of the Hegelian idealism. Nor was this the only defect of that idealism: unquestionably it was also wrong in regarding that which can only be the ultimate goal of a knowledge approaching towards completion, as already attained or attainable. But in view of the universal idolatry of experience which prevails at present, and which is all the cheaper and all the safer now that the importance and indispensableness of its object are visible to all mankind, I will at least close with the avowal that I hold that much reviled ideal of speculative intuition to be the supreme and not wholly unattainable goal of science, and with the expression of my hope that German philosophy will always arouse itself afresh, with more of moderation and reserve, yet with no less enthusiasm, to the endeavour, not merely to *calculate* the course of the world, but to *understand it*.

APPENDIX [1].

237. In the case we have just considered, a very plausible supposition, viz., the resolution of a motion, led to a correct result, though the conditions of that result really lay in quite another field; there are other cases in which a correct though not quite complete supposition leads to results which are apparently wrong but which can be made right by interpretation. Let a heavy rod whose length is $2a$ and weight W lean against a perfectly smooth vertical wall and make with the perfectly smooth horizontal plane on which it stands the angle ϕ. It will necessarily slip down unless the foot which tends to move away from the wall encounters some lateral check. The amount of this resistance, or, which is the same thing, of the thrust S exerted against it by the sliding rod, is expressed by the equation $S = \dfrac{W}{2} \cot \phi$. If the rod stand upright, $\phi = 90°$, $\cot \phi = 0$, and therefore $S = 0$; the rod balances itself freely upon its foot, exerts no horizontal pressure at all, and needs no lateral check, and can dispense with the vertical wall. As ϕ diminishes, i.e. as the rod slopes, $\cot \phi$ increases, and with it the thrust; but when ϕ becomes 0, and the rod lies horizontally upon the ground, the thrust according to the formula is infinitely great, while a glance at the facts show us that it must be nothing. This apparent contradiction is easily removed. When we propounded the problem we thought of course of a continuous horizontal plane capable of resistance stretching from the foot of the rod to the vertical wall; but this part of the supposition did not enter

[1] [See Editor's Preface.]

at all into the small calculation by which we arrived at the formula $S = \dfrac{W}{2} \cot \phi$; here we thought only of the single point at the foot which had to carry the weight of the rod; between this point and the wall lay nothing that this calculation took count of. In other words the *general* formula treats the two walls simply as geometrical loci, of which in calculating each particular case we consider only the two points at a distance of $2a$ from each other upon which the forces in question act in this case. Now, if we do not go beyond what is involved in this calculation, at the moment when ϕ becomes equal to o there is a gap between the foot of the rod and the vertical wall, equal to the length of the rod, and through which it would fall when there is no perpendicular force to support its weight. It can now no longer be said to exert a thrust S; but S signified not only this thrust but also the horizontal force, which in the first place counteracts this thrust, but which also forms the only obstacle that prevents the rod from slipping down into the horizontal position in which its weight no longer meets any resistance. Now that S becomes infinite when ϕ becomes equal to o means that a force acting horizontally towards the vertical wall would have to be infinitely great in order to prevent the rod from falling through the gap; in other words, as infinite forces are never found, there is no horizontal force that could produce that result. We must not be misled by the fact that in practice this result is often attained by squeezing bodies together in a horizontal direction; for this result is then due to the roughness of the surfaces with which the squeezing and the squeezed bodies come into contact, and to the compressibility of the latter which by slight alterations in its shape furnishes points of support which before were wanting.

INDEX.

Abstraction, 41, 205.
Accident and Substance, 78.
'Actual Reality' (*Reale Wirklichkeit*); *see* Reality, ii. 286.
Adjective, 17–8.
'*Ad contradictoriam*,' 109.
'*Ad subalternantem*,' 107, ii. 29.
'*Ad subalternatam*,' 109.
'*Ad subcontrariam*,' 109.
Affirmative Judgments, 63.
Analogy, 137, 322, 328.
— 'strict,' 328.
— incomplete, ii. 29.
— and Induction, cpd., ii. 33.
— and Hypothesis, ii. 95.
Analysis, opp. Synthesis, ii. 167.
Analytical Judgments, 82, 130.
'*Anders-sein*' explained, 264.
Anschauung ('Intuition' or 'Perception'), *note*, ii. 309.
'*An-sich-sein*' explained, 264.
Apagogic (indirect) proof, 307, 317.
Apodeictic Judgments, 65.
Apodosis, 123.
'*A posteriori*' Synth. Judgments, 82.
'*A priori*' Synth. Judgments, 82, ii. 295.
— Ideas, ii. 229.
— meaning of, ii. 309 ff.
Apprehension (Synthesis of), 37.
— Immediate; *see* Intuition.
Archimedes, 319.
Aristotelian Sorites, 128.
Aristotle, 53, 54, 64, 114, 121, 134, 256, 297.
— (on Platonic Ideas), ii. 215.
Assertorial Judgments, 65.
Augustine, ii. 226.
Axioms, 301.

Begriff; *see* Concept.
'Being for itself' (*Für-sich-sein*), 265.
'Being in itself' (*an-sich-sein*), 264.
Bernoulli's method, 316.
Boole, 277 ff.

Calculus of Chances, ii. 109 ff.
— Logical, 277 ff.
Categorical Judgment, 72, ii. 37.
Categorical character of Classification, 188.
Cause, opp. Conditions, 125.
— opp. Ground, ii. 37.
'*Cessante causa*—,' ii. 43.
Chains of Inference, 128.
Circle, the proper definition of, 216.
Circulus in definiendo, 214.
Circulus in demonstrando, ii. 2.
Clara perceptio, 222.
Classification, 163.
— by combination, 163, cp. 278.
— natural, 178.
— by development, 180 ff.
'*Cogito, ergo sum*,' ii. 226.
Coherence of world of Thought, 91, 95.
Coherent (Ideas), 1.
Coincident (Ideas), 1.
Collective proof, 315.
Colours (names of), 28.
Combinatory classification, 164 ff.
Comparison, 27.
Compensation in Abstraction, 42.
Concept, 157 ff.
— (prior to Judgment), 23, cp. ii. 27.
— Imperfect, 39.
— ('*notio*'), 44.

334   *INDEX.*

Concept, Singular, 46.
— Logical, 47.
— Universal, 51, ii. 264.
Conditions, 89.
— opp. Cause, 125.
Conjunctions, 21.
Consequence, 89, 125.
— opp. Effect, ii. 37.
Constitutive Concept, 154, 168.
Construction, 207, 305.
Content (of a concept, *materia*), 44, 51, and *see* pp. 15-6.
— (presentation of to mind), ii. 259.
— has 'Validity,' ii. 211, 269.
Contradiction, 101.
— principle of, 80.
Contradictory opposition, 108.
Contraposition, 112.
Contraries, 143.
Contrariety, 101.
Contrary opposition, 108.
'*Conversio pura*,' 109 ff.
— '*impura*,' 109.
Coordinated, 44.
Coordinated cases, ii. 111.
Copula, 58, 61.
— of Categorical Judgment, 78 ff.
Copulative Judgment, 99.
— Premisses, 126.
Current of Ideas, 1.

Darwin, 248.
De dicto simpliciter, ii. 5.
De dicto secundum quid, ii. 5.
Deductio ad absurdum, 319.
Deductive proof, 308 ff.
'*Definiendo angustior*,' 215.
— '*latior*,' 215.
Definitio, 211.
Definition, 209.
— Nominal and Real, 213 ff.
— Genetic, 222.
Descartes, ii. 179, 226.
Description, 208.
Descriptive Definition, 221.
δευτέρα οὐσία, ii. 216.
Dialectic, Plato's, ii. 222, 330.
— Hegel's, 191, ii. 330.
διαφορά, 53.
Dictum de omni, 100, 330.

Differentiae specificae, 53, 209.
Ding (*see* Thing and *Sache*), has existence, ii. 208.
— opp. 'Content' and 'objective' (*sachlich*), but = 'external object' (*Gegenstand*), ii. 270.
Direct Proof, 307.
Disjunction, Incomplete, ii. 12.
— and Probability, ii. 110.
Disjunctive Judgment, 68, 99, 102.
— Law of Thought, 102, 330.
— Premisses, 126.
Disparates, 104, 143, 149, 228.
Distincta perceptio, 222.
Distinction, 26.
Duality, the Principle of, 286.

Effect, opp. Consequence, 94, ii. 38.
'*Effectuum naturalium*,' ii. 47-8.
εἶδος, 51.
Eleatic dialectic, ii. 201.
Ellipse, equation of, 172.
Episyllogism, 128.
Equal; *see* 'Like.'
Equation of the Ellipse, 172.
Equations, constitutive, 154.
Equilibrium, problem of conditions of, 336.
Essential marks, 161.
Evidence, transmission of, ii. 117.
Excluded Middle, principle of, 100, 102.
Existence, Judgment of, 74.
— opp. Validity, ii. 209, 267.
Expectation, mathematical, ii. 123.
— moral, 376, ii. 125.
Experiment, ii. 39.
Explanation, opp. Classification, 188.
— Incomplete, ii. 10.
Explanatory theory, 188.
Extent (of a concept, '*ambitus*'), 44, 51.

Fact; *see Sache.*
— and Law, ii. 79.
— knowledge of (*Erkenntniss der Sache*), ii. 186.
Fallacia falsi medii, ii. 4.
False premisses, ii. 1.

Fichte's *Zeitschrift* quoted, 100.
Fiction, dist. Hypothesis, ii. 90.
Figures of Syllogism, 116, 123.
Figure, second, 134.
— third, 137.
'*Für-sich-sein*' explained, 265.

Galen, figure of, 120.
Gauss (principle of least constraint), ii. 323.
'General' (Generic) opp. Universal Judgment, 97.
General term (mathematical), ii. 79.
γένος, 51.
Genus, 44, 51.
Genus proximum, 209.
'*Geschichte der Aesthetik in Deutschland*' (Author's), 262.
Goklenius, Goklenian Sorites, 128.
Grammar cpd. with Logic, 20.
Gravity, 90.
Ground and Consequence, ii. 37.
Ground, ii. 38.

Hegel, 47, 54, 262.
Hegelian Dialectic, 262, ii. 330.
Heraclitus, ii. 200.
Herbart, 94.
Hume, ii. 295.
ὑποτυπώσεις, Pyrrhonian, ii. 196.
Hypotheses, subsidiary, ii. 100.
Hypothesis, dist. Postulate, ii. 90.
Hypothetical Judgment, 65, 89, 99, ii. 37, 68.
— Syllogism, 123.
— character of Explanation, 188.
Hysteron Proteron, ii. 3.

Idea ('*Idee*,' see ii. 202 *note*), 168, ii. 202 ff.
— ('*Vorstellung*'), meaning of, 31.
Ideal, 180.
Ideas, Coherent and Coincident, 1.
— opp. Impressions, 13.
— (opp. *Begriff*), ii. 265.
Identical ('*gleich*'), ii. 254.
Identity ('*Identität*'), principle of, 99, ii. 296, 329.
— ('*Gleichheit*'), ii. 260, and *see note*, ii. 254.

ἴδιον, 54.
Immediate Inference, 106 ff.
Imperfect concepts, 39.
Impersonal Judgment, 72.
Impressions (opp. 'Ideas'), 13.
Incommensurables, Inference concerning, 148.
Indirect (apagogic) proof, 307, 317.
Induction, cpd. w. Analogy, 136 ff., ii. 33.
— Complete, 315.
— Imperfect, ii. 32.
'Inductive,' 308.
'Inductive Logic,' ii. 22.
Inference and Disjunction, 106.
— Immediate, 106.
Innate Ideas ('*Ideen*'), ii. 229 ff., 311 ff.
Intuition (*Anschauung*), ii. 309 ff.
Inverse Ratio of Extent and Content, 51.
'Investigation of the Laws of Thought' (Boole's), 277 ff.
Ionians, philosophy of, 252.

Jevons, 297.
Judgment (and Concept), 23, 56.
— (Real significance of), ii. 273.
'Justification' of a conception, 304.

Kant, Classification of Judgments, 61 ff.
— on Categorical Judgment, 78
— Analytical and Synthetical Judgments, 82, 130.
— Synthetical Judgments, 84.
— Synthetical Judgments, *a priori*, ii. 295.
— his Categories, ii. 220.
— Matter and Form, ii. 233.
κατηγορεῖν, 77.
Kepler, ii. 69.

Language, a logical, 272.
Laplace, ii. 131.
Law, meanings of, ii. 68.
— and Rule, ii. 71.
— of Nature, ii. 68.

Law, and Facts, ii. 83.
— Faith in, ii. 292.
Leibnitz, 272.
Like ('*gleich*'); see *note*, p. 327, and *note*, ii. 254.
Limitative Judgments, 63.
Line without mass, 352 ff.
Linnaean classification, 166.
Locke on Innate Ideas, ii. 311 ff.
Logical; a logical language, 272.
— the calculus, 277 ff.

Major premiss, 130.
Mark, meaning of the term, 47.
Marks, essential and unessential, 161.
Material ('*sachlich*,' opp. '*formal*'), 279.
Mathematical Truth and Law of Identity, ii. 297.
Mathematics and Logic, 35, 147.
Mean, arithmetical, ii. 143.
Measurements, correction of, ii. 143.
Mechanical Physics, 90.
Metaphysics (Aristotle's), ii. 215.
Method of least squares, ii. 145.
Middle concept, 114.
Middle term, ambiguity of, ii. 4.
Minor premiss, 133.
Minority, the 'winning minority,' ii. 151.
Modality of Judgments, 64, 112.
— True, 66.
'*Modus ponendo ponens*,' etc., 125.
Moods, 117 ff.

Naming, 25.
Natural Classification, 178.
Negative Judgments, 63.
Newton, ii. 47-8.
νοητὸς τόπος, ii. 213.
Nominal Definition, 213.
Nominalism, ii. 267.
Numbers and Things (Pythagorean doctrines), 255-6.

Objectification, 14, 140.
Objective ('*objectiv*'), Objectivity ('*objectivität*'), 14-5, cp. ii. 203.
Objective ('*objectiv*,' opp. '*subjectiv*'). ii. 279.
— (*sachlich*), ii. 253, 260.
Observation, ii. 38.
Occurrence, opp. Existence, ii. 208, 289.
'*Operationskreis des Logikcalcüls*' (Schröder), 278 ff.
Opposition of Judgments, 108.
'Order of the day,' ii. 161.
ὁρισμός, 211.
'Other being' ('*Anders-sein*'), 264.
οὐσία, ii. 211.

Parallelogram of forces, proofs of, 355 ff.
Paralogisms, ii. 14.
Part of a concept, 47.
Particular Judgments, 62, 84.
Pendulum's swing, time of, ii. 88.
Perception (synthesis of), 37.
— and the Impersonal Judgment, 74.
Personal error, ii. 74.
Petitio principii, ii. 2.
Philosophical calculus (Leibnitz), 272.
Picture in the mind, opp. Conception, ii. 26, cp. ii. 264.
Plato, 56, 76, ii. 210.
— (the Meno), ii. 312.
— (the Theaetetus), ii. 201.
Platonic 'Ideas,' ii. 202 ff.
— 'Dialectic,' ii. 330.
Polylemmas, 127.
Porphyrius, 54.
Position, 26.
Postulate, dist. Hypothesis, ii. 90.
Predicate, 58, 77.
Premisses, 114.
— Hypothetical, 126.
— Establishment of, 133.
Prepositions, 21.
Presentation, the act of, ii. 259.
Principium exclusi tertii, 100, 102.
Principles of Analogy discussed, 322 ff.
'Principles of Science' (Jevons'), 297.
Probability, ii. 109.

Problematic Judgments, 65, 68 ff.
Progressive proof, 307.
Projections, ii. 76.
Proof, forms of, 307 ff.
Proofs by exclusion and by limitation, 318.
Property, 54, 78.
— and Thing, 78.
Proportion, Inference by, 150 ff.
Prosyllogism, 128.
Protagoras, ii. 201.
Protasis, 123.
πρώτη οὐσία, ii. 216.
Proving too much, ii. 10.
Proving too little, ii. 10.
'*Pseudomenos*,' ii. 17.
Psychology, ii. 332.
'Pure case,' ii. 37, 67.
Pythagoras, 251 ff.

Quality of Judgments, 63.
Quantification of the Predicate, 297.
Quantitative variations of Causes and of Effects, ii. 61 ff.
Quantitative Ideas, 33.
Quantitative Judgments, 83.
Quantity of Judgments, 62.
'*Quaternio terminorum*,' 115, ii. 4.

Real, Reality; *see* Actual (*Wirklich, Wirklichkeit*), ii. 208, cp. pp. 14-5.
— (of external world, '*real*'), ii. 187, 286.
— ('*real*,' opp. '*formal*'), ii. 279.
Real Definition, 213.
Realism, ii. 267.
'Reason' and 'Condition;' *see* 'Ground,' 93.
Receptivity of Thought, 35.
— and Spontaneity, 36, ii. 233.
Reduction, 122.
— to impossibility, 122.
Refutation, 314.
Regressive proof, 307.
Rehnisch, 100.
Relations, reality of, ii. 260.
Remotive Judgment, 99.
— Premisses, 126.

Resolution of forces into components, 364.
Rotatory forces, 340, 347.
Rule, ii. 71.

Sache, see *Ding*, 'of those things (*Sachen*), the given thinkable contents,' ii. 273.
Sachlich, see 'Material,' 'Objective,' 'matter of knowledge (*sachlich*), although not things (*dinghaft*),' ii. 268, *see note*, ii. 270.
Schröder, '*Operationskreis des Logikcalcüls*,' 278 ff.
Self-evidence, may be spurious, 301.
Sensations, disparate groups of, 228 ff.
Sextus Empiricus, ii. 183.
Similar, Similarity ('*Aehnlich*,' '*Aehnlichkeit*'), defined, 327.
Singular Concepts, 45.
Singular Judgments, 62, 70.
Socrates (in Plato), 224, ii. 202.
Sophisms, ii. 14.
Sophists, ii. 201.
Sorites, 128.
Space, of more than three dimensions, 231.
Spatial Intuition, ii. 310.
Species, 44, 50.
— Perfect and Imperfect, 170.
— of two genera, 170.
Specific difference, 53.
Spectrum analysis, ii. 51.
Speculative Thought, 195.
State, 54.
Statistics, ii. 84, 139.
Subalternation, 107.
Subcontrary opposition, 108.
Subject, 58, 76.
— Grammatical and Logical, 60.
Subordination, 44, 49.
Substance and Accident, 78.
Substantive, 17.
Substitution, Inference by, 143.
Subsumed, 44.
Subsumption, 49.
— Inference by, 129.
Sufficient Reason, Law of, 91.

συμβεβηκός, 54.
Syllogism, 114.
— Subsumptive, 129.
— Aristotelian, criticised, 135.
— Real significance of, ii. 276.
Symbols, 146.
Synthesis of Apprehension, 37.
— of Perception, 37.
— opp. Analysis, ii. 167.
Synthetical Judgments, 82, 84, 131.
— (*a priori*), ii. 295.

Tabula rasa, ii. 232.
Taylorian Theorem, 369-374.
Things, the peculiar 'reality' of, 14 ff., cp. ii. 208.
Thing and Property, 78.

Thought (opp. 'current of ideas'), 3, 13.
τρόποι, sceptical, ii. 194.
Type, 179.

Ultimate Concepts, 55.
Universal ('first Universal'), 30.
— Judgments, 62, 97.
— Laws, 186.
— conception, ii. 265.
Universals which are not concepts, 46, 53.
Universality and Necessity, ii. 240.

Validity, ii. 209, 267.
Verb, 17-8.
'*Vorstellung*;' *see* Idea.

Zeno, on motion, ii. 14.

THE END.